SUBJECTIVITY WITHOUT SUBJECTS

SUBJECTIVITY WITHOUT SUBJECTS

From Abject Fathers to Desiring Mothers

Kelly Oliver

ROWMAN & LITTLEFIELD PUBLISHERS, INC.
Lanham • Boulder • New York • Oxford

ROWMAN & LITTLEFIELD PUBLISHERS, INC.

Published in the United States of America
by Rowman & Littlefield Publishers, Inc.
4720 Boston Way, Lanham, Maryland 20706

12 Hid's Copse Road
Cumnor Hill, Oxford OX2 9JJ, England

British Library Cataloguing in Publication Information Available

Library of Congress Cataloging-in-Publication Data

Oliver, Kelly, 1958–
Subjectivity without subjects : from abject fathers to desiring mothers / Kelly Oliver.
p. cm.
Includes bibliographical references and index.
ISBN 0-8476-9252-3 (cloth : alk. paper). — ISBN 0-8476-9253-1 (paper : alk. paper)
1. Feminist theory. 2. Feminist psychology. 3. Subjectivity. 4. Women—Identity. 5. Men—Identity. 6. Group identity. I. Title.
HQ1190.058 1998
305.42'01—dc21 98-35602
CIP

Printed in the United States of America

∞ ™ The paper used in this publication meets the minimum requirements of American National Standard for Information Sciences—Permanence of Paper for Printed Library Materials, ANSI Z39.48–1984.

For Russell Oliver,
(February 27, 1913–August 22, 1997),
my grandfather,
whose intellectual curiosity
and generosity
fostered my own need for philosophy

Contents

Acknowledgments

I would like to thank Maureen MacGrogan for her continued support of my projects and her encouragement on this one in particular.

Four of the chapters in this book have been previously published in journals, and I would like to thank *diacritics, a review of contemporary criticism, Journal of Value Inquiry,* and *Praxis International* for giving me permission to reprint those articles here: a version of chapter 2 appeared in *diacritics* 27, no. 1 (Spring 1997): 45–58; a version of chapter 4 appeared in *diacritics* Summer 1991: 43–63 as "The Crisis in the Paternal Function"; a version of chapter 6 appeared in *Journal of Value Inquiry* 29, no. 4 (December 1995): 521–32; and a version of chapter 7 appeared in *Praxis International* 11, no. 1 (April–July 1991): 178–94.

Introduction

In the 1990s, debates in feminist theory have often centered around the advantages and disadvantages of "postmodern" theory for feminism. With various caveats and qualifications, feminists end up taking sides, for or against postmodern theory. The most contentious issue is the politics of identity linked to the so-called deconstruction of the subject central to the work of theorists such as Foucault, Deleuze, and Derrida, among other mostly French philosophers and their followers. On the one hand, these theorists in various ways have shown that the modern subject is the illusory creation of conservative forces, an idea shared by many feminists concerned that the ideal of an autonomous self-determined subject as a male subject serves patriarchy. On the other hand, at points it seems that these theorists undermine not only the modern subject but also any center of agency or identity, including identities used by progressive movements such as the women's movement and the civil rights movement to call for political change. So, it seems that while challenging the notions of subject and identity that support the status quo, postmodern theory also undercuts the possibility of an alternative subject or identity that might change the status quo.

In fact, the problem has been articulated as one of agency. If there is no unified subject, then who is the agent of political action or change? Without the subject how can we have agency? And without agency, how can we take action? More than this, even if we can take action, how can we come together as groups in order to make a difference without identity politics? How can we fight the status quo in the name of something other if any appeal to a name is illegitimate or conservative? These are the questions that force feminists to choose sides, for or against identity politics. Rather than choose sides, however, perhaps we need to explore the dynamics of identity. After all, it seems premature to accept or reject identity politics until we understand how identity works and what is at stake in the politics of identity.

In this book I come at the problem of identity from various angles, always with an eye to avoiding those extreme notions of identity that force choosing one over the other. I mean this in two senses: accepting or rejecting identity politics and choosing oneself over another (or vice versa). As an alternative to theories that fix the subject or identity in ways that perpetuate conservative agendas to maintain the status quo, I suggest dynamic notions of subjectivity that neither sacrifice the ability to act nor reinscribe an oppressive identity, that neither sacrifice oneself nor others.

My concern throughout this book is to theorize identity and subjectivity as open to otherness rather than closed off from it. Identity and subjectivity become oppressive when they close themselves off from others. Traditional theories of the metaphysical or autonomous subject are not the only theories to close subjectivity off from others. Current theories of identity based on abjection or exclusoin of otherness also can work to normalize discrimination and oppression. By analyzing the repressed others of contemporary notions of paternity and maternity, especially the othered body, and by suggesting alternative ways to conceive of self-other relations and the subjective identity at stake in them, I hope to begin to develop a theory of subjectivity as openness to others.

By thinking of subjectivity as fluid, I hope to navigate between two extremes that plague contemporary attempts to theorize difference: at one pole, the position that I can understand anyone just by taking up their perspective, which makes communication unencumbered; and at the other pole, the position that I can understand no one because of radical alterity that prevents me from taking up their perspective, which makes communication impossible. The first assumes that we are absolutely identical, which erases our differences, and the second assumes that we are absolutely different, which erases our communion. Both presume a certain solidity of the subject. Both work with an oppositional notion of identity and difference. And, both seem to presume that communication requires recognition.

The Hegelian legacy of recognition as a struggle to overcome otherness is still with us. Throughout this book I explore the usefulness and limitations of the notion of recognition and its flip side, abjection, in developing a theory of identity that opens the subject to otherness or difference. Most notions of recognition presuppose that what is recognized is something familiar or identical. For this reason, theories of recognition usually fall short in accounting for compassionate relations with difference. Here, I suggest moving from a notion of recognition to a notion of witnessing in order to theorize relations with difference and otherness that are neither hostile nor assimilating but rather loving or welcoming. While certain notions of recognition require that the subject see something in the other and acknowledge it, certain notions of witnessing require acknowledging something that cannot be seen, witnessing to the impossibility of recognition.

The book has three sections: Abject Fathers, Desiring Mothers, and Subjects without Subjectivity. In general, the three chapters in the first section, in various contexts—continental theory, popular culture, and film—diagnose representations and theories of male identity and masculinity as controlled, disciplined, and authoritarian as the flip side of an abjected male body. In general, the three chapters in the second section, in various contexts—continental theory, law, popular culture, and film—diagnose representations and theories of female identity and femininity as out of control, undisciplined, and without law as the flip side of a repressed maternal authority that founds personal identity. In general, the four chapters in the third section, in various contexts—continental theory, science, and film—attempt to reinscribe subjectivity otherwise than the subject-object, self-other, mind-body, masculine-feminine, paternal-maternal dualisms that continue to haunt contemporary theories.

Each section ends with a chapter on film that is intended not only to exemplify the theories discussed in earlier chapters but also—especially the last chapter on Varda's *Vagabond*—to challenge and expand the theoretical discussions of identity and otherness. My hope is that the discussion of films will make the theories more concrete and accessible, especially in a classroom situation where it often helps to show films or give other types of audiovisual embodiments of complex theoretical notions.

Abject Fathers

In the first chapter, "The Morality of American Manhood, Responsibility, and Virility," I diagnose recent calls for a return to paternal responsibility at the Million Man March in 1995 and the Stand in the Gap Promise Keepers rally in 1997. I analyze the ways in which paternal responsibility is linked to virility—"real men are responsible men"—and virility is an issue of control, an issue that is complicated by race. I show how the Promise Keepers trade individual identity and responsibility for group identity and absolution of responsibility. I argue that the movement is motivated by an attempt to reclaim patriarchal authority and that its moral convictions are merely justifications for that attempt. I suggest that, although on the surface much of the rhetoric is the same in the Million Man March and Nation of Islam and the Promise Keepers movements, the effects and contexts of that rhetoric are radically different. Whereas the Million Man March attempts to combat stereotypes of black men as irresponsible with positive images of responsibility, the Stand in the Gap rally attempts to absolve white men of their responsibility for social problems, especially sexism and racism.

The second chapter, "Fatherhood and the Promise of Ethics," examines the link between God and paternity in the work of Ricoeur, Levinas, and Derrida. I present the work of these three French theorists in a dialectical relation in which Ricoeur maintains that the father is a universal symbol, Levinas insists that the father is singular and unique, and Derrida suggests that the father operates between the universal and singular, which is the paradox of ethics. I argue that all three of these theorists leave us with a notion of paternal authority that, like the men's movements discussed in chapter 1, work to reinforce patriarchy against recent challenges from the women's movement and feminists.

In chapter 3, "Abjection in Fassbinder's *Despair* and Polanski's *The Tenant*," I use Kristeva's theory of abjection to diagnose the main characters in each film. I argue that both main characters, Herman in *Despair* and Trelkovsky in *The Tenant*, suffer from delusional self-fragmentation as a result of their struggle with otherness. Caught in a Hegelian master-slave fight to the death, each character kills either the other or himself. In both films, the force of otherness is located in the body, particularly the female body, which is used as a screen to filter the abject male body. In a general sense, all three chapters in this section analyze ways in which the female body is abjected and then either erased or disciplined by various patriarchal notions of masculinity and paternity.

Desiring Mothers

In chapter 4, "Kristeva's Imaginary Father as a Screen for the Desiring Mother," I read *against the grain* Kristeva's notion of the imaginary father from *Tales of Love.* Although on the surface Kristeva presents the imaginary father as an alternative to Lacan's father of law and threats in order to reinscribe the authority of the paternal function, I use her texts to develop my hypothesis that behind the screen of paternal authority is the maternal body with its own outlaw authority. Narcissism as Kristeva describes it in *Tales of Love* can be read as a process of moving deeper within the maternal body, from identifications with maternal breast to maternal sex to maternal womb and conception. Ultimately, the imaginary father represents the mother's love, which is possible only if she is a desiring subject who is not reduced to the maternal body. I argue that the mother's love is the necessary support for the abjection of the maternal body, which Kristeva sees as necessary for subjectivity.

In chapter 5, "Recognition, Witnessing, and Identity: Drucilla Cornell on Family Law," I use Cornell's analysis of the politics of adoption in order to problematize the relationship among recognition, witnessing, and identity. Cornell maintains that law must recognize "the equal protection of the imaginary domain in the name of citizen's equivalent chance to become a person, to interiorize and cohere the identifications that make us who we are into a self." Until law recognizes each one of us as equal citizens, Cornell concludes that feminists have an obligation to witness to the injustices of patriarchy by recognizing our differential positions in relation to its institutions. I argue that the type of recognition involved in the legal recognition of citizens is very different from that involved in the feminist witnessing Cornell describes. In fact, feminist witnessing demands the recognition of the impossibility of recognizing. For this reason, theories of witnessing may take us farther than theories of recognition in developing notions of identity that are not built on the exclusion of others. I extend my analysis of witnessing in the last chapter of the book, "Beyond Recognition: Witnessing the Other Otherwise in Varda's *Vagabond*."

In chapter 6, "Face to Face with the mOther: Alterity in Bergman's *Persona*," I once again use Kristeva's theory of abjection to diagnose the relationship between the two main characters in Bergman's film *Persona*. Like Fassbinder's Herman and Polanski's Trelkovsky, Bergman's two main characters, Elisabeth and Alma, are both involved in a violent struggle with the other over her own identity. Yet, in this film maternity works as the limit case to undermine the Hegelian master-slave scenario in which one or the other must be sacrificed. In the end, unlike Trelkovsky or Herman, Elisabeth and Alma work through their struggle and return to themselves stronger than before. In a general sense, all three chapters in this section analyze various ways in which maternity calls into question traditional theories of subjectivity.

Subjectivity without Subjects

In chapter 7, "Fractal Politics: How to Use the Subject," I address head-on the problem of political agency after the deconstruction of the subject. Focusing on Derrida's and Foucault's challenges to the metaphysical subject, I try to respond to this challenge without sacrificing political agency. I suggest that chaos physics might provide a model for thinking of effects and agency without subjects, subjectivity without subjects. The movement of fractal patterns is similar to the movement of social patterns analyzed by Foucault. Just as disciplinary structures can multiply and reproduce themselves on various levels in different institutions, so too can resistance strategies. Chaos physics provides a model of an open system that allows for the possibility of even structural change. Subjectivity is such an open system.

In chapter 8, "Between Soma and Psyche: Kristeva and the Crisis in Meaning," I analyze some of the advantages and disadvantages of Kristeva's attempts to develop a theory of open subjectivity. Kristeva's corpus brings the body back into theories of subjectivity, yet it falls short, especially in terms of the abject paternal body. Kristeva's attempt to bring the body back to theory by maintaining both that the structures of language are already operating in the material of the body and that all language contains a bodily semiotic element is successful in bridging the gap acutely felt in contemporary theory between the body and language, experience and language. Yet, Kristeva's notions of the imaginary father (read *with* rather than against the grain) and a unique discourse for each analysand undermine her attempts by reinscribing a gap between meaning and language.

In chapter 9, "Subjectivity without Subjects: Circulation from Vision to Visions, "I begin to rethink space and vision in order to rethink identity and subjectivity. The predominant models of identity and subjectivity based on recognition and abjection presuppose empty space traversed by vision. Vision is imaged as a distancing sense that both separates us from others and our world and bridges the gap between us and our world. By challenging this notion of space and this notion of vision, we can begin to imagine a nonviolent subjectivity and identification. Neo-Hegelian theorists from Lacan to Kristeva and Butler leave us with necessarily violent scenarios of identification based on exclusion. By analyzing the notions of vision and space presupposed by these theories, I open up the possibility of alternative accounts of identification that do not require exclusion and violence. I suggest a theory of identity that leaves open the possibility of love even as it explains the existence of violence.

In the last chapter, "Beyond Recognition: Witnessing the Other Otherwise in Varda's *Vagabond*," I extend my analysis from the previous chapters by once again applying theories of abjection and identity to Varda's film *Vagabond*. The result takes us beyond theories of identity based on recognition and abjection to a notion of identity as witnessing to the other. Once again taking up the relationship among recognition, witnessing, and identity, I try to move beyond current notions of identity and subjectivity to imagine a relationship with another that is not based on recognition or abjection, inclusion or exclusion, but rather on a relationship across difference—a relationship beholden to difference.

I

ABJECT FATHERS

1

The Morality of American Manhood, Responsibility, and Virility

Some time in the mid–twentieth century, fatherhood became almost synonymous with responsibility. As the economic structure of the industrial United States moved the workplace farther from home, men left their families in order to provide for them financially. As they became the breadwinners, men became responsible for family finances and ultimately the family itself, its material as well as moral and spiritual survival and growth. Middle-class women stayed at home to take care of the house, the children, and the needs of the breadwinner. Parental duties were defined by the geography of industrial capitalism and its inheritance, patriarchy.

Although the nuclear family with Mom at home and Dad at work was a postwar fantasy, it is a fantasy that dies hard. In spite of the facts that many children are raised by single parents, mostly moms, and even when there are two parents they usually both work outside the home, the fantasy of the nuclear family and paternal breadwinner is making a big comeback. For the last several years politicians have been harping on family values and the need to honor the family as the cure-all for social ills, now seen as evidence of moral decay caused by the fall of that short-lived nuclear family. Recent celebrations of paternal responsibility and authority continue to make headlines with the Million Man March in October 1995 and the Stand in the Gap Promise Keepers revival in October 1997.

Of course, for centuries fathers' duties have been described in terms of their natural authority in the family. These recent revivals are attempts to bring us back in time, a nostalgia for patriarchal authority. John Locke describes the father as the "master of the family," the *natural* ruler of the family "as the abler and the stronger" (1980, 44). Jean-Jacques Rousseau also defines the father as the natural authority in the family: "For several reasons derived from the nature of things, in the family it is the father who should command. . . . [A] husband should oversee his wife's conduct, for it is important to him to be assured that the children he is forced to recognize and nurture belong to no one but himself" (1987, 112).[1]

Hegel also maintains that although man's natural place is as leader in the family, he must enter the public social sphere, while woman's natural place is at home serving her man. In the *Philosophy of Right*, Hegel says that man has his "actual substantive life in the state" and woman has her "substantive destiny in the family" (1952, 114). Whereas men are capable of higher intellectual life, women inhabit a realm of feelings; "women correspond to plants because their development is more placid and the principle that underlies it is the rather vague unity of feeling" (263). Women are "educated" into this natural realm of feeling "who knows how?—as it were by breathing in ideas, by living rather than by acquiring knowledge. The status of manhood, on the other hand, is attained only by the stress of thought and much technical exertion" (264).

In the twentieth century, Sigmund Freud continues the argument that men are naturally more civilized than women who belong at home with the children:

> [W]omen soon come into opposition to civilization and display their retarding and restraining influence—those very women who, in the beginning, laid the foundations of civilization by the claims of their love. Women represent the interests of the family and sexual life. The work of civilization has become increasingly the business of men, it confronts them with ever more difficult tasks and compels them to carry out instinctual sublimations of which women are little capable. (1961, 50)

Like Locke, Rousseau, and Hegel before him, Freud identifies the father as the first authority, on which the authority of all subsequent government develops. "A Prince is known as the father of his country; the father is the oldest, first, and for children the only authority; and from his autocratic power the other social authorities have developed in the course of the history of human civilization" (1967, 251).

Movements such as the Million Man March and the Promise Keepers turn the focus back to fathers as authorities and leaders in the family; they propose that social change will take place only when each man changes his ways and becomes a responsible father and husband. They presume that reinstating paternal leadership and authority in the family will address social problems at their source, the torn moral fibers of the country, so that mending individual strand by strand will make the entire social fabric stronger. Although in both cases these groups gathered in Washington, D.C., to show their political force to the nation and its leaders, neither of them focused on social, institutional, or governmental responsibility or institutional change in favor of personal responsibility and individual change.

The focus on fathers as both natural authorities and individuals as the seat of change are part of the Calvinist evangelical religious heritage that has been a formative part of American conceptions of family. The Promise Keepers movement has been compared with the Great Awakening spirited by Jonathan Edwards, not just because it is a sweeping popular evangelical revival but also because it puts family at its center, the father at its head, and believes that social change will follow. Also, like Edwards's movement, the Promise Keepers praise a form of self-discipline in the name of Christ. Like Edwards's movement, they convert using emotional sermons against lustful passions that distract men from fulfilling their God-given duties and responsibilities. Although departing from Christianity, the Nation of Islam uses the same kind of techniques with an appeal to Allah rather than Christ.

From Jonathan Edwards to Ralph Waldo Emerson, American philosophy, profoundly Christian, even evangelist, was also deeply Platonic.[2] Edwards proposes two moralities, one natural, which is corrupted because of original sin and human pride, and the other divine, which rescues the natural through reason: "there is the most sweet harmony between Christianity and reason" (Edwards 1959, 286 f.). Although Emerson finds divine perfection in the natural, like Edwards, he too believes that Platonic reason and the balanced soul are possible for all men who must take it upon themselves to perfect their God-given faculties. The combination of the evangelical notion of the possibility of rebirth through Christ and the Platonic notion of the possibility of perfecting one's soul through the triumph of reason over passions gave birth to the American ideal of self-improvement.[3]

The possibility of self-improvement became heroically embodied in Abraham Lincoln and Frederick Douglass, who pulled themselves up by their bootstraps to become self-made men. Both Lincoln and Douglass saw passion as the downfall of democracy and freedom and reason as the hope for equality and unity. In his 1838 address to the Young Men's Lyceum, Lincoln warned that "passion has helped us, but can do no more. It will in future be our enemy. Reason, cold, calculating, unimpassioned reason must furnish all the materials for our future support and defense" (Lincoln 1953–1955, 115). Historian Daniel Walker Howe argues that "when Lincoln declared that America would stand or fall by *'the capability of a people to govern themselves,'* he meant this in both a political and a psychological sense" because he saw

America's greatest enemy as its own "undisciplined passion" (1997, 143, 142).

Frederick Douglass also saw undisciplined passions as the cause of slavery and discrimination: "The forces against us are passion and prejudice, which are transient, and those for us are principles, self-acting, self-sustaining, and permanent" (1994, 937). Douglass says that in slavery "reason is imprisoned here, and passions run wild" (1994, 493). This is why for Douglass, as for Lincoln, the triumph of reason over passions requires temperance, especially in relation to alcohol.[4] In his speech "Self-Made Men," Douglass addressed the subject of manhood itself. Although he did not use the contemporary rhetoric of *real men,* the suggestion is that real men have character built through self-discipline, temperance, and hard work. Real men make the best of themselves and are upstanding morally.

Echoing the nineteenth-century ideal of self-made men and self-improvement, the appeal to manhood and its nature were central elements of both the Million Man March and the Stand in the Gap rally. In both cases, men were called on to stand up and act like men. Both movements emphasize that real men are responsible men. Real men take responsibility, which brings with it paternal authority ordained by God, because real men are also godly men.

The supposition is that men have not been acting like men. By shirking their responsibilities, perhaps they have been acting like women. Certainly, in the case of the Promise Keepers that point has been made explicit when Promise Keepers' speakers claim that women have assumed the role rightly given by God to men, the role as leader and authority in the family. To stand up and be real men, men must reclaim their authority within the household by taking it back from their women. In "Seven Promises of a Promise Keeper," Tony Evans advises Promise Keepers to take back their authority by approaching their wives and saying, "Honey, I've made a terrible mistake. I've given you my role. I gave up leading the family, and I forced you to take my place. Now I must reclaim that role. . . . Give it back! God never meant for you to bear the load you are carrying."[5]

The Promise Keepers: From Sinners to Winners

The Promise Keepers promise to give us a "New Man," a postfeminist sensitive but manly man, modeled after a sensitive but manly God. Participants at rallies sport T-shirts saying "Real Men Love Jesus," "Real Men Pray," and "Jesus Is Life . . . The Rest Is Basketball." At rallies they are repeatedly asked to tell the man next to them things such as "God is a very secure guy." Speakers tell them that God holds out his hand and says, "Wanna be friends?" God is just one of the guys, and Jesus is like a big brother who will help you out as long as you surrender your life to him. But God is not a wimp or a sissy, and his followers should not be, either. Speakers at Promise Keepers' rallies incite the crowd to chant with them by calling them wimps and telling them to act like men. Different sections of the bleachers compete to see who can yell the loudest in the name of Jesus. In football stadiums across the country hundreds of thousands of men have gotten together to do cheers for Jesus. Their leaders have convinced them that they can be Christians and tough guys, that real men are godly men, and that true masculinity comes through surrender to God. "Promise Keepers are sinners in the hands of a loving, macho God who is eager to forgive them their transgressions, restore their manhood and fix their broken lives and families" (Spalding 1996, 260).[6]

This "gospel of guyhood" attempts to redefine manhood in the face of what sympathizers see as the bewildering state of contemporary men, caught between feminist demands for more sensitivity and old macho stereotypes. The Promise Keepers—with a magazine called *New Man*—try to bridge this gap by calling on men to reclaim their patriarchal authority but to do so tenderly. They must become "tender warriors" engaged in a "culture war" in which the enemy is presumably any progressive social movement.[7]

They call on men to fight the images of feminized men presented in the media and elsewhere by taking authority from women, "the weaker vessel" (Spalding 1996, 260). "Tony Evans, a popular Promise Keepers preacher . . . writes that America is losing its families because of feminized American males who have abdicated their roles as spiritually pure leaders, 'thus forcing women to fill the vacuum' " (Allen 1997, 10). But some conservatives think that the Promise Keepers themselves, "with all their hugging and crying," threaten to "feminize" American males. Hanna Rosin writes in the *New Republic* that "the real threat is that the Promise Keepers . . . represent the mass culmination of an embarrassing phenomenon: the feminization of the American right" (1997, 11).

Obviously, conservatives, most Promise Keepers among them, see femininity as the nation's greatest danger. They seem to think that "when men act like women and women act like men, the nation goes to hell." They reduce all social problems to this "mix-up" in gender roles: Men must lead and women must follow. The presumption is that women as heads of households have led the nation down the wrong path, so it is time for men to get us on the right track again. One Promise Keepers speaker, Steve Farrar, says that "when you take the major pressing issues that are facing us—violence, teen pregnancy, broken families—and reduce them to their lowest common denominator, you're going to find a lack of male leadership at the root" (Gilbreath 1995, 20). The presumption, then, is that female leadership has led to violence, teen pregnancy, and broken families.

The Morality of Patriarchy

Promise Keepers claim that the problems facing the nation are moral and not political. In their foundational literature, "Seven Promises of a Promise Keeper," evangelist Luis Palau says, "What else does society hold? Some 1.6 million elective abortions last year. More than a million out-of-wedlock births. Broken families. Brutal violence on the streets and in the media. Drug addiction. . . . The problem is in the heart, not just the outward behavior. . . . Political campaigns . . . do nothing about the inner condition of human depravity" (Allen 1997, 10). All social problems are reduced to matters of individual morality. Politics is erased in favor of something more personal and "real," relationships among godly men and a personal relationship to Christ.

But what is the politics of this Promise Keepers' morality? What kind of morality is based on the principle of manliness as paternal authority? It sounds like nothing more than a morality of patriarchy. It is not just that the Promise Keepers' morality is in keeping with patriarchal values; rather, the Promise Keepers' morality is meant to justify patriarchy. Their morality is meant to justify the hierarchical chain of paternal command. The morality they espouse is the morality of manhood and men's God-given right to rule. The "sins" that their leaders spend most of their time fighting in their war on culture are those that challenge patriarchy and its hierarchical paternal order, specifically abortion and homosexuality.

Certainly a woman's right to choose to have an abortion challenges male command. Paternal authority requires that men control their women and children. In the name of the so-called right to life, Promise Keepers want to take us back to an era when women and children were treated as the property of men. Men's manliness is at stake in their ability to control women and children, born and unborn. Some of the Promise Keepers' leaders go so far as to suggest that men should have the ultimate control over contraception; after all, their virility is at stake.

Homosexuality also challenges the hierarchical authority structure of patriarchy. Homosexuality leaves us without "one proper male leader" either by pairing two males and thereby subverting hierarchical leadership or by pairing two females and doing away with male leadership altogether. Of course, Promise Keepers believe that homosexuality is a sin like so many others that can be "cured" through faith. Any gay men who attend Promise Keepers meetings are under pressure to "convert" to heterosexuality/Christianity, which for the Promise Keepers amount to the same thing.[8]

Women's authority in the household also challenges patriarchical authority. Promise Keepers like to quote Ephesians 5:22: "as the church submits to Christ, so also wives should submit to their husbands" (New men for Jesus 1995, A21). Certainly women-headed households fly in the face of the morality of manhood. In this case, paternal authority has been usurped by women, and Promise Keepers seem especially nervous about maternal authority. Sometimes the movement seems like nothing more than an attempt to escape from maternal authority in order to resuscitate and incorporate paternal authority. Freud saw patricide as necessary to the formation of social order and authority, but it seems that matricide is the fundamental necessity for reinstating paternal authority in an era when women have taken steps to win their freedom and independence.

The threat of maternal authority, and the attempts to do away with it and replace it with paternal authority, are evident in Ed Cole's speech at Promise Keepers rallies. Described by one reporter as "General Patton addressing his troops," Cole incites the crowd to yelling contests by telling them that after he says, "When I became a man," they are to say, "I put away childish things." After the crowd's first attempt, Cole scolds them, "Not bad for wimps. Now let's try it like men!" Then he goes on to command the crowd: "Act more like a man! Act more like a man! Why? Because when a man acts like a child it forces his wife to act like his mother. And when a man forces his wife to act like his mother, she does two things for him. She makes decisions for him and she corrects him. Now there's a problem with that! When a MAN acts like a CHILD and forces his WIFE to become his MOTHER, the problem is—you can't make love to your MOTHER! . . . Turn to the guy next to you and say 'I think he's talkin ta you again' " (Spalding 1996, 260).

Even the incest taboo is explained in terms of asserting paternal authority. Real men do not have sex with their mothers because her authority undermines their own. Real men cannot have a woman making decisions for him or correcting him. Real men, it seems, have real problems with maternal authority. The very fact that they have mothers, that they were born out of women's bodies, seems to threaten their masculinity. While the prohibition against incest, championed by the Promise Keepers, is ultimately justified through their rhetoric of paternal authority, by the same logic, the phenomenon of incest (in most cases father-daughter incest) can be seen as an attempt to reinstate masculinity and virility—that is, paternal authority—in the face of some feminine or maternal threat to it. After all, sex is another of man's God-given rights through which he can exercise and maintain his place in his kingdom. Perhaps that is why Promise Keepers founder, ex-football coach Bill McCartney, defended two of his football players against charges of date rape by saying, "Rape by definition is a violent act and I don't think that's what we're talking about here" (Spalding 1996, 260). The presumption is that date rape, by definition, is not really rape. Perhaps, then, it is just men exercising their God-given authority over women—manly men proving their virility?

Feminists seem to be another moral enemy of Promise Keepers. At one Promise Keepers rally the entire stadium burst into chants of "Je-sus, Je-sus, Je-sus," shaking upraised fists at a plane flying overhead with banners that read "Only weak men are afraid of strong women" and "Promise Keepers, losers and weepers" (Gilbreath 1995, 20). Given their stands on abortion, male leadership, and gay rights, it is no wonder that they see feminists as one of their enemies. Not only do Promise Keepers refuse to allow women to participate in their events as anything other than volunteers handling food and concessions; they also refuse to allow women pastors to participate in their evangelical group meetings on every level (Swomley 1997, 8). They claim that they want to unite all Christian religious factions, with the exception, it seems, of those in which women have authority. In response to one of his feminist critics, Promise Keeper William Murchison derides feminists, saying, "as we know from experience, facts only infrequently intrude between gender feminists and the truth" (Murchison 1996, 5).

The Promise Keepers' rhetoric about *forcing* women to take men's roles reinstates masculine authority by asserting that even when they give up their authority it is through their own agency and no one else's. All choices are men's; they are the only agents. Yet, the Promise Keepers advocate reclaiming authority through gentle force; they are "tender warriors." They advocate a kinder, gentler patriarchy because it will be more effective. Their speakers are explicit about the efficacy of morality, telling men that they cannot maintain their leadership in the family if they abuse drugs and alcohol, cheat on their wives, or abuse their kids. These "sins" are morally wrong because they undermine a man's authority at home. His wife and kids will turn against him, and his family management will be ineffective. These "sins" make a man impotent, which is why real men, manly men, are sexually pure and temperate.

The New Manly Godly Man

The rhetoric of manhood and the sports and military images that dominate Promise Keepers events suggests that their version of paternal responsibility is wrapped up with virility. To be responsible is to be in control. One reporter who attended a Promise Keepers event writes:

> Watching the men at Oakland Coliseum stomp, cheer and celebrate their manhood I can't help thinking of the catchy title of Mariah B. Nelson's recent book about sports, and sexism, *The Stronger Women Get, the More Men Love Football.* Clearly, Promise Keepers represent a reaction to the progress of women. . . . I found it frustrating to listen to speaker after speaker blame men for their failure to act as the leaders "God equipped them to be." Why must a secure sense of manhood depend on men being in control? Isn't it possible that the notion that "men must run things" is in part to blame for the breakdown of marriages, families and the notion of what it means to be a man? (Spalding 1996, 260)

Promise Keepers meet in football stadiums and sports arenas because men feel more comfortable there than in church. They do not use any of the trappings of a conventional church. Instead they have former military men and sports figures, along with ministers, all wearing coaching jerseys, speak to the crowd. The men in the stadium behave in many of the same ways they do at sporting events: cheering; yelling; throwing Frisbees, footballs, and foam airplanes; listening to rock music; slapping each other; and giving high fives. Promise Keepers even use the scoreboard to indicate the number in attendance by putting up "Jesus: 48, 832, Satan: 0." Speakers, especially Promise Keepers founder, Coach Bill McCartney, continually use sports metaphors urging men to become winners by playing on God's team.[9]

More frequent, however, is the use of military metaphors to pump up the men in the stadium. Coach McCartney ends each rally by honoring pastors, saying, "Men, we're in a war! We need great leadership! We need a unity of command. We need all our leaders to come together with one heartbeat" (Spalding 1996). In a Promise Keepers video, the coach tells his followers, "Many of you feel like you have been in a war for a long time, yet the fiercest fighting is just ahead. God has brought us here to prepare us. Let's proceed. It's wartime" (Swomley 1997, 8). Speaking to over forty thousand pastors (no women allowed) in Atlanta's Georgia Dome on Pat Robertson's *700 Club,* when asked about the future of the Promise Keepers, the coach responded, "Psalm 2:8 says, 'Ask and I will give you the nation for your inheritance, the outermost parts of the Earth for your possession' " (Hoffer 1996).

Promise Keepers leaders see themselves as a "Godly army" preparing to "take back the nation for Christ" by force. One of Promise Keepers directors, Rev. James Ryle, told a reporter that "he regards Promise Keepers as the fulfillment of the Bible's prophecy of a great force that will destroy sinners and infidels in the period preceding Armageddon. Never before have 300,000 men come together throughout human history except for the purposes of war" (Conason 1996, 10). Promise Keepers cofounder Dave Wardell told the *Denver Post,* "We want our nation to return to God. We're drawing a line in the sand here" (Bellant 1995, 28).

What could be more macho than fighting a war, joining an army or a sports team? Promise Keepers' appeals to manhood and real men, their call to reclaim authority from women, their constant use of military and sports metaphors, their assemblies in sports arenas, their sporting wardrobes, all indicate that what is at stake is masculine virility. The Promise Keepers' notion of paternal responsibility is nothing more than the exercise of the virile subject's will to possess and control his environment.[10] As some reporters have noted, in an age when men are confused about what it means to be a man, the Promise Keepers provide a strong image of manhood tied to responsibility as control or leadership and virile images of sports and war—patriarchy as the answer to male bewilderment.[11]

Accountability as Following Orders

Perhaps even more striking than the Promise Keepers' military metaphors and ideas of taking over the nation and possessing the earth are their use of a military chain of command and their perverse notion of individual responsibility as submission to that command. After they leave the stadium, Promise Keepers are asked to organize accountability groups at the local level. These groups of a few men each have a "key man" who reports to the next in command in the Promise Keepers hierarchy. One Promise Keepers spokesman, Chuck Stecker, says:

> I believe with all of my heart that the military structure that we know and love so well is perfect for the accountable relationship which God is calling us to in Promise Keepers. That same structure, whether it be at the squad level for the army right up or whether it be at the detachment level, squadron level, and so forth, is exactly what we need. I believe that accountable relationships build readiness. Quite frankly, having served in a Ranger battalion, if a squad leader did not know where his soldiers were, his Rangers, he was not doing his job. And in order to be able to know those things he had to be in accountable relationships with them in order to develop that. (Swomely 1997, 8)

Promise Keepers' key men, then, are like squad leaders setting up accountability structures in order to prepare troops for battle. Each individual Promise Keeper is accountable to the group and to his squad leader. In turn, each squad leader, or key man, is accountable to his superior, an "ambassador" who reports to headquarters in Colorado. Promise Keepers work through local churches, and Coach McCartney claims that they plan to "go into every church whether they like us or not" (Swomely 1997, 8). McCartney calls the clergy the "commissioned officers" in the Promise Keepers' army.

Just what do Promise Keepers mean by *accountability*? Accountability groups are designed to keep men on the straight and narrow by asking them to confess to other group members who will "help" them mend their ways. The national coordinator for local leaders and cofounder Dave Wardell explains how the system works: "I can go home and maybe still be the same guy after the conference. But if I have another guy calling up, holding me accountable, asking 'How are you treating your wife? Are you still cheating on your income taxes? Are you looking at your secretaries with lust?' it makes a difference. I don't think a woman would get in my face, toe to toe with a guy, whereas a guy could tell me, 'I don't like it. And if you don't listen to me, I'll punch your lights out' " (Bellant 1995, 28). Men are held accountable to follow orders from their superiors. Accountability means submission to the chain of command.

Promise Keepers' notion of responsibility is similarly paradoxical. Combining evangelical and military techniques (which history teaches us have often amounted to the same thing), Promise Keepers begin by using personal responsibility against men, telling them that they are to blame for society's problems because they are worthless sinners. Like the boot camp sargeant who belittles his privates into humble submission so that he can build them up again from the bottom up, Promise Keepers break down men so that they can build them up again in the service of God's army. The first step is to make men feel bad about themselves, who they are, and what they have done. The next step is to offer to take away their pain and problems if they only submit to the group and its leaders.

First, attendees at Promise Keepers events are held personally responsible, and then they are absolved of their responsibility. By submitting to the organization's hierarchical authority structure, they go from sinners to winners. One reporter describes that process:

> The Promise Keepers are men schooled in the mega church movement—that watered down, gushy religion now sweeping America. Mega church preaching works on the same principles as the recovery movement: it fa-

> vors public, mechanized confessions of sin, and a good cop, bad cop routine, by which you are chastised for your inadequacy and then comforted by a therapeutic God. (Rosin 1997, 11).

The rallies are themselves exercises in crowd control since speakers continually command attendees to stand up, to sit down, to repeat prayers or chants, to turn to their neighbors and chastise them or hug them. The leaders issue orders and the members follow them.

Surrending personal autonomy and freedom are consistent with both the sports team and military models employed by Promise Keepers. Teamwork requires that every individual work for the good of the team. And the military will work only if each individual surrenders to the chain of command. Ultimately, then, the call for personal responsibility and accountability is rhetoric used to make members obedient to orders from their higher-ups. The leaders of the group claim to report to the commander in chief, God himself, whose absolute authority justifies their own. In the end, the Promise Keepers movement is a theocracy that undermines notions of responsibility and accountability consistent with democratic values.

After personal responsibility has been used to break down members by blaming them for social problems (always referred to as personal sins) in step 1 of the process, in step 2 members are absolved of all responsibility for social problems. One Promise Keepers speaker, Jeffrey Johnson, absolves attendees at the rally by saying, "That bitterness you find on your job: you didn't make it bitter; it was bitter when you got there. That bitterness in your community: you didn't make it bitter; it was bitter when you got there. . . . The racism in this world: we didn't make it racist; it was racist when we got here. The sexism in the world: we didn't make it sexist: it was sexist when we got here" (Hetherly 1997, 14). The reward for giving themselves over to God is that they no longer have to take responsibility for social problems, especially those problems from which they benefit most as white men, racism and sexism.

Racial Reconciliation

The sixth promise of a Promise Keeper is "to demonstrate biblical unity by reaching across racial and demoninational lines." At rallies, attendees are remonstrated for committing the "sin" of racism. They are asked to find a man of color in the stadium and hug him, asking for his forgiveness. The vast majority of men who attend rallies are white, so at this moment the few men of color in the audience are surrounded by white men eager to ask their forgiveness. True to their models of sports and the military, Promise Keepers preach racial "reconciliation." Traditionally, sports and the military have been two places where men of color have opportunities comparable to white men. Both of these institutions rely on men working together across racial differences to win. Promise Keepers founder Coach McCartney made racial reconciliation part of his agenda because his football training taught him that he needs unity to win.

If men are to reclaim their patriarchal power, then all men need to unite in the culture war against homosexuals, feminists, and ultimately all women. "Power in America has traditionally been accorded to straight, white, Christian men. . . . Every time the demand arises that the people who hold power and privilege in society share it, those in power make an effort to redefine who 'we' are as opposed to 'them.' What happened here [in the case of the Promise Keepers] is that the boys' club has expanded to include people of color. When push comes to shove, what's more important, race or gender?" (Hoffer 1996). Or, perhaps we should ask, which is more threatening to patriarchal authority, race or gender?

Racial reconciliation appears to be the Promise Keepers' most progressive aspiration. But, what do they mean by *reconciliation?* Examining what they call their "next frontier in reconciliation" is telling. In its July 1997 newsletter, Promise Keepers writers report on a meeting of Messianic Jewish leaders that it sponsored in Atlanta. According to the newsletter, converting Jews to Christianity is the "next frontier in reconciliation" (Swomley 1997, 8). It becomes obvious that reconciliation does not mean embracing differences; rather, it means assimilation. Promise Keepers, however, are clear that when talking about racial reconciliation they do not mean integration. Promise Keepers president Randy Phillips told the Colorado Springs *Gazette Telegraph* that "the goal is not integration . . . the goal is reconciliation through relationships" (Hetherly 1997, 14). Attendees at rallies are told to pledge to enter into a relationship with a man of another race. It is the "some of my best friends are Negros" approach to racism.

Joe Conason diagnoses the choice of the word *reconciliation*:

> Promise Keepers has deliberately chosen the word "reconciliation" as its rhetorical focus on race rather than the word, "equality." The warm and fuzzy rhetoric of "reconciliation" conceals some subtexts: The notion that only changes in peoples hearts will make a difference is a means of avoiding demands for jobs, community self-determination, freedom from police and criminal violence, and access to housing and educational opportunity. Were the economic program of the conservative backers of this organization—as exemplified by the agenda of the Republican freshmen—ever to be put into practice, the social and economic infrastructure

> of communities of color would be eliminated. This is fundamental to understanding the essentially regressive racial politics that underlie Promise Keepers' carefully coiffed image. (1996, 10)

Many of the Promise Keepers' critics have pointed out that hugs will not stop racism. In the words of Mandy Carter, field representative for the National Black Lesbian and Gay Leadership Forum, "We are concerned that Promise Keepers call for racial harmony but do not speak to its 96 percent white membership about the racial advantage that whiteness gives them in this society. Institutional racism is not healed by hugs" (Swomley 1997, 8). It is also dubious that hugs and pledging to enter into a relationship with a man of another race will actually change hearts.

Like so much else about the Promise Keepers, their 1997 march on Washington is regarded by some of their membership and sympathizers as their *competitive* response to the Million Man March two years before. One Promise Keeper reports that "in 1995 . . . Promise Keepers drew 700,000 men to stadiums in 13 different cities; which was either more or fewer, depending on whose statistics you believe, than Louis Farrakhan attracted to Washington D.C. for the Million Man March. In 1997 the statistical comparison with Farrakhan takes on real relevance. Promise Keepers plans in Washington a prayer and worship event. The anticipated attendance: 1 million" (Murchison 1996, 5; see also Van Brema 1995, 62). Contrary to the Promise Keepers' rhetoric of reconciliation, this view certainly paints a picture in black and white.

The Million Man March and the Nation of Islam: Rescuing the Black Man

Although the Promise Keepers' Stand in the Gap rally was a mostly white event and the Million Man March was a mostly black event, on the surface they have more in common than their location. Two years before men attending the Stand in the Gap rally made their seven promises, participants at the Million Man March took a pledge to be more responsible fathers and husbands. Hugh Price, president of the National Urban League, called the march "the largest family-values rally in the history of America" (Lacayo 1995, 32). Like the Promise Keepers, the organizers of the march, Nation of Islam leader Louis Farrakhan and former National Association for the Advancement of Colored People secretary Benjamin Chavis, asked women to stay at home and watch their children and pray while their men attended the march. According to its organizers, the purpose of the march was for African-American men to "atone for their sins." And, like the Promise Keepers, speakers concentrated on personal responsibility rather than institutional responsibility or social reform. One reporter describes the agenda:

> Farrakhan's call included a demand for "atonement" that African-Americans should recognize "wrongs done and make amends," and apologize for all offenses "against the Creator." The march agenda spoke relatively little about contemporary public policy issues, such as affirmative action, immigration and welfare reform. Instead, it emphasized the need for blacks to assume "personal responsibility" for their own circumstances, and challenged African-American males to provide leadership for their families and communities. (Manning 1995, 14–17)

Real Men Are Not Stereotypes

Like the Promise Keepers' event, the march has been criticized because it excluded women and promoted patriarchal visions of men, women, and families. Part of the pledge taken at the march was "I pledge from this day forward I will never abuse my wife by striking her or disrespecting her, for she is the mother of my children and the producer of my future." With the rhetoric, women are reduced to mothers and producers of men's futures—he must respect her for the sake of *his* children and *his* future. But, the real purpose of the march was not so much to reinforce patriarchy as to combat stereotypes of black men with more positive images of black men making commitments to families and self-improvement. Like the Promise Keepers' rally, the Million Man March included rhetoric of *real men* and *manliness*. One marcher says that "we have marched to tell ourselves and the nation that we want to be real men. Real men don't attack their loved ones. Real men don't shirk their duties" (Dyson 1995, 1100). More than this, we might say that real men are not stereotypes. Even Minister Farrakhan said the purpose of the march was to show the nation and black people a different image of black men.

Although the exclusion of women from the Million Man March seems suspect to most feminists, many commentators have justified the men-only march by pointing out that the stereotypes of black men as violent, dangerous, and irresponsible need to be expelled. The men who gathered for the Million Man March were not so much trying to create a New Man as combat an old image of black men by showing the country and each other that there are different types of black men. Clarence Page put it this way: "Since black men, particularly young black males, are the most feared and loathed creatures on urban streets today, we need self-esteem more than most" (Fineman 1995a, 32).

With one in three black men in their twenties in jail, paroled, or on probation (primarily a result of racism in the legal system, especially among police), black men need to affirm that they can in fact take responsibility for their own destinies, that they are not criminals (The Farrakhan distraction 1995, 36). Jesse Jackson points out that black men "are projected as less intelligent than we are, less hardworking than we work, less universal than we are, less patriotic than we are and more violent than we are. Indeed, the courteous and celebratory mood of the crowd [at the march] was a direct rebuke to the white Washingtonians who stayed away from their workday routines in fear" (Outmarching the hatred 1995, 521). As one reporter noted, "the emotional heart of the march, it seemed to me, was not atonement but affirmation: look at us, and look at our sons. We are not your stereotype" (Klein 1995, 48).

The media response to the Million Man March, especially when compared with their response to the Promise Keepers Stand in the Gap rally, indicates that combating stereotypes and media racism is an uphill struggle. It is striking how critical the media are of the Million Man March and how forgiving they are of the Promise Keepers. Most of the conservative and liberal press alike saw the Stand in the Gap rally as a group of harmless men promising to be better fathers and husbands (What is wrong with that? they asked), whereas most of the press criticized the Million Man March. Conservatives jumped all over Farrakhan and his anti-Semitism, homophobia, and separatism, but they praised the Promise Keepers in spite of the fact that its leaders are also anti-Semitic and openly homophobic. Liberals, many of whom do make the same arguments against the Promise Keepers, criticized the march for being sexist and not addressing institutional racism.

One conservative went so far as insisting that "we must now call a spade a spade" by focusing on all the advances made by blacks instead of their hardships; he suggested that blacks should quit whining, that they do not "recognize what they have achieved," and that this attitude shows a "lack of gratitude" that fuels white resentment—as if blacks should be grateful to whites for having civil rights (Patterson 1995, 24)![12] Others called Farrakhan a "wicked man"; insisted that you cannot separate the message from the messenger, so to focus on the positive aspects of the march or Farrakhan's role in it is like saying that "Hitler was nice to pets"; and called his speech "mumbo jumbo will hoodoo you" (Wieseltier 1995, 56; Alter 1995, 44; An elegy for integration 1995, 108). Yet, these same magazines praise the Promise Keepers' leaders and ignore the outrageous and inflammatory things they have said. What I would call the angry white men who make up the Promise Keepers' clientele (paying $50 to $80 to attend their rallies) are seen by the media as harmless boys promising to be good, while the demand for recognition from black men who have been rendered invisible by racism is seen by the media as threatening and corrupted by the philosophy of Louis Farrakhan.

Million Man Responsibility and Promise Keepers' Accountability

I agree with liberal critics who point out that the rhetoric of taking paternal responsibility and wanting to be *real men* does not address the racism that leaves so many African Americans in poverty. Racism, social and economic inequality, inequalities in education, and discrimination in every sector of society are all erased by the rhetoric of personal responsibility. The problems of inner-city violence and drugs that are attributed to the fact that black women are the heads of households and fathers are missing are not the result of personal irresponsibility. In this case, reducing social problems to personal responsibility blames those who suffer from racism for the symptoms of a racist society.

Like the Promise Keepers' call for paternal responsibility, this invocation of paternal responsibility as paternal authority seems to be another call for reinstating patriarchy and virile subjectivity, with one important difference: historically black men in America have not been the patriarchs; they cannot *re*claim their paternal authority because historically it has not been fully theirs. Moreover, as many commentators have noted, the Million Man March was less about the patriarchal values espoused by its organizers and more about creating hope and an affirmation of black men.

The Promise Keepers' movement, on the other hand, is *primarily* motivated by aspirations to restore a crumbling patriarchy and reclaim paternal authority; it is more than anything a reaction to the gains made by women toward achieving their own self-sufficiency and freedom. The "demonic" culture that threatens the Promise Keepers are those elements in American culture that challenge patriarchal authority. Although the Nation of Islam, like most religious movements, is also patriarchal, it is not moved by merely patriarchal motivations; and, in spite of the ban on women at the Million Man March, it is not just a reaction to gains made by women. Aside from the Million Man March, women are usually involved in the Nation's activities, if not its leaders. And, the primary motivation of the Nation of Islam seems to be empowering black Americans and improving their social and economic conditions.

The call for responsibility at the Million Man March operates differently than the call for responsibility by the Promise Keepers. As I argued earlier, the Promise Keepers' call for responsibility ultimately collapses into their need to absolve themselves of responsibility, especially for social problems. The Promise Keepers ignore the fact that their ancestors were responsible for sexism and racism and that they are the beneficiaries of that legacy. Personal responsibility is merely part of the rhetoric that motivates surrender to the hierarchy and God and the absolution of all responsibility. Responsibility is then replaced with accountability, which operates not through self-control but the control of the group and group leaders over group members by threatening to "punch their lights out."

The call for responsibility at the Million Man March is a response to a history that denies black men responsibility. Their ancestors were slaves who were not even regarded as human let alone persons or citizens. As such they were treated like animals who were incapable of responsibility or self-government. Although black men today do have rights as persons and citizens, they are still believed to be irresponsible, now in a moral rather than metaphysical sense. The march was an attempt to combat stereotypes of the irresponsible black man by presenting a positive image of black men taking responsibility and making commitments. More than this, the sense of solidarity that resulted from the march helped give black men a sense that they are agents of their own destiny, that they are responsible not only in a moral sense but also in a metaphysical sense. And, out of the affirmation of their responsibility, their agency—so long denied in American history—hope was born.

While black men are struggling for an empowering sense of subjectivity and agency, white men who turn to the Promise Keepers are suffering from threats to the power that they have too long enjoyed. For this reason, it is radically different for black men to claim responsibility than it is for privileged white men to hold each other accountable for the sake of maintaining their power. Some of the rhetoric may be the same, but its effects and contexts are significantly different.

Purification Techniques for an Abjected Body

On the surface, however, there are resonances between the values espoused by the Nation of Islam and its leaders and those espoused by the Promise Keepers and their leaders. For example, the battleground for the Nation of Islam, like the Promise Keepers, is the nation. Just as Promise Keepers' leaders look forward to the day when their army takes back the nation for Christ, the Nation of Islam looks forward to the day when it receives the nation from Allah. Both movements focus on family values and devotion to God. Although both movements have their roots in American religious evangelism and traditions of self-improvement, their relations to the axis of power in America are radically different, their historical trajectories are radically different, and therefore the politics of their moralities are also different in some important ways.

The Nation of Islam has its roots in two Depression-era movements, the Moorish Science Temple led by Noble Drew Ali and the Universal Negro Improvement Association led by Marcus Garvey. Both of these movements were responses to the poverty of black Americans who had moved north after the abolition of slavery only to find more hardship and despair. Noble Drew Ali's message that "Christianity is for the European (paleface); Moslemism is for the Asiatic (olive-skinned). When each group has its own peculiar religion, there will be peace on earth" prefigures the Nation of Islam's move toward a new nationality and the connection between nationality and religion (Lee 1996, 20). Like the Nation of Islam after it, the Moorish Science Temple maintained that white rule will end by divine intervention. The Universal Negro Improvement Association, on the other hand, was a back-to-Africa movement that stressed black independence through self-sufficiency (Lee 1996, 21). The Nation of Islam has continued significant economic relations with Africa and the emphasis on self-sufficiency.[13]

The original beliefs of the Nation of Islam as put forth by its founders, Wallace Fard (seen as Allah on earth) and Elijah Poole (who became Elijah Muhammad, Allah's messenger), include the beliefs that blacks are the chosen people; whites are devils who will be punished for their wicked ways, especially their enslavement and persecution of blacks; blacks must become aware of their chosen status before the fall of white America will take place; and blacks must cleanse themselves both externally and internally by following a strict diet and refraining from smoking, drinking, abusing drugs, gambling, and committing adultery (Lee 1996, 30). Elijah Muhammad predicted that the fall of America would occur in the 1960s, but when it did not happen, the Nation of Islam's focus started to move away from its millenarian doctrine and toward the doctrine of self-improvement. In 1969 Minister Louis Farrakhan (who was already becoming one of the Nation's most important spokesmen) told the *New York Times* that the purpose of the Nation of Islam was "to give the black pride in himself and love for himself as the first stage. The second is that he should start to build for himself—we are in the second stage now" (Lee 1996, 48).

Although the Nation of Islam rejects Christianity as white religion and embraces Muslimism as the religion of people of color, in some ways its movement is more akin to eighteenth- and nineteenth-century American evangelical Christian movements than the Promise Keepers movement. The Nation of Islam, like most evangelical movements, defines its fight in terms of good and evil and preaches purity and temperance. Although purity and temperance are heuristic strategies for becoming self-sufficient, they are also virtues in themselves. More than this, for the founders of the Nation of Islam, self-improvement comes only through strict self-discipline and an ascetic lifestyle. Evil works through weak bodies that give rise to weak morals. Elijah Muhammad explained the evil behavior of whites using the myth of Yakub, who did genetic experiments to transform the black population into whites; the result was that "as they [grew] lighter and lighter they grew weaker and weaker. Their blood became weak, their bones became weak, their minds became weaker, their morals became weaker" (Lee 1996, 29). The moral of this myth is that weak bodies make for weak souls. Members of the Nation of Islam avoid evil, particularly the wickedness of white decadence, by purifying their bodies. Like eighteenth- and nineteenth-century evangelical movements, the Nation takes the Neoplatonic view that one purifies the soul by disciplining the body.

Although, like other evangelical movements, the Promise Keepers promise self-improvement, followers do not advocate strict self-discipline; rather, they employ a hierarchy of discipline that works through members' self-confessions (accountability) and the "punch your lights out" threats from key men. Even while Promise Keepers preach purity and define their fight in terms of good and evil, they see themselves primarily engaged in a "culture war" over appropriate or godly notions of manhood and leadership and not a battle against bodily corruption. Moreover, their ideals of moral purity are not set out in terms of prohibitions but vague goals of paternal responsibility and racial and religious unity. Although Promise Keepers are supposed to feel remorse and ashamed for their sins, they are not engaged in the same kind of battle against the temptations of the flesh as the Nation of Islam or the eighteenth- and nineteenth-century evangelical movements. Also, although those sins are the work of Satan and the forces of evil, that evil does not work through a weak body that gives rise to a weak morality but through a demonic culture that preys on men's lack of confidence and authority.

Why is the body so absent in the Promise Keepers movement and so central in the Nation of Islam? First, while the black body, especially the black male body, has been abjected and vilified in our culture, the white body, specifically the white male body, does not exist. Whereas black male bodies are displayed in various ways, both defiled objects and sources of violence and feminized objects of beauty, white male bodies rarely show up anywhere except sports or medical discourses.[14]

Even the sacrificed body of Christ is absent from Promise Keepers gatherings—a crucifix is never seen at a Promise Keepers rally.

It is not surprising that bodies are absent from Promise Keepers' discourse since it is precisely the connection between the white male body and power that they try to deny. Paternal authority comes from God and not from the physical world; white men's authority is not bodily. If they admit that their power is based in the white male body, then the challenges levied by the women's movement and civil rights movement hit home. But, by ignoring and denying the body, white men ignore and deny that they are the beneficiaries of sexism and racism; they deny their responsibility. They want the power and authority historically covertly assigned to the white male body without taking responsibility for it. The Promise Keepers movement itself can be seen as an attempt to compensate for the ways in which progressive movements have exposed the abject white male body.

On the other hand, it is not surprising that bodies are central to the Nation of Islam. The focus on strict control over the body is, as I argued earlier, a traditional American evangelical ideal. But more than this, the body of the black male in particular is itself contested territory. Historically, in the slave trade black men and women suffered physical torture, abuse, and murder. Black men were the victims of lynching as a result of the perceived threat of the black male body. Today although slavery and lynching are illegal, black men are still threatened with physical abuse and murder: black men make up the largest group of victims of violent crime; black men have a higher unemployment rate and get paid less than white men; black men make up 74 percent of drug-related prison sentences even though they make up only 13 percent of America's drug users; one out of three black men in their twenties is in jail, paroled, or on probation; the death rate from heart disease, among others illnesses, is higher for black men than white men.[15] The statistics go on and on. As Spike Lee suggests in his film *Get on the Bus,* black men are an endangered species.

So, the struggle is one for survival, literally. The Million Man March was a response to the real physical threats to black men that confront them on many fronts. Rather than see themselves as victims, they stood up for their responsibility and self-government. With the Million Man March they tried to counterbalance the abjected black male body imagined by American culture and portrayed in the media. The Nation of Islam's prescriptions of strict discipline for the body also can be seen as responses to the abjected black body. These disciplinary techniques are not only survival mechanisms (to prevent drug abuse, alcoholism, and physical violence against each other) but also rituals through which to purify bodies that have been abjected by racist American culture.

2

Fatherhood and the Promise of Ethics

In *On the Genealogy of Morals,* Nietzsche describes Judeo-Christian morality as a result of the resentment of the weak who affirm themselves only by hating others: "slave morality from the outset says No to what is 'outside,' what is 'different,' what is 'not itself" (1967, 36). God in all his forms and the pious adherence to religion, philosophy, or science are the creation of weak wills who need something transcendent in order to justify and redeem earthly life. The master morality, on the other hand, is not so much the affirmation of difference or an embrace of others as a noble indifference to what is outside, different, not itself.

At the turn of the nineteenth century, Nietzsche mourned the death of God as the end of security and a stable horizon, but he also celebrated the death of God as the beginning of the power of man and the value of earthly life. At the turn of the twentieth century, our earthly life is in fact threatened by the power of man to destroy as well as create life. As man harnesses the power of the earth he can both destroy the world and all of its inhabitants and create and populate the world with designer life forms. Technological advances make the slave morality's "no" to what is not itself into the threat of the literal annihilation of entire civilizations. So, at the turn of the twentieth-century ethics takes us face to face with the other. Noble indifference is no longer possible. Looking for an ethics of what is outside, different, not ourselves, we insist on the piety of the other, or at least the divinity or wonder of the encounter with an other. We try to imagine piety without pity.[1] God, dead as the source of truth, beauty, and knowledge—dead as the One—has been resurrected as the wholly other—reborn as ultimate difference.

Here, I want to look at three tales of ethics that return to God in order to attempt to overcome the slave morality's need to annihilate difference. In each of these three texts ethics is framed by father-son relationships, most strikingly the relationship between God and Christ and the relationship between God and Abraham. Ethics and fatherhood are wed in Paul Ricoeur's (1974) *Conflict of Interpretations,* Emmanuel Levinas's (1969) *Totality and Infinity,* and Jacques Derrida's (1995) *The Gift of Death.*

Both Ricoeur and Levinas reject the Freudian/Lacanian association between father and law and instead associate fatherhood with promise. For Ricoeur, fatherhood promises equality through contracts, while for Levinas, fatherhood promises singularity beyond the law. The tension between equality and singularity, between law and something beyond the law, is what is at stake in Derrida's *The Gift of Death.* There, Derrida describes ethics as a paradox between the universal and the individual, between equality and singularity. Kierkegaard's reading of the story of Abraham and Isaac from Genesis is the centerpiece of Derrida's analysis. If we read *The Gift of Death,* with its focus on this story of a father and son, in relation to Ricoeur and Levinas on the question of fatherhood, it reads as the culmination of a dialectical tension between the two. And, if we read the Abraham story as a legend about father-son relations rather than just a parable of faith, *The Gift of Death* appears to uncover not just the paradoxical logic of ethics but also the uncompromising logic of patriarchy and paternal authority.

Paternity Begets Fraternity

In "Fatherhood: From Phantasm to Symbol," Ricoeur describes fatherhood as a battle of wills struggling for recognition. He brings together what he calls the different perspectives of psychoanalysis, phenomenology, and religion to rearticulate the Oedipal situation as a *process* of recognition (rather than a *structure*) that moves from the father as phantasm to the father as symbol and replaces images of real murder with symbolic sacrifice. Through his dialectical analysis, Ricoeur himself attempts to articulate a recognition of fatherhood that moves us away from the phantasm of the father as castrator to the symbol of the father as compassionate. Relying on Hegelian dialectics, Ricoeur outlines a movement from psychoanalysis's fantastic image of an omnipotent father who must be killed so that the son might live, through the *Phenomenology of Spirit*'s master-slave dialectic, to the Christian religious representation of the loving father sacrificing himself through his son for the sake of all his children. In this higher stage of the dialectic of paternity, the murder of the father is replaced by his sacrifice. Oddly, however, in Ricoeur's dialectic we end up stuck at the level of the master-slave fight to the death, in which, without the Hegelian resolution, the only options available to ensure the recognition of the father by the son (or the son by the father) are murder or suicide. Whereas Hegel insists that recognition comes only when the master and slave are willing to risk death but also realize the necessity of avoiding it, for Ricoeur, recognition requires death, symbolic if not imaginary. Unlike Ricoeur, Hegel knows that mutual recognition cannot be maintained if one of the parties is dead.

For Ricoeur, recognition does not necessitate avoiding death but rather moving away from the realm of the family and the body to the level of the social and the law. In order for the father-son relationship to be one of mutual recognition, the father must sacrifice his absolute authority so that the son might also participate in it. The goal of recognition is equality, which can be achieved only through social contracts that abstract from the particulars of embodied familial relations. Designation, necessary for recognition, is a social operation. It is removed from the realm of the bodily drives that motivates the Oedipal scenario. Designation requires the sublimation of bodily drives into abstract laws that can equalize bodies by turning them into symbols.

The move from psychoanalysis to Christianity is a move from a domestic family to a social family: Through God the father's sacrifice of his son, we all become members of the Christian family; we all become children of God. For Ricoeur, God is not the Father because he gives the law. Rather, the law, the covenant or contract, enables him to be recognized as father (1974, 49). Ricoeur implicitly rejects the Lacanian association of the Father with the Law or the Name. He claims that there is no name of the father, that "Father" is not a name but a designation (1974, 485). And the father's proper name is of little significance to his function as father. So, too, the father is not the Lacanian "no" or the Freudian prohibition. Rather, the law or covenant is a promise and not a prohibition. Moreover, law does not originate with the father but makes his recognition possible. The son does not originate from the father, but the father originates through the designation *father* by the son. The father becomes father only in answer to the call of his son.

For Ricoeur, *God* is the original father, but not until he has been properly designated as "Father" by *his* son. It is only after Christ calls him "Father" that God is frequently referred to as "Father" in a significant way in the Bible. Ricoeur points out that when God is referred to as "Father," it is in passages that are not the typical narrative sagas of the Old Testament but prophetic texts that announce something. He suggests that in the Old Testament God can be identified as the Father of Israel through God's covenant with Israel. The covenant, that Israel is chosen by God, is both law and promise. The covenant is a divine contract of sorts, but in the New Testament it becomes the promise of eternal life and the kingdom of heaven. Christ calls God his *father* as a reminder of this covenant. Ricoeur argues that in this sense, the biblical God is not a father because he begets man or creates man or because he is an origin; rather, he is a father because he is a promise. He is the promise of compassion.

For Ricoeur, the father-son relationship becomes one of mutual knowledge and recognition when in Matthew 11:27 Christ says, "All things are delivered unto me of my Father: and no man knoweth the Son, but the Father; neither knoweth any man the Father, save the son, and *he* to whomever, the Son will reveal *him*." Ricoeur interprets this passage as the articulation of the mediation necessary for the recognition of the father: "there is fatherhood because there is sonship, and there is sonship because there is community of spirit" (1974, 491). The father is recognized by the son *through the laws of the community*. The son's designation, "father," is made possible by those laws that promise the end of murder. In Matthew 11:27 Christ articulates his relationship to his father in terms of the community and a promise of revelation. The son reveals his father *to the community*, and it is this designation by the son that institutes fatherhood.

For Ricoeur, the institution of fatherhood requires the sacrifice of the son for the sake of the father's other children. Mediated by contracts, the unique relationship between father and son can be annulled such that the force of that relationship applies equally to all other children. Paternity gives way to fraternity. Ricoeur's essay suggests that God's promise, his covenant or law, is fulfilled with the sacrifice of his son, which in turn equalizes all God's children in his eyes. Through the fulfillment of the covenant, through Christ, all of God's children are brothers. In other words, the contract takes priority away from the bond between father and son; that bond is sacrificed for the sake of equalizing relationships. The father promises that law will replace blood and that the law will make all men brothers. Ultimately, then, God's law is the promise of equality guaranteed through contracts, both divine and social.

The marriage contract works as the link between the divine and the social. Sanctioned by God, the marriage contract is recognized by the larger secular social community. The father is a father in the family community, which is first recognized as a community through the marriage contract, which is recognized both by the larger religious and secular communities (Ricoeur 1974, 480). The marriage contract mediates the father-son relationship, makes its social, and promises equality through contracts.

Ricoeur, however, overlooks the failure of contracts to provide equality. Although he moves the recognition of fatherhood from the family into the social to formulate a notion of recognition between father and son as equals that does not reproduce the power hierarchy of the Oedipal scenario with its murderous revenge, he does not analyze the inequities in these legal and social contracts that might make this type of recognition impossible. Contracts assume equal parties but cannot create them; rather, the assumption of inequality merely serves to cover over significant inequalities. To claim that contracts ensure quality, Ricoeur must assume that all of the parties to a contract enter the agreement as equals.[2] For although contracts attempt to ensure equality on some levels, they cover over inequalities on many other levels. For example, the marriage contract (not to mention the social contract in general), which for Ricoeur is the contract that defines fatherhood, has a history of defining its parties unequally. Men and women have not been equal parties to the marriage contract or the social contract in general. When Ricoeur discusses mutual recognition and equality, they are always only between fathers and sons, fathers and sons who become brothers through the social contract that excludes full participation by, or recognition of, their mothers and sisters.

We might wonder about the mother of God, Mary. Is she not mother until recognized by the son? Or, is she mother when recognized by the Father, God? Who recognizes her? Her pregnant body suggests motherhood prior to the son's designation. And, if the Father is not father until designated by the son, who is the father of her child before the son's acknowledgment? Is her designation and recognition of the child's father irrelevant?[3]

It is ironic that Ricoeur defines the father-son relationship in terms of symbolic contracts that ensure recognition when we consider that many father-child relationships in the United States are mediated by real contracts, child custody contracts.[4] In the United States, state welfare agencies spend much of their time trying to track down fathers to collect child support. The contracts that mediate these relations do not necessarily result in equality or recognition. In fact, the legal and economic mediation in the relation between father and children can lead to further alienation and resentment.

Finally, Ricoeur denies the significance of embodiment or physical generation in favor of abstract law/promise. He adds that to recognize the father with the mother through their contractual union is also to recognize them through their sexual union. Certainly, fatherhood and motherhood are dependent on sexual union (or technological intervention). For Ricoeur, sexuality that conceives the family is recognized as the "carnal dimension" of the contract (1974, 480). Although he acknowledges the "carnal dimension," he insists that it can only lead to murder. To prevent murder, we must move beyond bodies and fantasies to symbols. "Begetting is a matter of nature, fatherhood of designation. It is necessary that the blood tie be loosened, be marked by death, in order that fatherhood be truly instituted" (471).

However, Ricoeur overlooks that even God's law is founded in blood. God's promise, the covenant, is a promise made on the basis of blood and constantly reaffirmed through blood, blood as a sign of generation and of fertility. There is no law, no covenant, without blood. The story of Moses, the receiver of the law, is full of blood: the Passover blood, Zipporah's circumcision of Greshom, the ox blood after the tablets are given. The promise that Ricoeur identifies with Christ and God's sacrifice that replaces murder is marked by blood, Christ's blood, which is symbolized by wine in the Eucharist. God's law, especially as promise, cannot be separated from the body and the blood.

For Ricoeur, the dialectic of fatherhood reaches its highest stage when the body becomes symbol, blood becomes wine. Then fatherhood is no longer the murderous Oedipal fantasy but a symbol mediated by social laws that guarantee the equality of brothers. Murder gives way to sacrifice, hatred to compassion. Paternity begets fraternity. But isn't this just another repetition of the psychoanalytic story? In *Totem and Taboo,* Freud describes social fraternity as the result of brothers banding together to murder their father, eat his flesh, and stay together through their shared and repeated guilt (1913). The Oedipal situation inaugurates the social that makes sublimation and repression through guilt possible and necessary.

Christian compassion and its foundation in promises, laws, and contracts take on a different hue when viewed in light of Nietzsche's *On the Genealogy of Morals.* There Nietzsche describes Christian compassion as the ultimate cruelty, beginning with legal contracts and ending with unpayable debt and eternal guilt that result from God's sacrifice. In his analysis, the sacrificial economy produces more guilt than murder ever could. Rather than equalize the father-son relationship or make all men brothers equal to Christ, God's sacrifice increases the paternal authority that commands the sons' obedience and guilt. The promise of equality is nothing more than the bloody ransom offered in exchange for a body already become corpse—piety as payment.

Paternity as Infinite Singularity

Like Ricoeur, Emmanuel Levinas proposes a notion of paternity that cannot be reduced to law or threats but must be a promise. Like Ricoeur, he proposes an ontology of paternity that takes us beyond the Freudian psychoanalysis of paternity, which he claims reduces sexuality and paternity to pleasure and egology. Unlike Ricoeur, however, for Levinas, the promise of paternity is not a promise of recognition and equality but a promise of nonrecognition, strangeness, an open future, infinity, singularity. The promise of paternity is not Ricoeur's promise that from a dead father the son will inherit his designation, that the son will also be recognized by his son as father, or the Freudian promise that the son will inherit his power. It is not a promise from the past, a promise that returns to itself. Rather, the promise of paternity, as Levinas describes it, is a promise of an open future, the promise that the son is to his father. Although in Levinas's analysis there is an analogy between death and paternity, fatherhood requires neither murder nor sacrifice. Paternity is a special case of alterity that can inform all other relations. It is the only relation in which the self becomes other and survives.

For Levinas, paternity does not reestablish the Hegelian battle of the wills, each seeking recognition from the other. Ricoeur's notion that it does takes us back to a tragic egoity that enables unity at the expense of multiplicity: there is only one king, father or son. For Levinas, paternity does not return us to a battle of wills that reinscribes the subject and turns the self back onto itself even in the operation of self-dispossession and abandonment. Rather, paternity opens up a different structure of subjectivity that opens the self onto the other. The structure of the subject in an erotic relationship moves the self beyond the ego and its exclusivity.

Paternity begins with Eros and fecundity. Yet, Eros and fecundity are ontologically anchored in paternity. For Levinas, Eros and fecundity have their telos in paternity. Eros is possible because of sexual difference, which is neither a contradiction between two nor a complementarity between two. Eros is an event of alterity, a relationship with what is absent in the very moment at which everything is there. Even in an experience that seems to completely fill the universe with itself, the caress seeks something other. The caress is not directed toward another body; rather, the caress is directed toward a space that transcends through the body and a time that Levinas describes as a future never future enough (1969, 254). In the erotic relationship the caress is directed toward the future, the forever and always of promises of love, a future that is never future enough to fulfill such promises.

The relationship with the other is such a promise, a promise that cannot be fulfilled, a paradoxical promise whose fulfillment would destroy the promise. And this promise is time. For Levinas, time is not constituted as a series of nows; it is not constituted in the present or by an ego. Rather, time is the absent promise in the relation with the other; it is the not-yet, the always still to come. It is the time of love, the infinite engendered through finite beings coming together. "Love seeks what does not have the structure of an existent, the infinitely future, what is to be engendered" (Levinas 1969, 266). Love seeks what is beyond any possible union between two. Love seeks the "trans-substantiation" that engenders the child (266). Engendering the child is an inherent element in the structure of the erotic relationship; the erotic relationship is defined as fecundity. The caress and voluptuosity are analyzed within this context of fecundity. Paternity, made possible through a relationship with the feminine, opens the masculine subject onto infinite time and returns him to the ethical relationship.

For Levinas, in the masculine erotic relationship, the other beyond the subject's control is the feminine other; fecundity necessitates a relationship with a feminine other. This feminine other is a prerequisite for moving outside oneself: "But the encounter with the Other as feminine is required in order that the future of the child come to pass from beyond the possible, beyond projects. This relationship resembles that which was described for the idea of infinity: I cannot account for it by myself, as I do account for the luminous world by myself" (1969, 267). The transsubstantiation of the father by the son is only possible by virtue of the feminine other. Man needs woman to beget a son. More than this, it would seem, the infinite time opened up between father and son through paternity is possible by virtue of the movement through the cyclical, nonlinear time of the feminine. Paternity moves the (male) subject outside time through the mediation of another time, the cyclical time of life. Paternity conquers "father time" by moving through the feminine.

Paternity opens the subject onto infinite time in various ways. The discontinuity of generations brings with it inexhaustible youth, each generation replacing the one before it. In addition to this chronology that stretches indefinitely through time, the ontology of paternity sets up the subject within infinite time. The space between the father and the son opens up infinite time. Not only the discontinuity of generations that promises continued youth but also the transsubstantiation of the father in the son opens the subject to an other. "[T]he father discovers himself not only in the gestures of his son, but in his substance and his unicity" (Levinas 1969, 267). In this way the father discovers himself in the son and yet discovers that his son is distinct, a stranger.

Through the transsubstantiation of the I, Levinas says that paternity accomplishes desire. It does not satisfy desire, which is impossible, but accomplishes it by engendering it and by engendering another desiring being, the son. Paternity engenders desire, which is the infinite time of the absolutely other. The time of the other is infinite as compared with the finite time of the self. In relationship with the child, the subject is opened onto infinity: "The relation with the child—that is, the relation with the other that is not a power, but fecundity—establishes a relationship with the absolute future, or infinite time" (Levinas 1969, 268). Paternity, with its generation and generations, literally opens onto infinite time, a time beyond death. That future is the infinite desire that is present as a desire for desire itself infinitely extended into a future that is never future enough. What Levinas calls goodness is associated with the infinity of desire engendered by paternity. "In paternity desire maintained as insatiate desire, that is, as goodness, is accomplished" (272). Paternity is the link between desire and goodness, Eros and ethics. Since unlike need, it can never be satisfied, erotic desire is accomplished in engendering a son, a son who embodies desire. In this sense, desire engenders itself (269). For Levinas, the desire of the caress in the erotic relationship is ultimately resolved in paternity: "This unparalleled relation between two substances, where a beyond substances is exhibited, is resolved in paternity" (271). From the beyond, from desire, two substances create another desiring substance, the son.

More than the continuation of the substance of the father in the son, as the word *transsubstantiation* might suggest, paternity is a form of transsubstantiation of subjectivity itself. Paternity transforms subjectivity from the subject as "I-can" who sees himself as the center of meaning and values—the constitutor of the world—to a subject beholden to, and responsible for, the other. This form of transsubstantiation takes us beyond substance. The subject or I is not a substance but a response. The paternal subject is not Husserl's, Sartre's, or Ricoeur's virile "I know," "I-can," or "I-will" but a response to the other who opens up a radically different time, a time beyond the "I know," "I-can," or "I-will." Levinas says the relationship with the son through fecundity "articulates the time of the absolutely other, an alternation of the very substance of him who can—his trans-substantiation" (1969, 269).

The relationship of paternity is unique in that the I breaks free of itself without ceasing to be I; it is the only relationship in which the self becomes other and survives (Levinas 1969, 278). The I breaks free of the ego, of what ties it to itself, so that it can reach out to another, even become another, become other to itself. This process of becoming other to itself opens up the possibility beyond its own possibilities, an openness to an undetermined future. "Fecundity is part of the very drama of the I. The intersubjective reached across the notion of fecundity opens up a place where the I is divested of its tragic egoity, which turns back to itself, and yet is not purely and simply dissolved into the collective. Fecundity evinces a unity that is not opposed to multiplicity, but, in the precise sense of the term, engenders it" (273).

In Levinas's analysis the father discovers himself in the gestures, the substance, the very uniqueness of his son. This discovery of himself in the son is not Ricoeur's recognition; the father does not recognize himself in his son but discovers himself, finds himself, for the first time. Paternity engenders the father as much as it does the son. Fecundity gives birth not only to the son but also to the father. In relation to his son, who is both himself and not himself, the father discovers his own subjectivity. As he realizes that his son is distinct, a stranger, he discovers that he too is distinct, even a stranger to himself.

Rather than establish the equal and mutual recognition of father and son—or brothers, for that matter—Levinas's notion of paternity establishes the uniqueness of the subject in relationship with an Other. The father-son relationship is not one of law-bound recognition but of outlaw singularity. What Levinas calls "paternal election," which chooses from among equals, makes unique precisely by recalling the non-uniqueness of the equals among which *this one* was chosen. The father chooses the son after he has had no choice. His love *elects* this particular child in his uniqueness as the loved one, the one meant to be. In this regard, Levinas suggests that all love for another person must approach paternal love insofar as that love elects the loved one from among all others. This love makes the loved one unique and this love necessary rather than contingent.[5] This love is not just for a limited time only but for all time, for a future never future enough, for infinite time.

At this point, we might wonder why the relationship with the lover does not provide the same kind of uniqueness as the father-son relationship. Strangely enough, it seems that for Levinas the feminine lover is neither radically other nor the same, and both are required for the uniqueness identified with the father-son relationship. It is as much the son's sameness as the son's difference that engenders the uncanny otherness experienced by the father in this relationship. Although the feminine lover may be unique and chosen by the lover, she is neither other nor the same because she is not fully human. For Levinas, the fecund relationship with a woman has its goal in the child, more particularly, a son. The paternal relationship, however, is higher than the lovers' relationship because it is social. The lovers' relationship takes place at the level of laughter and caresses and not language proper. Levinas describes the beloved woman as "silly" and "infantile," her face fading into animality; making love with her is like playing with a "young animal" (1969, 263).

For Ricoeur and Levinas, paternity is always described as a father-son relationship. Even for Derrida in *The Gift of Death*, the paradox and promise of ethics are represented in the story of a father-son relationship, the story of Abraham. But, if fatherhood is a promise for the future, could this future be a daughter? Or does this future have to be a son? Three-quarters of the way through *The Gift of Death,* Derrida makes a short detour through woman that suggests these questions. He comments on the absence of women:

> It is difficult not to be struck by the absence of woman in these two monstrous yet banal stories [Abraham and Bartelby]. It is a story of father and son, of masculine figures, of hierarchies among men (God the father, Abraham, Isaac . . .). Would the logic of sacrificial responsibility within the implacable universality of the law, of its law, be altered, inflected, attenuated, or displaced, if a woman were to intervene in some consequential manner? Does the system of this sacrificial responsibility and of the double "gift of death" imply at its very basis an exclusion or sacrifice of woman? (1995, 75–76)

Derrida raises these provocative questions about woman as if to trouble his own text, which (apart from these questions) also avoids woman. At least Kierkegaard worries about Sarah.

Recall that for Levinas the father discovers himself in the son, who is both himself and a stranger. Levinas emphasizes that it is the otherness of the son that pulls the father out of himself toward infinity. Yet, it is the *sameness* of the son that allows the movement without shattering the father's subjectivity altogether. Ultimately, it is the sameness between father and son that allows for the father to discover himself and his uniqueness through his son. The father identifies with his son. And paternal love is the father's election of this son from among equal "brothers." Paternal election makes biology irrelevant. So, it is not just the biological substance of the son that makes him like and unlike his father; it is something about the son qua son. Should we interpret Levinas literally in his discussion of the paternal election of a son? If so, paternal election provides not only an image of the father's choice of this particular child but also the image of the father's choice of a son in particular. The father chooses this son, and that election makes him unique; in turn, the son's uniqueness makes the father unique. Through their relationship, they both are singular. Yet, the discovery of their singularity has its basis in their sameness.

How can the son be an absolute other if he is also the same? Is it the son's difference or his sameness that restructures the I through paternity? Wouldn't a daughter be a stranger child? Because of sexual difference and the nonlinear, cyclical effects of feminine time, wouldn't the daughter be other enough to open up an infinite future? For Levinas, desire is possible only in a relationship with an absolute other.

Paternity engenders desire and thereby returns the erotic relationship to the ethical. And, yet, doesn't this paternal desire fall back into need if the son returns the father always to himself?[6]

For Levinas, it seems to go without saying that the father chooses a son rather than a daughter. If the father cannot elect a daughter, however, then the ethics of paternity is an ethics of sameness, a subtle version of the slave morality that cannot say "yes" to difference. The singularity engendered by paternity is the singularity of the masculine. And, in spite of its illusion that it can, ultimately, without difference, without daughters, mothers, wives, the same cannot maintain itself.

The Paradox of Ethics Uncovers Paternal Authority

> But the distance of the commentary is not neutral. What he comments upon is consonant with a whole network of affirmations which are his, or those of him, "he."
>
> —Derrida, "At This Very Moment . . ."
> (in Bernasconi and Critchley 1991)

Negotiating sameness and difference or equality and singularity is at the center of Derrida's *The Gift of Death.* Whereas Ricoeur presents the father-son relationship as a relation of mutual recognition through law that ensures equality, and Levinas presents the father-son relationship as a discovery of oneself through a relation to the other that ensures singularity, Derrida discusses a father-son relationship that puts equality and singularity into conflict. Whereas for Ricoeur, relations are necessarily mediated by contracts, laws, and ethics, for Levinas, ethics is prior to the law and makes law possible. For Derrida, however, ethics is a paradox between law and the impossibility of law. Derrida suggests that the father has a duty to his son through the law, which allows for designations as well as names; but the father also has a duty that cannot be named or designated, an absolute duty unmediated by law. These two duties, the duty to respect the equality before the law and the duty to respect the singularity of the individual, conflict. This conflict is the heart of the story of a father caught between his Father and his son, the biblical story of Abraham.

Although it remains in the background of Derrida's analysis, it is significant that Abraham is *promised* a son, Isaac, in his old age. Because his wife Sarah is too old to conceive, Isaac is a miracle. God promises that Abraham will have a son who will be the father of many generations of Israel. For Abraham, Isaac holds out God's promise of generations to come. So, why does God ask Abraham to sacrifice Isaac? Does the promise of fatherhood, the promise of generations, require sacrifice? God, the Father, asks his son for a sacrifice. In Kierkegaard's analysis in *Fear and Trembling,* Abraham must give up the ethical or the law for the sake of a higher religious realm (1954). Abraham is in the paradoxical position of believing in the promise of Isaac and believing that he will kill Isaac. Abraham believes the impossible; he believes in what Kierkegaard calls the paradox of faith. So, Abraham is the father of faith. For Kierkegaard, this paradoxical belief moves Abraham out of the realm of ethics and into the realm of religion or faith. For Derrida, this paradoxical belief is the core of ethics, which necessarily straddles the universal and the individual (what Kierkegaard calls the ethical sphere and the religious sphere).

Out of the focus of either Kierkegaard's or Derrida's texts is another crucial factor: *At least* two father-son relationships are present in this story, Abraham-Isaac and God-Abraham. Once we see the relationship between God and Abraham as another father-son relationship, then we read a different story. Derrida reads Abraham's relationship to God as the relationship to the wholly other, while he reads Abraham's paternal relationship to Isaac as a relationship of duty to family and law. This is Abraham's conflict. Does he do his duty to his son, family, and society and not commit murder, or does he sacrifice that which he loves to the Absolute, to God? If piety is dutiful obedience, the Abraham story shows both the impossibility and the necessity of piety. Derrida characterizes the dilemma in terms of an absolute duty to God that conflicts with an ethical duty to Isaac, his family, and society. In my exploration of Derrida's analysis of the Abraham story, I will investigate what happens when we reinterpret the relationship between God and Abraham as another father-son relationship.

The Gift of Death is about the aporia of ethics, responsibility, secrecy, sacrifice, death, gift giving, and faith. At the beginning of *The Gift of Death,* Derrida uses Jan Patočka's *Heretical Essays on the Philosophy of History* to link secrecy and responsibility. Following Patočka, Derrida concludes that "the history of the responsible self is built upon the heritage and *patrimony* of secrecy, through a chain reaction of ruptures and repressions that assure the very tradition they punctuate with their interruptions" (1995, 7, my emphasis). The secret is a secret inherited from the father, the patrimony of secrecy. The secret is the mystery of orgiastic practices that are repressed and incorporated by/into philosophy. And, as Patočka makes it out, the secret or mystery itself is maternal. Describing the way in which Plato incorporates the mystery, Patočka says that "the cavern is a vestige of the subterranean place for gathering of mysteries; it is the lap of the earth-mother. The new thinking inaugurated by Plato involves the desire to forsake the lap of the earth-mother in order to set out upon the pure 'path of light,' hence to completely subordinate the orgiastic to responsibility" (Derrida 1995,

11). The earth-mother, it turns out, is kept secret by the patrimony from fathers and sons.

Derrida tells us that for Patočka, the demonic mystery is hidden within responsibility and that this mystery is associated with "orgiastic irresponsibility" (1995, 20). The awakening from the mystery is the ability to keep a secret. The idea is that if one is to keep a secret, one needs to have a sense of responsibility and conscience. Now, if we recall that the mystery and orgiastic irresponsibility are associated with earth-mother and that the secret is a patrimony, then the awakening is the ability of fathers to keep the maternal element a secret. The secret of life is that it originates with mothers and the earth. The secret passed down from father to son is the secret gift of life given by the mother and the earth. But this secret is not articulated. Rather, this is the type of secret rendered invisible through practices of repression and incorporation within the patriarchy. In order for fathers and sons to take responsibility, the mother's gift of life must not be spoken. In order for fathers and sons to become responsible subjects, they must forget that earth-mother is responsible for their very lives. Only if "she" is irresponsible can they be responsible.

In Derrida's text, the father (Abraham/God) gives the gift of death, which turns out to be the same as the gift of life. The gift of death is the willingness to sacrifice that which one loves for an other, to give up one's own life or the life of one's son, in this case, for an other. Abraham is willing to sacrifice Isaac (whom he loves, as Genesis reminds us several times) to God. And God sacrifices his son, Christ, for the lives of all of his children. In Christ's case, the gift of death is put forth as a gift of life.[7] Still, to equate giving one's life for another, or dying so that another might live, or sacrificing that which one loves for the other, with the maternal gift of life is to incorporate and repress that fundamental gift. The rituals and ceremonies of sacrificial sons render invisible the secret maternal sacrifice. There is no gift of death, however, without the gift of life. In this story, as in many others, the power to give death is the father's. The father can believe that the gift of death, within *his* own power, is the same as the gift of life. He can believe that by giving death it is *he* who gives life. But, as Irigaray says, this belief covers up the truth.[8]

In order for the father to be responsible, the mother cannot be. But, as Derrida maintains, the father's responsibility is a paradox. It puts him in an impossible spot. Because of the contradiction at the core of responsibility, he is always guilty and never responsible enough.

> Guilt is inherent in responsibility because responsibility is always unequal to itself: one is never responsible enough. One is never responsible

> enough because one is finite but also because responsibility requires two contradictory movements. It requires one to respond as oneself and as irreplaceable singularity, to answer for what one does, says, gives; but it also requires that, being good and through goodness, one forget or efface the origin of what one gives. (1995, 51)

Responsibility requires that one respond as oneself and respond as all others, as the universal; responsibility requires both confessing that one's actions originate with oneself and forgetting that one's actions originate in oneself.

Of course, if we reinterpret Derrida's remarks in light of my hypothesis that the secret of responsibility is the life-giving mother, they take on a new meaning. The life-giving mother is the secret origin of the gift of life that must be forgotten. The guilt inherent in responsibility could be the guilt involved in the matricide that makes it possible for the father/son to claim responsibility (for life). He must respond as if he alone is responsible; he is singularly responsible (otherwise the responsibility is not his). Yet, he must forget or efface the origin of that which he gives because that which he gives, the gift of life/death, is also from the mother; he must forget that at its origin he alone is not responsible (for life). Within the frame of Derrida's text, this contradiction is the aporia of responsibility. Responsibility requires both substitution and nonsubstitution: "For responsibility . . . demands on the one hand an accounting, a general answering-for-oneself with respect to the general and before the generality, hence the idea of substitution, and, on the other hand, uniqueness, absolute singularity, hence nonsubstitution, nonrepetition, silence, and secrecy" (1995, 61).

In other words, responsibility has two sides that come into conflict with each other. On the one hand, to hold someone or yourself responsible is to account for and justify his/her/your actions. On the other hand, to be absolutely responsible implies that you alone are responsible, that you have a unique relationship to your obligation that cannot be accounted for, justified, or explained; your responsibility, if it is truly yours, is unique and cannot be understood in terms of any universal laws, principles, or language. Absolute responsibility requires secrecy because the "secret" obligation defies words; it cannot be spoken even if one were to try.

When Abraham is called by God, he answers, "Here I am," presenting himself to do God's bidding.[9] His words say everything and nothing about his response to God. Because he is answering to God, the Absolute, out of an absolute responsibility, the appropriate response for Abraham is silence. If, however, he were testifying in a court of law, out of a general responsibility Abraham would be required to speak.

In one case the appropriate response is to speak; in the other the appropriate response is to remain silent.

This is why when Abraham speaks, he does so (according to Kierkegaard) ironically. When Isaac asks his father, "Where is the ram for the sacrifice?" Abraham replies, "God will provide." He neither lies nor justifies the situation to Isaac—he says both something and nothing at the same time. Irony is what is said and not said at the same time. So, it is not by accident, in an apparent digression on woman in the middle of this text, that Derrida quotes Hegel saying, "Woman is the eternal irony of the community"—she is what is said and not said.

Ethics is "an insoluble and paradoxical contradiction between responsiblity *in general and absolute* responsibility" (Derrida 1995, 61). General responsibility requires the sacrifice of absolute responsibility, and absolute responsibility requires the sacrifice of general responsibility. Moreover, various philosophers have told us that both require the sacrifice of women. For example, Hegel describes how general responsibility, or ethics, requires the sacrifice of the family, including woman, wife, and sister:

> Human law in its universal existence is the community, in its activity in general is the manhood of the community, in its real and effective activity is the government. It *is, moves,* and *maintains* itself by consuming and absorbing into itself . . . families presided over by womankind, and by keeping them dissolved in the fluid continuity of its own nature . . . it creates for itself in what it suppresses and what is at the same time essential to it an internal enemy—womankind in general. (1977, 288)

And, for Freud, women are opposed to civilization and any sort of general responsibility or law of society:

> Women soon come into opposition to civilization and display their retarding and restraining influence. . . . The work of civilization has become increasingly the business of men. . . . His constant association with men, and his dependence on his relations with them, *even estrange him from his duties as a husband and father.* Thus the woman finds herself forced into the background by the claims of civilization and she adopts a hostile attitude towards it. (1961, 50–51, my emphasis)

In these scenarios, duties to law, ethics, and society conflict with duties to women and families.

With Derrida's reading of the Abraham story (following Kierkegaard), we have another conflict of duties between duties to women and family—now seen as part of the law or ethical—and duties to the Absolute, God. Abraham must leave his family behind. He must be willing to destroy his family for the sake of his absolute responsibility to God. It is almost as if generalizing a law of family relations or sexual relations requires reinstating a higher duty so that women and families will once more be sacrificed. If man's first duty is not to his society, which requires the sacrifice of women and family, then it is to his God, which requires the sacrifice of women and family.

Yet, in Derrida's reading of (Levinas's reading of) Kierkegaard's reading of Genesis, God is not *really* outside the family scene. Rather, in Derrida's text God is also figured as a father. The duty to God as father is not a duty to an absolute and wholly other. Abraham is also a father, and through fatherhood he shares something with God. In fact, Abraham inherits the patrimony of secrecy, which he must pass on to his own son, from God.

According to the story told by Derrida and Kierkegaard, Abraham's duty to God the Father is absolute and cannot be justified. Why? Why can the Father command without justification? Why is the Father's authority without question or accountability? Within patriarchy, isn't it always the father's prerogative to issue commands without justification? When the son happens to talk back and ask, "Why?" as in the case of Moses, his Father threatens him with death. The father does not have to justify himself. When the child asks, "Why?" it is enough for the father to say, "Because I am your father—that's why." Is the command from the Patriarch really the command from the wholly other that resonates from Levinas's texts through Derrida's? Insofar as God is figured as Father, he is not wholly other; rather, he is essentially the same in his relation to his son.

Abraham's conflict is not only a conflict between general responsibility to all Others and absolute responsibility to the wholly other God. It is a conflict between duties to Father and son. He has a duty to protect and love his son. He has a duty to obey and love his Father. His Father commands him to sacrifice his son. Ultimately, it is for the sake of his son, for the sake of his patrimony, that Abraham obeys God the Father. Piety protects patrimony. If the son obeys the father's absolute yet outlaw authority, it is because one day he will be the father and inherit that authority. This is the promise of paternity within patriarchy. Once we read God as a Father, isn't the Abraham story another version of Freud's Oedipal drama in which the son must defer to the father's authority, must castrate himself, to avoid castration? This autocastration is the ceremony that seals the promise that the father's omnipotence is to be passed on to his son. As Kierkegaard says, Abraham is "great by reason of his power whose strength is impotence" (1954, 31). The son's impotence is demanded in the face of the Father's potency, but the son's impotence buys him the patrimony of potency.

Derrida indicates at one point that Abraham's sacrifice of law and family, of everything that is his own, moves him outside economy. But, if his sacrifice is made at the command of the ultimate Patriarch, God the Father, then the son is only protecting what is his own by giving in. His sacrifice is made in the name of fatherhood, for the sake of preserving the authority of fatherhood. He sacrifices the present for the future, his own future and the future of his son. The paradox is that God asks Abraham to sacrifice his son, his heir, for the sake of paternal authority and his/His heirs. The paradox is that Abraham is both father (to Isaac) and son (to God) at the same time. He has the authority to take Isaac up Mount Moriah, bind him, and raise the knife over his head. Isaac goes along with it because Abraham is his father, whom he obeys and loves, just as Abraham goes along with his Father, God, whom he obeys and loves. So, Abraham is the father of faith. But, Isaac, the son, also has faith in his fathers. He is the one who lays his life on the line with his obedience and faith. The Abraham story is a lesson in the son's obedience to paternal authority. The father's responsibility for the gift of life, his authorship, is acknowledged through the son's obedience. Piety designates authority.

Derrida can suggest that the gift of life and the gift of death amount to the same because ultimately it is the father's gift of the death of the mother that promises life to the son. The son submits to the father because of the promise that someday he will inherit everything and take over the position of the patriarch. The promise of fatherhood is made through the sacrifice of mothers and their daughters. We hear the echo of Derrida's haunting questions:

> Would the logic of sacrificial responsibility within the implacable universality of the law, of its law, be altered, inflected, attenuated, or displaced, if a woman were to intervene in some consequential manner? Does the system of this sacrificial responsibility and of the double 'gift of death' imply at its very basis an exclusion or sacrifice of woman? (1995, 76)

If the dutiful reverence for the father that we call piety were extended to the mother, could it promise an ethics without murder or sacrifice? An ethics that says "yes" to what is outside, what is different, what is not itself? Is there piety without God? Is there God without patrimony? Can the patrimony from father to son acknowledge matrimony without guilt or pity? Is piety for the One necessarily pity for the Other? Is there compassion without guilt and resentment?

3

Abjection in Fassbinder's *Despair* and Polanski's *The Tenant*

In this chapter I analyze films by Rainer Werner Fassbinder and Roman Polanski using Jacques Lacan's notion of misrecognition and Julia Kristeva's notion of abjection. My analysis will center on figures of abject males, Herman Herman in Fassbinder's *Despair* and Trelkovsky in Polanski's *The Tenant*. Both films present images of self-disintegration and abjection. In the case of *The Tenant* the abject is explicitly feminine. In the case of *Despair* the feminine represents that abject body from which Herman is trying to escape.

The Psychoanalytic Frame

In "The Mirror Stage," Lacan describes a misrecognition at the heart of self-recognition. He proposes that what he calls the "mirror stage" is the first stage in self-recognition and self-consciousness, or more specifically the development of the ego (1977). Lacan concludes that the ego in all its structures is characterized by misrecognition (*méconnaissance*), which begins in the mirror stage (1977, 6). The infant recognizes itself in the mirror only by misrecognizing itself. The mirror stage presents the infant with an Ideal-I, an ideal of narcissistic omnipotence, which is a fiction in relation to its total incompetence in reality (2). The infant sees in the mirror an image of wholeness, unity, control, and agency with which it identifies in spite of the fact that its own experience includes none of these characteristics. In this way, the mirror image "symbolizes the mental permanence of the I, at the same time as it prefigures its alienating destination" (2).

Lacan suggests that the discrepancy between the infant's own experience of fragmentation and incompetence and the mirror image of unity and agency produces the experience of alienation fundamental to self-consciousness. Alienation is the product of the misrecognition at the heart of self-recognition. And, alienation from the other, whether it is our own image as other or another person, gives rise to aggresivity in all interpersonal relationships. We are stuck at the level of Hegel's master-slave scenario, constantly struggling to regain ourselves against the other.

Julia Kristeva locates the alienation and splitting constitutive of self-identity at an earlier stage before the mirror stage. She maintains that even before the infant gets any sense of itself as a self or any other as an object, it inhabits a world of abjects. The abject does not have the clear-cut borders of either subjects or objects. It is only by traversing this world of abjects that the infant becomes a subject that sets up borders between itself and others. Still enjoying the narcissistic identification with its parent(s), what Kristeva calls the imaginary father, the infant facilitates the weaning process by abjecting its mother's body, specifically her breast. In fact, what the infant rejects as abject is the lack of boundaries or borders between her body and its own body. The abject challenges borders; so in the process of becoming a self or individual, the infant rejects that which challenges borders in order to set up its own.

As Kristeva describes it in *Powers of Horror,* both individual and group identity are formed by abjecting or jettisoning all characteristics that threaten one's own proper identity (1980b). So, anything that challenges borders, the in-between, must be eliminated, abjected, to become properly identified as an individual. This splitting off of everything distasteful to identity prefigures the splitting inherent in Lacan's mirror stage. But, this earlier splitting or jettisoning involved in the stage of abjection is more visceral than cognitive or recognitive. Without yet recognizing itself or the other, the infant is already involved in a process of exclusion that eliminates "improper" elements from its own fledgling identity.

If everything goes as it should, then abjection is a stage in ego development that gives way to the mirror stage and the onset of the ego proper. But, in Kristeva's analysis, if there is no loving support for abjection, then the identification between the mother and infant consumes the infant. Rather than abject the maternal body in order to become distinct, through its identification with the maternal body the infant abjects itself. If there is no support of what Kristeva calls the loving imaginary father, then the infant remains stuck in abjection identifying with an improper and unclean maternal body. Herself unable to separate from her intellectual fathers, in *Powers of Horror* Kristeva takes the male infant as the norm. The perilous situation caused by identification with the maternal body makes the male infant unclean, while it seems to be unavoidable for the female infant. Abjection, then, always involves disgust and/or fascination with a maternal body, often mistaken for the female body itself.

Fragmentation in Fassbinder's *Despair*

Fassbinder's *Despair* (1978) is set in Germany just before World War II. Dirk Bogarde plays Herman Herman, a Russian immigrant to Germany who owns a chocolate factory in Berlin. Early in the film we see Herman split into two Hermans, one taking pleasure in watching the other. What he calls his "disassociation" progresses throughout the film until the end when, completely delusional, he is suffering from fragmentation. Herman's disassociation becomes so extreme that he misrecognizes a carnival worker, Felix Weber, as his double. Herman pays Felix to put on his clothes and help him with a scheme. Unbeknownst to Felix, Herman plans to shoot him in order to collect his own insurance money (mistakenly believing that he and Felix look exactly alike). Of course, since he and Felix look nothing alike, his plan fails and he is eventually caught.

Despair opens with a scene of water dripping on broken eggshells; the scene is accompanied by sweet and cheerful music while we see some drink made of raw eggs being stirred. The harsh double of this sweet mixture is one of the last scenes, when Herman is hiding from the police in a tiny room in a broken-down hotel where water from the roof is dripping on broken porcelain in front of a cracked mirror in which we see Herman's fragmented image. What was once the pleasant, even luxurious, water sliding and bouncing off eggshells after they were cracked has become more like a monotonous Chinese water torture tormenting Herman in front of his fragmented image. Warmth and cheer have given way to stark despair. By the end of the film, Herman's pleasure in watching himself turns into painful paranoia.

From the scene in which we meet Herman and his wife Lydia, shot through a window, to the final fragmented reflection in the shattered mirror, *Despair* is full of mirrors, windows, and reflections. In fact, it seems that we see most of the characters in their reflections on glass. When Herman meets Felix at the carnival, it is in a fun house maze of glass and mirrors. From the beginning of the film, we see Herman living and working in a maze of glass. Both his house and his office have walls of glass, full of windows, and mirrors. So, even before we see Herman split in two watching himself, we see Herman splitting in his reflections.

The first scene in which Herman appears in two places at once happens after he and his wife Lydia are preparing for bed. We see Herman arranging the chair in the living room so that it has a perfect view through the bedroom door. When his wife wants to close the bedroom door, Herman refuses. Next we see Herman in bed with Lydia and another Herman sitting in the living room chair watching. Herman looks up to acknowledge the other Herman watching him. In this scene we see Herman in bed with Lydia and the double watching in the chair, while in the repetition of this scene later in the film, the audience is thrown off when we once again see Herman moving his chair preparing the vantage point of his double, and it turns out that Herman is watching while his double is in bed with Lydia. We discover that it is not really Herman but his imagined double in bed with Lydia (asking her to kiss his boots) when Herman (and the audience) is brought out of his fantasy by Lydia calling him to come to bed. By now, even the audience cannot be sure of Herman's location.

After returning from a meeting with Felix (the vagabond whom Herman insists is his double), Herman asks his secretary a rhetorical question that turns out to have a literal force for him. When he returns to his factory, his secretary tells him that Müller has resigned. Thinking that she means his employee Müller and not Chancellor Müller, Herman asks, "Do I own this factory or am I some tramp wandering the streets?" For Herman—who exclaims when he meets Felix, "The chromosematic scale is dotted to infinity but nature's pulled double"—this is an urgent question. Herman's self-alienation and disassociation have been projected onto his double. So, he must kill his double in order to overcome his self-alienation and reunify his split identity.

As Herman is preparing to fake his own death by killing Felix in his place, he tells Lydia a story about finding his long-lost twin brother so full of despair that he makes Herman promise to kill him. He tells Lydia that his brother is physically alive but morally dead, a liar, a cheat, a forger, a murderer, a poisoner of the woman who kept him, bent on self-destruction, and his last chance to regain his self-respect is through death if Herman will kill him and take his place. Herman tells Lydia this story so that she will not be afraid when the police come to tell her that he has been found dead. He wants to assure her (and himself) that it is not him but his brother, his double, his abjected alter ego, who has been killed.

Herman, himself a liar, forger, and eventually a murderer, projects these qualities onto his double and kills off the double to rid himself of the abjected qualities. By killing the double, Herman attempts to regain his own self-respect, regain his self-unity, and overcome his alienation. But, as it becomes clear to Herman that his plot has failed and that the man he killed was not his double after all, he becomes more fragmented and delusional. In a replication of the mirror stage,

Herman misrecognizes himself as whole and in control of his own agency in his "double," Felix, while he experiences himself as fragmented. Once his misrecognition is exposed, he loses any sense of wholeness or control. Cut off from the illusory source of his own agency, Herman imagines that he is an actor in a movie absolved of any real responsibility.

Becoming the Other in Polanski's *The Tenant*

Roman Polanski's 1976 film *The Tenant* also confronts its audience with images of fragmentation and splitting, which lead to the deterioration and ultimate death of the film's protagonist, Trelkovsky (played by Polanski). As in Fassbinder's *Despair,* the opening shot of *The Tenant* introduces its main characters as shadowy images behind panes of glass. The opening shot tracks along the inside of a claustrophobic courtyard surrounded on all sides by walls and windows. Behind one of these windows we see the figure of a woman who later becomes the figure of a man, Trelkovsky, foreshadowing the transformation to come.

The movie begins with Trelkovsky trying to rent an apartment whose present tenant, Simone Schule, threw herself out the window and is now laying in a hospital bed. Banking on her death, both the manager and Trelkovsky make the arrangements for him to take over the apartment as soon as she *vacates.* To assess his chances of getting the apartment, Trelkovsky visits Simone in the hospital. There he meets one of her friends, Stella. Thinking that Trelkovsky is also a friend of Simone's, Stella confides in him and they start an affair of sorts. Shortly after the visit, Simone dies and Trelkovsky moves into her apartment, which still houses some of her things.

The other tenants' sensitivity to noise and their constant complaints produce a surveillance effect that makes Trelkovsky self-conscious about his every move and eventually leads to paranoid delusions of conspiracies against him. By the end of the film, he thinks that the other tenants are trying to turn him into Simone Schule and force him to throw himself out the window. The audience is implicated in Trelkovsky's paranoid frenzy because Polanski continues to blur any sharp distinctions between paranoid fantasy and reality. It is never entirely clear what is Trelkovsky's fantasy and what is real. Morning after morning we see Trelkovsky stop at the café across from his apartment to have his coffee and Galloise. But the attendants in the café always insist that he sit where Simone sat, drink hot chocolate as Simone did, and smoke Marlboros because that is what Simone smoked. They seem to be trying to turn him into Simone. And so begin his disassociation and fragmentation.

A striking turning point in the film (reminiscent of the scene in *Despair* in which Herman occupies the position of his double watching himself in bed with Lydia) occurs when Trelkovsky, who has a view of the bathroom from his apartment window, looks up from the bathroom to see himself looking down from his apartment window. This vivid split consciousness, this self-consciousness always watching itself, marks the first step toward fragmentation and disassociation. Both these films suggest that it is a short step between self-consciousness in the philosophical sense and self-consciousness in the everyday paranoid sense of watching oneself to the point of paralysis. Once we step out of ourselves to engage in self-reflection, where do we stop? The psychic splitting necessary for self-conscious reflection can continue ad infinitum. Once the splitting starts, what can stop it?

The Tenant is a meditation on the way in which fragmentation dislocates the ego. At one point Trelkovsky asks, "At what precise moment does an individual stop being who he thinks he is?" How many pieces can he break into and still be himself? He says, "If you cut off my arm, I say me and my arm. . . . but if you cut off my head, do I say me and my head or me and my body?" He asks, "What right does my head have to claim to be me?" Exactly where in his body is *he* located? Already embarrassed of his body at the beginning of the film, Trelkovsky cannot admit that he has to go to the bathroom and tells Stella that he has to make a phone call instead. As the film progresses, he becomes increasingly alienated from his body.

In a scene later in the film, he wakes up with a tooth missing, not realizing that he pulled it himself during the night. By the end, his nights are filled with dressing in Simone's clothes and painting his fingernails, while his mornings bring shock and horror at what has happened during the night. Trelkovsky has become the tenant of his own body, at its mercy. He is haunted by images of bodily disintegration: mannequin heads appear in almost every room, in one scene he sees his own head bouncing in the courtyard, and he finds a tooth hidden in the wall. And in the end, when he throws himself out the window, his body survives and he has to drag himself up the stairs to do it again.

Having become the other, having become Simone, Trelkovsky attempts to kill off the otherness within himself by killing himself. Whereas Herman kills the other in an attempt to kill off his abject alter ego, Trelkovsky kills himself. Both these films leave us with a Hegelian fight to the death between self and other in which the options are limited to murder or suicide. In the case of Trelkovsky, the otherness that threatens his life is feminine otherness. Trelkovsky dresses up as a woman and throws himself out the window. We could say that to kill off the feminine in himself, he kills himself. As he becomes more feminine—to the point of looking in the mirror dressed as a woman, rubbing his stomach, and saying, "I think that I'm pregnant"—he also becomes more violent in reaction to the increasing violence of his paranoid hallucinations. Ultimately, this violence—both his own and that of the others—is all directed at Trelkovsky in drag.

Femininity as a Cover for the Abjected Male Body

In *The Tenant* the feminine appears as a temptation to bodily lust, a lust that will be punished by bodily disintegration. At Simone's funeral, while Trelkovsky is lusting after Stella, the preacher is delivering a threatening sermon promising the complete putrefaction and disintegration of the body when "worms shall consume thy eyes." Trelkovsky's own lust lead him to paranoid shame. He is constantly being watched in his lust for Stella (whether by a little girl at the funeral or by a man in the movie theater). It is after a night together that he completely breaks down into paranoid delusion that ends in his suicide. In *The Tenant* the punishment for succumbing to the feminine appears to be consumption and death.

In *Despair* the feminine is also reduced to the body and the object of male lust. Whereas Herman always appears clothed, even in the bedroom scenes, his wife, Lydia, is almost always nude or partially nude. Her fleshy curves become one of the central props in the film. She is nothing but body and affect, while he stands outside his body and watches at a controlled distance. Herman is constantly calling her a "stupid woman." He says that "intelligence would take the bloom off her carnality," and he compares her brain to the cream centers of his chocolates. Herman says that he is the smart one and Lydia is the stupid one; he is the mind and she is the body.

Herman and Trelkovsky can be interpreted as two different manifestations of the same phenomenon. Herman appears controlled and disciplined; he is master of his own body. Trelkovsky appears ashamed and distrustful of his own body; his body is a constant threat. Both Herman's discipline and Trelkovsky's shame are manifestations of a fear of a body out of control. On the surface this body out of control would appear to be the female body, loathed and dominated by Herman, fascinating yet threatening to Trelkovsky. But this abject female body is merely the projection of a male body more terrifying yet. By projecting their fears of a body out of control onto the female body, these male characters do not have to face their own bodies out of control. The identification of the body with the female and the subsequent abjection of that body—both fascinating and horrifying, on the border between human and animal—are means of controlling their own abject male bodies.

As Kristeva explains, to set up your own clean and proper identity as a self, it is necessary to jettison certain threatening elements from your own identity. Those elements are the borderline qualities that threaten any identity, in the first instance associated with the maternal body and its threats to autonomy. In Western culture, in general, masculine identity has been constructed through a disassociation from the body that is possible only by feminizing the fleshy material of the body itself, especially in fluidity. Everything about the body that is threatening for maintaining the borders of identity, everything that is in between animal and *man,* has been associated with the female body and feminized so that the male body is purified through a masculine identity that excludes everything feminine and threatening. As I have argued elsewhere, even sperm and male bodily fluids become solidified and purified through the feminization of the body and the abjection of the female body.[1]

Herman attempts to control his own body by disowning it, associating the body and its inferiority with his wife Lydia and dominating her (to the point that we see him imagining making her kiss his boots while she lies naked in bed). Trelkovsky, on the other hand, can never completely sever his identification with the female body even while he abjects it. Like the phobic whom Kristeva decries in *Powers of Horror,* Trelkovsky abjects the maternal and the feminine and yet continues to identify with them. The questionable borders of his self-identity become based on an identification with what is made repulsive and disgusting—the feminine and maternal—to the point that he has to kill himself to overcome the threats from this abject and all-consuming maternal body.

Alien Characters

These male characters' abjection of the female body is complicated by the fact that both of them are themselves foreigners, abjected others, within their dominate cultures. Trelkovsky is a Pole living in a Paris suspicious of foreigners. Herman is a Russian Jew living in Berlin just before World War II. Political and social identity are explicit themes of Fassbinder's *Despair.* Although Herman is increasingly surrounded by Nazi soldiers in uniform, he seems oblivious. When one of his employees shows up at work in a uniform, Herman asks whether he has joined the Boy Scouts and comments that the brown uniform will match the chocolates. When he is asked about his political views, he says that it is impolite to express political opinions. And during a conversation about politics among his insurance agent, his wife, and her cousin, in which the names of the various factions of the right are being ridiculed, Herman says that he does not think about politics because he has just insured his life. Yet, as a Jew in Germany during World War II, it seems that Herman's life cannot be insured.

Herman (and the audience) gets a startling premonition of things to come when visiting a chocolate factory in Dusseldorf, which Herman is interested in purchasing. He sees chocolate men moving around in circles on a conveyor belt. Those with imperfections are handpicked from the belt and thrown into a box. Herman stops to stare at the box of little chocolate human figures, broken and mangled in a pile. After this incident, Herman confesses to the owner of the factory that he joined whatever army was in power in Russia and that he forged his papers to get out of the country. Once Herman tells the owner that his mother was a Rothschild, the owner tells him to keep his "fucking shekels" because he has decided not to sell his factory to Herman at any price, presumably because he has realized that Herman is a Jew.

Later Herman seems disturbed by a group of Nazi soldiers throwing bricks at a Jewish butcher's shop and the reaction (or lack of it) of two rabbis playing chess at a café across the street. Still, Herman seems too absorbed by his own personal fantasies to realize what is going on around him. One day tasting some chocolates at his factory, his assistant, the Nazi Müller, is pounding on the wall complaining about the reparation payments that the Germans have to make after World War I and the fact that there are still French soldiers on German soil. Herman's only response is "This is too bitter"—the chocolates or Müller's reaction? In spite of Herman's seeming oblivion to the political and social situation surrounding him, it is hard to avoid asking how much of his alienation is caused by his alien status.

Both *Despair* and *The Tenant* can be seen as representations of the inner alienation experienced by foreigners who try to maintain the integrity of their self-identity in the face of being excluded by the culture within which they live. On the surface they seem to fit in. They try to learn the language and pass as natives (Herman prides himself on knowing German better than his wife does). But, inside they suffer alienation to the point of disassociation, fragmentation, and ultimately self-destruction. In turn, their own sense of abjection is projected onto the female body that must be dominated or killed to sustain their own sense of self-identity.

II

DESIRING MOTHERS

4

Kristeva's Imaginary Father as a Screen for the Desiring Mother

Since her earliest writings, Julia Kristeva has attempted to bring the semiotic body, replete with drives, back into structuralism. This attempt has also marked her point of departure from Lacanian theory. She argues that Lacan's bracketing of the drives "castrates" Freud's discovery. Kristeva, protecting the father of psychoanalysis from this castration threat by his most prodigal son, reinscribes the drives in language. Her tactic is to reinscribe language in the body, arguing that the dynamics that operate the symbolic are already working within the material of the body and the presymbolic imaginary. She concludes that these dynamics must therefore be material or biological as well as symbolic. In other words, her strategy is to trace the signifier through the body to reinscribe the body in language at the same time.

For Kristeva, this body, which sets up and harbors the symbolic (at the same time that it threatens it), is the maternal body. The maternal body *prefigures* the law of the father and the onset of the symbolic. Reading "against the grain" of her writing, Kristeva's texts take us deeper into this maternal body. In her earlier writings she is concerned with recovering a repressed maternal body, which is associated with the child's relation to its mother's breast. Later she becomes concerned with the abject maternal body, which is associated with the child's relation to its birth and the mother's "sex."

For Kristeva, within Lacanian theory the living body is sacrificed to desire. It becomes only a sign. As she passionately argues, when language is not mixed with drives and actually requires the repression of drives, this subjugation to the law of the signifier turns the living person into a sign, and signifying activity stops. Kristeva claims that the exemplary subject of Lacanian desire is the masochistic neurotic engaging in autocastration and bodily mutilation or the completely catatonic body of the clinical schizophrenic (1974, 132).

Kristeva does not argue that Lacan is wrong about the function of the mirror stage or castration. Rather, she emphasizes that Lacan's account does not analyze what is heterogeneous within the symbolic (1980a, 276). Lacan's account of the mirror stage emphasizes the image of the body as other, the body as symbol reflected in the "mirror." It throws us into a hall of mirrors where we can no longer identify the "real" of the body; the real body is impossible. Yet, as she suggests, Lacan's account covers over the fact that without the body there would be no reflection in the mirror. She maintains that with *material* rejection we cannot explain the transition from the presymbolic to the symbolic. We cannot explain what motivates the move through the mirror stage to the symbolic. Lacan, of course, posits the castration threat as the motive. But to experience this threat in the first place, the child must take a position as a subject in the mirror stage. It must recognize that it is and yet is not its image. The child must "see" the gap between its body and its image, the other. Kristeva persuasively argues that this move is already thetic and symbolic, that the mirror stage requires a negation of the other to identify as a subject or self. Negation is already a judgment, which is made only from a position. It is already thetic. In other words, in Lacan's account, we seem to be moving in circles: the child takes a position as subject so that it can negate its image to take a position as subject. "To say 'no' is already to formulate syntactically oriented propositions that are more or less grammatical" (1974, 122). For Kristeva, rather than prefiguring the symbolic, the mirror stage appears to already be symbolic.

How then do we get to this symbolic in the first place? If the mirror stage is already symbolic, then we certainly cannot use it as an explanation for the onset of the symbolic. Kristeva argues that the only way to explain the transition from presymbolic to symbolic is to acknowledge the material element, which is heterogeneous to the symbolic. Rejection is not unique to the symbolic.[1] Rather, it operates first in the semiotic body. For example, Kristeva reinterprets Freud's fort/da game: While Lacan sees a negativity that functions through the metonymy that marks the beginnings of symbolization, she sees a negativity that is still primarily gestural and kinetic—the bodily act of throwing and retrieving the reel (1974, 170).[2]

Negativity moves through the symbolic because it moves through the corporeal. It operates in living matter prior to the symbolic (1974, 123). And, for Kristeva, it acts not only as lack but as excess. If the symbolic is merely founded on a lack, then there is all the more reason for avoiding it altogether, for taking refuge in neurosis and psychosis. In Kristeva's account, however, material negativity is founded on excess. Anality is the primary example. When there is too much waste, some must be expelled. In anality, rejection precedes the symbolic (1974, 151).

Moreover, in anality, separation and rejection are pleasurable (1974, 151). Not only anality but also orality causes pleasure, which is an added motivation for speaking. As Kristeva describes it, the move from presymbolic to symbolic is not purely motivated by a castration threat or sense of lack. Rather, it is excess and pleasure that move the child into the realm of the symbolic. Here she challenges the Lacanian notion of the stern father of the law, who performs the function of the paternal third party who forces the child to move away from the maternal body and into the symbolic. Kristeva's theory subverts the Lacanian notion of the paternal function.

While for Lacan the material of language points to an unconscious that is structured like a language, for Kristeva it points to an unconscious that is heterogeneous to language. In *Black Sun* she says that "the unconscious is not structured like a language but like all the imprints of the Other, including and most particularly those that are most archaic, 'semiotic,' it is constituted by preverbal self-sensualities that the narcissistic or amorous experience restores to me" (1987a, 204–5). The unconscious is structured like the alterity already within the maternal body and the maternal function. The maternal body, with its rejections and reduplications, becomes a model for the unconscious and for the link between drives and symbols.

Taking the maternal body as a model, Kristeva returns to the Freudian theory of drives, which she maintains provides "a bridge between the biological foundation of signifying functioning and its determination by the family and society" (1974, 167). She is interested in this drive toward heterogeneity and how through jolts of matter it eventually produces the speaking subject. The material signifying process, or drive process, is both biological and social. For Kristeva, it cannot be reduced to either one or the other.

The material of language points back to the semiotic maternal body, which both gives rise to it and destroys it. It points to the maternal music in language. Is this unconscious, Kristeva's unconscious, beyond both Freud and Lacan because, as she says in *Tales of Love,* neither of them liked music (1987c, 192)? Or because of repression of the primary identification with their mothers? Or, ultimately, because they are not mothers?

Back into the Mother's Body

The Maternal Body or the Mother's Breast

Kristeva emphasizes the maternal function in and prior to the child's insertion into the symbolic. For her, material rejection operates according to a maternal logic that prefigures the law of the father. This law before the law of the father is the law of the mother's body, which regulates the oral and anal drives (1974, 27). The law of the father, then, is prefigured in the body of the mother. In the signifying process, Kristeva identifies this law before the law of the father with the semiotic *chora,* the organizing principle of which is the maternal body. She defines the *chora* as "a nonexpressive totality formed by drives and their stases in a motility that is as full of movement as it is regulated" (1974, 25). In a footnote in "Le sujet en procès," Kristeva describes the *chora:*

> [T]he *chora* is a womb or a nurse in which elements are without identity and without reason. The *chora* is a *place* of a *chaos* which *is* and which *becomes,* preliminary to the constitution of the first measurable body . . . the *chora* plays with the body of the mother—of woman—, but in the signifying process. (1977, 57)

This *chora,* this distant place, is not without regulation and is therefore the prototype for both the place of enunciation (the subject) and the place of denotation (the object) (1980a, 285). Maternal regulation sets up paternal prohibition. The mother regulates and monitors the child's body, what goes in and what comes out. Thus, the child's drives are regulated in relation to the mother's body. Kristeva maintains that the first sounds the child makes mimic this mother-child dyadic bodily relationship.[3] In fact, she suggests that some of the infant's first sounds are holdover muscle reactions from the infant's previous intrauterine experience (1980a, Place names).

For Kristeva, it is the mother's breast that satisfies the archaic oral drives and represents the maternal regulation, as the mother gives and takes away the breast. Following Freud, she suggests that the infant *becomes* the breast through its incorporation. This breast is not an object for the infant but a "model," a "pattern" (1987c, 25). The infant's identification with this model or pattern of/through incorporation is not the *imitation* of an object or a pattern. Rather, Kristeva describes this identification as a *reduplication* of the pattern, which suggests that this archaic identification, a strange identification indeed, is biological, or at any rate semiotic. It is intrasymbolic only in a very primitive sense. It is as if here again Kristeva follows her logic of rejection backwards through the first semiotic negations to discover the first semiotic identifications.[4] This archaic semiotic identification with the mother's breast, which is merely a reduplication, becomes the first in a series of reduplications. It prefigures and sets in motion the logic of object identifications in all object relations, including discourse and love (1987c, 25).

Kristeva compares the infant's incorporation of the breast to the subsequent incorporation of "the speech of the other." She explains that through incorporating the speech of the other the infant incorporates the pattern of language and thereby identifies with the other. In fact, it is the incorporation of the patterns of language through the speech of the other that enables the infant to communicate and thus commune with others. And through the ability to "assimilate, repeat, and reproduce" words, the infant becomes like the other: a subject (1987c, 26).

For Kristeva, the operator within this structure—the logic of reduplication, put in motion by the first identifications with the mother's body—sets up the logic of the psyche: repetition. The logic of reduplication itself becomes a pattern reduplicated by the psyche. Like her earlier notion of the logic of material rejection (with which she explains how we separate ourselves from others), the logic of reduplication reproduces itself differently on different levels. Patterns are reduplicated on level after level until thresholds are crossed—the semiotic gives way to the symbolic, biology becomes culture—but like fractals in geometry, the patterns are recognizable. What the logic of reduplication provides, which the logic of rejection did not, is a theory of identification. With her theory of narcissism, Kristeva can explain not only how we break away to become individuals but also how we come together to commune and love. In fact, she uses her notion of primary narcissism to reconceive the process of becoming a subject as a process that does not involve a break motivated by a threat that cuts off the possibility of love without fear.

But, for Kristeva, to become autonomous, the child must break out of this identification with the breast by abjecting its mother. It must move from an identification with the mother's nourishing breast to an identification with its own birth and the horrifying maternal sex, to an identification with an abjected and threatening mother.

Birth or the Mother's Sex

The abject threat comes from what has been prohibited by the symbolic, what has been prohibited so that the symbolic can be. The prohibition that founds and yet undermines society is the prohibition against the maternal body, whether it is the Oedipal prohibition against incest imagined by Freud, the prohibition against the mother's desire or *jouissance* imagined by Lacan, or the prohibition against the semiotic *chora* imagined by Kristeva (all of which Kristeva suggests are directed against the maternal body [1980b, 14]. The maternal body is what is off limits. For Kristeva, primary drive pleasure, which is associated with the mother's body, threatens the symbolic, which is why it is repressed. It threatens to uncover the process that leads to the appearance of unity and thereby expose that unity as merely one moment in the process. The unity of reason or consciousness cannot admit that it is part of a process that alternates between unity and the fragmentation and repetition of drives (1974, 148). To admit this, of course, is to admit that it is not unified. This is why the maternal body must become "abject," so that the child can become a subject proper.

The abject is not an object that corresponds to an ego; rather, it is what is excluded by the superego: "To each ego its object, to each superego its abject" (1980b, 2). The abject is disgusting. It makes you want to vomit. It is what is on the border, what does not respect borders. It is neither one nor the other, undecidable. The abject is not a "quality in itself." Rather, it is a relationship to a boundary and represents what has been "jettisoned out of that boundary, its other side, a margin" (1980b, 69). The abject is what threatens identity; it is neither good nor evil, subject nor object, ego nor unconscious, but something that threatens these very distinctions.

On the level of personal archeology, abjection shows up as the struggle to separate from the maternal body. This body, "having been the mother, will turn into an abject. Repelling, rejection; repelling itself, rejecting itself. Ab-jecting" (1980b, 13). The child tries to separate but feels that it is impossible. The mother is made abject to facilitate the separation from her. At this point the mother is not-yet-object and the child is not-yet-subject. The mother cannot tell whether this other in her *is* her or not, and either alternative seems equally impossible. The child in this abject relation to its mother is not yet separated from her but is no longer identical with her.

"Abjection is therefore a kind of *narcissistic crisis*" (1980b, 14). It is the "realization" that the primary identification with the mother is a "seeming," a fake. It is the beginnings of separation prior to the mirror stage. Or, as Kristeva maintains, it is the separation before the beginning. This abjection which calls the child's primary narcissism to account is founded in *birth itself.*

> Abjection preserves what existed in the archaism of pre-objectal relationship, in the immemorial violence with which a body becomes separated from another body in order to be—maintaining that night in which the outline of the signified thing vanishes and where only the imponderable affect is carried out. . . . This means once more that the heterogeneous flow, which portions the abject and sends back abjection, already dwells in a human animal that has been highly altered. . . . Significance is indeed inherent in the human body. (1980b, 10)

Human life, human society, is founded on the abject separation of one body from another at birth, a separation, like subsequent ones, that is labored but necessary. This primary separation, which founds and prefigures symbolic separation, is prior even to the maternal authority that separates the infant's body into drives and satisfactions. The prototypical abject experience is the experience of birth itself. It is at the birth of the child, and not before, that the identity of the human subject is most visibly called into question. Before the umbilical cord is cut, who can decide whether there are one or two subjects?

Birth is preidentity, presubject, preobject. Birth is an unruly border and therefore abject. It makes sense, then, that this not-yet-subject/not-yet-object is associated with the archaic mother: "defilement is the translinguistic spoor of the most archaic boundaries of the self's clean and proper body. In that sense, if it is a jettisoned object, it is so from the mother" (1980b, 73). The most archaic boundaries of the clean and proper self, of course, are those regulated by maternal authority, in particular anal and oral drives. Food, not yet the body, is taken in through the mouth. Feces, no longer the body, are expelled through the anus. The boundaries between body and not-body are controlled by the mother. As I have indicated, for Kristeva, both the subject and society, which depend on the symbolic, depend on the repression of this maternal authority. The symbolic, in setting up a parceling order, represses the parceling order set up by the maternal authority over the infant's body (1980b, 72). Kristeva revives the maternal function within traditional psychoanalytic theory. She problematizes the borders of the maternal and paternal functions, thereby, in a sense, "abjecting" the traditional paternal function. And certainly she pushes any crisis in that paternal function to its limit.

On the level of personal archeology, abjection becomes a kind of perverse protection in the face of primary repression. The not-yet subject with its not-yet- or no-longer-objects maintains "itself" as the abject. Abjection is a way of denying the primal narcissistic identification with the mother, almost. The child becomes the abject to try to avoid both separation from, and identification with, the maternal body—both equally painful, both equally impossible. If the abject "is a jettisoned object, it is so from the mother." The child *is this jettisoned object,* the waste violently expelled from the mother's body. The "subject" discovers itself as the impossible separation from, identification with, the maternal body. It hates that body but only because it cannot be free of it. That body, the body without borders, the body out of which this abject subject came, is impossible (1980b, 6). It is a horrifying, devouring body (1980b, 39);[5] it is a body that evokes rage and fear.

Kristeva says that the maternal body enrages because it carries the child (1988, 138). The rage is directed not just against the outside of the maternal body, which nourishes and weans; it is also directed against the inside of the maternal body, and especially the inside that becomes outside, the child among other things. This rage and fear are affects that mediate primary narcissism and the words that have not yet been acquired. They protect the "subject" against a complete collapse into primary narcissism; yet, at the same time, they show the crisis caused by the loss of union with the maternal body.

"Why abject?" asks Kristeva. "Perhaps because of maternal anguish, unable to be satiated within the encompassing symbolic," she answers (1980b, 12). Within the economy of the phallus, only the child authenticates the mother. So why should she let it go? Within the economy of the phallus, and the only available discourse on motherhood, the mother's is always an abject joy. She can rejoice in the abject—violent and painful—birth of her child.

And the child is left in an awkward position between birth and birth (between its birth and the realization of its birth),[6] repulsed by and yet mourning for this maternal anguish. If the mother's desire exists outside patriarchal discourse, if paternal discourse cannot account for it (e.g., the discourse of the virgin, or psychoanalysis, or even a certain feminism), then in order for the child to become its mother's desire, it too must fall out. If, within the patriarchal discourse, the mother's desire has no object, then in order for the child to become its mother's desire, it must take the place of no-object, the abject.

To put it in the terms of yet another metaphor, if within patriarchal discourse, especially psychoanalysis, woman is always and only man's other, then at most she can only pretend that she *is* the phallus (see 1986, 144). That is, she can only pretend to *be* the object of man's desire, his gratification, the phallus. She can have no gratification of her own, just as she does not *have* the phallus. Or, her only gratification, a masochistic *jouissance,* is to gratify another, to *be* the phallus. In these terms, then, the child must be the object of the phallus's desire—the hole, the hole out of which he came, "the adored and abhorred [abject] maternal sex" (cf. 1987c, 79, 369). The child identifies with the murky space between the inside and the outside of the maternal body.

Obviously, this identification with the border—or, more precisely, what breaks the border (between the inside and the outside of the body)—is going to have grave consequences for the Oedipal situation, in more ways than one. The child, the male child, feels rage against his mother because her carrying him in her womb compromises his identity. How can he become a man when "he" was once a woman? He was once part, now the expelled waste, of a woman's body. Even more curiously, how can he become a man and love a woman, that abject and threatening hole "represented" by his mother?[7]

In *Powers of Horror* Kristeva describes how the child, there always the male child, must split his mother in order to take up his masculine identity. The mother is split in two: the abject and the sublime (1980b, 157). Making the mother abject allows the male child to separate from his mother and become autonomous. If the mother is only abject, however, then she becomes the phobic object, and the child himself becomes abject. The Oedipal situation will be thrown out of alignment, on the brink of disappearing altogether. If the mother remains abject, she never becomes the object, and certainly not the object of love. The phobic substitutes the sign, in a denial of sexual difference, for the absent object (1980b, 45). Within the heterosexual story, the mother must also be made sublime so that the male child can take her, a woman, as an object of love. If she is only sublime, the child will not separate from her, will have no subject or object identity whatsoever, no primary repression and thus no secondary repression. In other words, the Other will have been completely foreclosed, never set up, and the child will be psychotic. He will still be unable to love a woman, or anyone else. For the psychotic, there is no one else, no object, no other(s). The sublime and abject must come together under the auspices of the paternal in order to produce the object of love (see 1987c, 368).

So, the son splits the mother, has his cake and eats it, too. But what about the daughter? Whereas the son splits the mother in order to unify himself, if the daughter splits the mother, she splits herself. In addition, the female does not have to divide the mother in order to take up her feminine identity. Taking up her gender identity requires that she abandon her mother as love object for the father (1988, 137). It would seem that for the female the mother need only be abject. But when the female makes her mother abject in order to reject her, she also makes herself abject, rejects herself, and not just temporarily. Kristeva maintains that when women do embrace the abject or even make themselves abject, it is in order to please a man, perhaps a pervert turned on by abjection (1980b, 54; 1988, 136). Feminine perversion, on the other hand, is very rare, because of the difficulty women have when they are in "combat" with their mothers (1988, 136–37).

Kristeva identifies two ways a woman can "get rid" of her mother. One possibility is that she never does get rid of her mother, but carries with her "this living corpse," the mother's body which no longer nourishes (1988, 137). Usually women close their eyes to this corpse; they forget about it. And they certainly don't eroticize it (1988, 137). The other alternative is that a woman forms a defense against the mother. Feminism is one such defense, and presumably, politics, art, and science are others. If a woman enters this "combat" with her mother without any such defense, Kristeva warns that it can lead to "fairly serious forms of psychosis" (1988, 137).

For both sexes, the battle to become autonomous is a battle with the mother. Primal repression, for both sexes, is a repression of the semiotic identification with the mother's body. In the traditional psychoanalytic account, primal repression is replaced and strengthened by a secondary repression—language. Language, in the end, comes through the law of the father, which guarantees that the primary prototype of the object, the mother, is signifiable even while she is desiring. Kristeva suggests that if we look closely at this thesis—that the mother is the first object—we see that "no sooner sketched out, such a thesis is exploded by its contradictions and flimsiness" (1980b, 32). For behind this mother-object is the mother's semiotic body, filled with drives and preobjects. Behind this mother-object is the anti-Oedipus, semiotic negativity, the logic of renewal, which takes us beyond and behind Oedipus and the unitary subject. Through a complex conception of the maternal function, Kristeva provides not only a discourse that can explain the child's move into the symbolic but also an alternative discourse of maternity. Her recuperated maternal function provides a support for both mother and child.

Although both Freud and Lacan acknowledge that the primary dyad is made up of mother and child, they emphasize the function of the father and his phallus. The Oedipal situation revolves around him and the big stick with which he enforces the law. He initiates the speaking being into language. In this scenario, especially Lacan's version of it, the third term (the father), or, more precisely, the fourth term (the symbolic), is not merely a satellite that circles the primary dyad. Rather, it is their sun, which while burning through the Milky Way that connects mother and child provides life and light to the speaking being. If this sun is eclipsed, the speaking being gives way to something subhuman, even animal.

Kristeva takes us back to the Milky Way of the primary dyad. She analyzes the pulses and jolts of this primary universe made up of only mother and child. In her scenario the father remains a third term which merely echoes with words the sounds already moving through this distant galaxy. The fourth term, which holds everything together and makes the human animal a speaking being, is material rejection, the fundamental alterity within, of which the symbolic is only one manifestation. Material (biosocial) rejection causes the animal to give way to the speaking being. And it is the mother's love that supports the move from material rejection to the symbolic "no" of Lacan's mirror stage.

Conception or the Mother's Womb

Even so, for Kristeva, the child can overcome the abject mother only through some paternal agency (1980a, 263). Although this paternal agency brings with it the need to symbolize, it is not Lacan's authoritarian father (1980b, 118, 44; 1986, 314). Rather, as Kristeva suggests in *Tales of Love,* it is the loving father who helps the child overcome abjection, and here she sets her loving father against Lacan's stern authoritarian father. By *Black Sun* they seem to be two faces of the same father, or at least collaborators. Here, not only must the loving imaginary father support the paternal function and the move to the symbolic; he must also be able to take the place of the stern Oedipal father (1987b, 23). In *Tales of Love* Kristeva claims to develop her notion of the imaginary father from Freud's "father in individual prehistory" in "Group Psychology and the Analysis of the Ego" (1921, 26). Her interpretation of Freud's father becomes her "loving father," and she chides Lacan for not seeing this loving father in Freud.

Kristeva argues that primary identification for Freud is with this "father in individual prehistory." As it turns out, this father is not really a father, or not only a father. Rather, the "father in individual prehistory," Kristeva's "imaginary father," is a combination of the mother and the father (the "father-mother conglomerate"; 1987c, 40). It has no sexual difference but has the characteristics of both masculine and feminine (1987c, 26, 40). The identification with this conglomerate is the vortex of primary identification within what she calls the "narcissistic structure," and this ordinary identification sets up all subsequent identifications, including the ego's identification with itself (33).

In "La vierge de Freud," Kristeva provides evidence for interpreting Freud's fantasy of a "prehistory" as a fantasy of a maternal semiotic meaning (1987d, 26). Here she argues that in Freud's text on Leonardo da Vinci we can read a "prehistoric," "unforgettable," "imaginary," "maternal function." From Freud's interpretation of the Catholic Virgin Mary, she extracts a maternal function that foreshadows the symbolic and meaning in the realm of the imaginary. She describes Freud's interpretation of the Virgin as a type of condensation in which he ultimately negates the maternal value of meaning, the semiotic, even when he exposes it. The maternal function described in "La vierge de Freud" bears an uncanny resemblance to the function Kristeva attributes to the imaginary father in *Tales of Love* and *Black Sun.* This "maternal function" is a "function which, already susceptible to meaning, reveals the archaic in signs and permits not only the elaboration but also the sublimation of introjective and projective fixations with 'the originary' " (1987d, 26). Here Kristeva reads Freud's fantasy of a prehistoric maternal as a maternal function already full of meaning, an imaginary formation somewhere between "the archaic and the symbolic," an imaginary mother (26).

In *Tales of Love* the identification with the prehistoric father-mother conglomerate—the originary—is an identification with an "imaginary father," a transference between the semiotic body and an ideal other who lacks nothing. Although it is both father and mother, it is called a father because, following Lacan, Kristeva identifies the symbolic with the father.[8] She explains this curiosity by arguing that even though the child's first affections are directed toward the mother, these archaic "object" relations are already "symbolic" and therefore associated with the father. This is to say that the logic of the symbolic is already within the maternal body. Although it seems strange, this combination is called a father because it is a metonymic relationship in the works. What she is suggesting is that the infant identifies, through an immediate transference that is pre-Oedipal, with the gap between the mother and her desire, which founds the Oedipal move and motivates the child's entrance into the symbolic: it is an archaic transference to the site of the symbolic in a preobjectal state. Here the father is not yet the father of the law of the symbolic. Rather, he is a presymbolic imaginary father who stands in as a support for the place of the mother's desire. The imaginary father is a metaphorical function that gives way to the metonymic paternal function; love gives way to desire.

Kristeva claims that the imaginary father allows an identification with the mother's desire for the phallus. In other words, the identification with the imaginary father allows an identification with the paternal function as it *already exists* in the mother. And this identification with the imaginary father also allows the child to "*ab-jet*" its mother's body and thereby separate from her. The separation from the mother's body is not tragic, however, because it is supported by the imaginary father, which is the mother's love itself. In my reading, the mother's love enacts the transference from the mother's body to the mother's desire and provides the needed support for the transference to the site of maternal desire. The transference to the imaginary father leads to a transference to the site of the mother's desire: her desire for the father, her desire to be satisfied, her implication in the paternal function. Insofar as the mother is primarily a speaking being, the other is already within her. That is, she is always already implicated in signifying systems. The mother-father conglomerate, then, is the combination of the mother and her desire. It is a father within the mother, a "maternal father."[9]

> The child, male or female, hallucinates its merging with a nourishing-mother-and-ideal-father, in short a conglomeration that already condenses two into one. . . . One soon notices, however, in the last instance (that is, if the couple truly becomes one, if it lasts), that each of the protag-

onists, he and she, has married, through the other, his or her mother. (1987c, 222–23)

In Kristeva's scenario, the husband is the phallic mother for the woman, while the wife is the mother who allows the man to remain a child. In the traditional story of Oedipal resolution the man finds his mother in his wife, while the woman finds her father in her husband. Moving through Lacan's twists in the Oedipal story, Kristeva argues that the woman finds her mother in her husband. She finally becomes the phallus (satisfaction) for her mother in the person of her (nourishing) husband. Thus,her Oedipal wish, to be the mother's phallus, is, like the man's, satisfied in marriage.[10] The woman, like the man, needs to couple to refind the lost mother; the mother is the "pedestal" of the couple, because the couple provides a reunion with the mother.

Once again it seems that the fantasy of a conglomerate mother-father, a fantasy of wholeness, is a fantasy of the reunion with the mother. Kristeva postulates the loving imaginary father as the archaic disposition of the paternal function preceding the symbolic, the mirror stage, and the Oedipal father (1987c, 22). She challenges traditional psychoanalytic conceptions of the paternal function and suggests that there are various paternal functions, not just Lacan's paternal phallus that lays down the law. As Kristeva sets it out, the imaginary father is not only a forefather to Lacan's father of the law but also a rival (1987c, 46). In *Tales of Love* she chooses the loving father over Lacan's stern father; in *Black Sun* she imagines a father who is both stern and loving, and for the infant, primarily loving.

Kristeva's claim to the loving father seems to be her claim to an inheritance that may have been given to Lacan, but is rightfully hers. As I have suggested, her claim to the loving father ideal is a claim to the loving mother. She takes her stand, separated from the mother but loved by the father (Freud?), to rival Lacan. Through this identification with the father, a father who loves like a mother, she can become the "imaginary" son, the rightful heir of psychoanalysis. Otherwise, she remains the abject mother outside the law and nothing but a threat to it, a position that calls into question her position as an analyst. As the abject mother, she cannot stand in for the father of the law, Lacan's stern father, and thereby engender the necessary transference to put the analysand back on track. She cannot be the place of that stern third party for whose sake the analytic relationship (like all others) exists. Thus, she postulates a loving third who gives herself up to the countertransference and loves the analysand like her child (see *In the Beginning Was Love*; Kristeva, 1988). Which is to say, she loves her own mother through the analysand, who "is" her child. So, through analysis, Kristeva seeks an identification with her mother, and this identification, the mother's with the mother, is the site to which the analysand transfers, the site of primary identification, which she calls the "imaginary father." The analyst, then, becomes the loving mother and not (merely) the stern father.

The Crisis in the Paternal Function

Kristeva qualifies the search for a primary identification itself by claiming that she is not trying to discover whether "daddy or mummy" is the primary object. Rather, she is looking for a way to treat her patients. She is looking for an identification that can provide, through the psychoanalytic transference, a sense of completion and wholeness that combines the maternal gratifications and the paternal prohibitions (1987c, 29). Thus, she invents the imaginary father who loves like a mother.

For Kristeva, the identification with the imaginary father sets up the emptiness within the narcissistic structure. The child finds itself between the mother and the imaginary father as that which is not the object of its mother's desire. The postulation of the imaginary father allows the child to imagine that the mother desires an other, "not I," and this "not I" sets up the space that eventually will be filled in by the father of the law, the symbolic. It seems that Kristeva has only a small bone to pick with Lacan over what she might call the "reduplication" of fathers that stand behind his one father of the law.

Kristeva argues, however, that the loving and not the stern father is necessary in order to serve at least two functions that protect the narcissistic space properly required to begin the process of becoming a symbolic subject: to offset devouring by the abject mother and to provide an imaginary secular replacement for a dead Christian god. Without the loving father we are abandoned by God and possibly devoured by abjection as well.

In *Black Sun* Kristeva calls the melancholic a radical atheist (5). The empty discourse of melancholia is a eulogy to the dead god, or at least a god who has abandoned his children. Working within a Christian imaginary, she seems to suggest that God is the word and as such still exists. However, God is also love and as such is dead. And without love the word is empty. Kristeva, herself mourning the loss of God the loving father, creates his secular substitute in the loving imaginary father. The function of a god who is the word and yet whose name cannot be spoken is taken over by the imaginary father, what she also calls the "cult of the irrepresentable" (1987c, 313).

The irrepresentable that makes representation possible is represented, strangely enough, by the imaginary father. Without the loving father, psychoanalysis, like religion, makes for masochism and/or paranoia (1987c, 311). We live in fear and under the constant surveillance of the stern father: superego or God of Abraham. This stern father cannot coax us away from our maternal shelter even if that shelter threatens to devour us, which is why we need the loving father as a support against abjection. Without "him," we are "extraterrestrials suffering for want of love" (1987c, 382–83). It is not a crisis in the law that has led to this suffering; rather, it is a lack of love:

> There has been too much stress on the crisis in paternity as cause of psychotic discontent. Beyond the often fierce but artificial and incredible tyranny of the Law and the Superego, the crisis in the paternal function that led to the deficiency of psychic space is in fact an erosion of the loving father. It is for want of paternal love that Narcissi, burdened with emptiness, are suffering; eager to be others, or women, they want to be loved. (1987c, 378)

Kristeva sees the crisis in paternity as the lack of love and not the lack of law. Thus, the contemporary analyst does not have to repair the analysand's relation to the law or the symbolic but must provide imaginary love to support that relation. She argues that if there were only the symbolic or Oedipal father, then there would be no way to offset the abject mother. Without the loving father, there is no way for the child to separate itself from the body of its abject mother. She suggests that the negation seen in borderline cases is not the repudiation of the name of the father but the inability to escape the abject mother (1987c, 50).

If the discourse of the borderline person seems empty, this does not necessarily mean that the law of the father has been foreclosed. Rather, the third party to whom the discourse should be addressed, the third party in/for whom the discourse becomes meaningful, is not necessarily the father of the law. The father of the law may well be in place; this is evidenced by the possibility of the discourse and the transference in the analytic situation (1987c, 50). But the discourse seems empty without the support of the primary identification with the loving imaginary father. "He" is the missing third; it is only in the context of "his" love that the symbolic has meaning.

In some sense, following my earlier reading, this loving third allows a reunion with the mother in a different guise and thereby facilitates the separation from the mother's body and a playful and sublimational entry into the symbolic. Without this loving third for whom we speak, we enter language with mourning and melancholy. We long for the lost maternal "thing" from whom we necessarily separate in order to enter the symbolic. If there is a loving imaginary father, who is really the mother's love in disguise, then our reunion with the mother comes through giving her up. To begin the process of becoming a subject we must abject the mother in order to separate from her. Without the support of the imaginary father—the mother's love—we will be devoured by abjection rather than become autonomous. We become abject, the in-between, the emptiness. We become the borderline between drives and symbols.

The borderline speaks of desire, but the discourse is empty, laden with drives that pass through repressive censorship because the words do not signify. The discourse is experienced as empty even though it is full of drives and affect representations. Thus, the structure of the metonymy of desire is in place, but the narcissistic structure of what Kristeva calls the "metaphor of love" is broken, not within the symbolic proper but earlier. The symbolic is set up on emptiness, an emptiness unprotected by the imaginary. For Kristeva it is an archaic transferential imaginary identification that moves the would-be subject away from the mother and into the symbolic. This imaginary third, the imaginary father, is the missing addressee in and for whom the translation of drives into language has meaning (1987c, 50).

Kristeva maintains that the imaginary is the ability to transfer meaning where it is lost (1987a, 103). The imaginary father transfers meaning to the lost maternal body. "He" reconciles the child to the loss of the maternal "thing" (1987a, 13). Kristeva argues that we must agree to lose the mother in order to imagine and name her, that the "link between pleasure and symbolic dignity . . . is insured by an imaginary father, as he leads his child from primary to secondary identification" (1987a, 41, 92–93). Imaginary pleasure is associated with the maternal body, while symbolic dignity is associated with the paternal (1986, 231; 1987d, 26).

For the child to move away from the maternal container, it must encounter the third party, the other; and this other, the third in the Oedipal situation, is the "Meaning of discourse" (1987c, 13). The child, then, must encounter the meaning of discourse as the other for/in "whom" it must speak, love, exist. Within the Lacanian framework, insofar as the other is also the desire for the phallus—the unfulfillable desire for satisfaction that keeps us talking—it is the mother's desire. The imaginary father is the maternal desire for the phallus (1987c, 40). It is the other already within the mother, not only in the real sense during pregnancy but also in the imaginary and symbolic senses. The other is, after all, primarily a speaking being.

For Kristeva, the mother loves the child through the third so that the child feels loved. Early in *Tales of Love* Kristeva maintains that the mother must love her child for the sake of a third party. If she does not, then she loves only herself. She is the classic narcissist, incapable of love. In other words, if she loves the child without any "diversion" toward an other, she is clinging to the child, hysterically demanding its love. She is loving the child as herself and is not, therefore, loving any other. Thus, the child believes that it is not loved, since its mother loved no *other* (1987c, 34).

Love, as Kristeva argues, is neither biology nor desire. Rather, it is the domain of the imaginary that moves between biology and desire, between the maternal body and the symbolic. Love, says Kristeva, is not a "narcissistic merger with the maternal container but the emergence of a metaphorical object—in other words the very splitting that establishes the psyche and, let us call this splitting 'primal repression,' bends the drive toward the symbolic of an other" (1987c, 31). The mother's love, rather than calling the child back to the maternal body, moves it toward the maternal desire, "toward the symbolic of an other." It is the mother's love that supports the move to the symbolic through "loving idealization," the function of the imaginary "father" (1987c, 33–34). The mother's love is the imaginary third. As early as "The Father, Love, and Banishment," Kristeva suggests that the mother's love is the "facsimile of the third person." Here she argues that not until Freud did motherhood

> by means of a language that "musicates through letters," resume within discourse the rhythms, intonations, and echolalias of the mother-infant symbiosis—intense, pre-Oedipal, predating the father—and this in the third person. Having a child, could a woman, then, speak another love? Love as object banished from paternal Death, facsimile of the third person, probably. (1980a, 157)

In an interview, Kristeva claims that it is not necessary to call the terms of the Oedipal situation "mother" and "father." She says that we could just as well call them "X" and "Y." In addition, she suggests that the sharp distinction between these two is breaking down. "There are contaminations between them." "This," says Kristeva, "is due to the crisis of the paternal function and the rendering of my 'X' and 'Y' ambiguous" (1984, 23). She endorses this "ambiguisation of identity." In another interview, she says that women can take the role of the third and fulfill the paternal function (1988, 139). Of course, the analyst is also a facsimile of the third party regardless of sexual differences. Thus, Kristeva breaks open the paternal function and the identification between the necessary third and paternal law.

In my reading, the movement between the abjected maternal body and the imaginary father or mother's love—which provides an incentive for the child to replace its demands on the mother's body with desires in language—suggests three terms prior to the Oedipal triangle of traditional psychoanalysis. On the "presymbolic" imaginary level that Kristeva describes, the narcissistic "subject" is the result of a transferential identification with the imaginary father, the seed of the ego ideal, which supports a separation from the abject mother. Kristeva's *prefigured* Oedipal situation operates between the narcissistic subject (the child), the abject mother (the mother's body), and the imaginary father (the mother's love) (1987c, 374).[11] These terms correspond to what I have called the mother's breast (maternal body), the mother's sex (birth), and the mother's womb (conception). In my reading, Kristeva sets up the *prefigured* Oedipal structure within the maternal function. Although these terms operate prior to the Oedipal complex and, in one sense, prior to the onset of the symbolic, their functions prefigure those of the three terms in the traditional Oedipal situation.

In traditional psychoanalysis, on the other hand, the ego is formed by pitting the superego against the id. On another level, it becomes the battle between the father and the mother in which, if the process is "normal," the father wins out and the desire for the mother is at best sublimated and at worst denied. I suggest that within Kristeva's texts, the paternal function is preceded and superseded by the maternal function. The imaginary father is more important than the traditional father of the law; "he" is merely a disguise for the mother's love. Even the Oedipal movement from the imaginary father to the stern Oedipal father turns out to be a move from the mother's love to the mother's desire.

"Herethics"—Loving the Other as/in Oneself

Kristeva reasks the question "What does woman want?" by asking, "What does the mother want?" She answers that the mother's desire is indeterminate; it is a desire for the phallus of the imaginary father, which could be her father or her child's father. In either case, it is a desire for the paternal phallus, which, within this Lacanian framework, represents gratification. What does any desire want? Gratification from an other. This is the lesson the child learns even on the semiotic level. What if the mother wants to be loved like a child herself? What if the mother creates a new kind of love that does not require the third party to stand in between holding apart and bringing together? A love outside the law.

Late in *Tales of Love* in a piece written prior to the rest, "Stabat Mater," Kristeva imagines this outlaw love. She imagines the mother's love for the child, which is a love for herself but also a willingness to give herself up, as the basis of a new ethics—"herethics" (1987c, 262–63). To imagine this "herethics," Kristeva suggests that it is necessary to listen to the mother and her music. Motherhood, she claims, needs the support of mother's mother (even in the person of a father, or imaginary father) (227); the mother's oscillating union/disunion with her child recalls her own union with her mother. When we listen to Kristeva, the mother, we see that her mother is present in her own motherhood: "Recovered childhood, dreamed peace restored, in sparks, flash of cells, instant of laughter, smiles in the blackness of dreams, at night, opaque joy that roots me in her bed, my mother's, and projects him, a son, a butterfly soaking up dew from her hand, there, nearby, in the night. Alone: she, I, and he" (247). Thus, the love that founds "herethics" is a daughter's love through identification with her mother. A mother's love is her reunion with her own mother, not only as a third party but also as herself. The child's transferential identification with the imaginary father is an identification with its mother's reunion with her mother, and it is this union which satisfies, makes one complete.

What does a mother want, especially in childbirth? She wants her mother. "The Paradox: Mother or Primary Narcissism," the subtitle of 'Stabat Mater," points to the mother as the site of the primary identification, which Kristeva calls the "imaginary father." If the mother loves an other, it is her own mother, and she loves her mother not only as an other but also as herself, now the mother. This love, which is narcissism—within patriarchal analysis "the inability to love"—is the basis of her "herethics."

Herethics is an ethics founded on the relationship between the mother and child during pregnancy and birth, one that sets up one's obligations to the other as obligations to the self and obligations to the species. It is founded on the ambiguity in pregnancy and birth between subject and object positions.[12] Pregnancy, says Kristeva, is an "institutionalized psychosis": Am I me or it? (1986, 297).[13] The other cannot be separated from the self, is within the self. It is not in its place—the place of the other—but rather in the place of the subject. This inability to separate self from other is a symptom of psychosis, the fundamental psychosis upon which any relationship is built. Only in pregnancy, says Kristeva, is this psychosis socially acceptable.[14]

How can we account for this other that resides in the maternal body without destroying the identity of the mother? And if our mothers have no identity, are we born out of a void? The mother's identity is questionable and as such points to the questionable identity of the subject itself. After all, is not the mother a subject, too? Kristeva argues that to suppose that the mother is the master of her gestation preserves her identity. In this case, she is the master of a process that is prior to the social contract of the group, a process that is presymbolic and therefore without identity. Thus, she risks losing her identity at the same time as she wards off its loss. It seems that we recognize that there is a presymbolic process out of which we are produced, but at the same time we deny it. We assure ourselves that "Mama is there" and that her presence in, and identity through, the process guarantees that everything is representable. Of course, this is to cover over "Mama's" questionable identity in this process. "In a double-barreled move," claims Kristeva, "psychotic tendencies are acknowledged, but at the same time they are settled, quieted, and bestowed upon the mother in order to maintain the ultimate guarantee: symbolic coherence" (1980a, 238).

Maternity, says Kristeva, is a bridge between nature and culture, between the drives and the symbolic. The other's body is the "pivot of sociality," "at once the guarantee and a threat to its stability" (1986, 297). The mother's body guarantees the continuation of the species and yet her questionable identity threatens the symbolic unity. Thus, maternity is impossible for the symbolic. Kristeva defines the maternal as "the ambivalent principle that is bound to the species, on the one hand, and on the other stems from an identity catastrophe that causes the Name to topple over into the unnameable that one imagines as femininity, nonlanguage, or body" (1987c, 235). The mother cannot be on the side of the drives or we are born out of something nonsocial and nonsymbolic; yet she cannot straddle the drives and the symbolic for the same reason, and she cannot be completely within the symbolic or we lose the child. The symbolic can deal with the other only as myth and fantasy (the virgin mother, the denigrated woman), which covers over this psychotic process and undecidable identity.

The mother knows better. While the child's relationship to the other may eventually set up the place of the other (through the primary maternal authority over the body, which leads to the mirror stage, and castration in the Oedipal situation) as the place of desire, which ensures symbolization, the mother's relationship to the child is another story. Kristeva suggests that the child may be the mother's first experience of an other. After all, in our culture, woman *is* the other, and if, as Lacan maintains, there is no other of the other, then woman has no other. For woman it is the one and not the other that is taken for granted. The birth of the child, however, "constitutes an *access* (excess) toward the Other" (1980a, 279). The mother experiences her being as a being for an other, which argues Kristeva, is a woman's only access to the other and therefore to love (1980b, 10; 1980a, 279).

The mother's experience of the child as other, then, is not a relation to the phallus and, by definition, unfulfillable desire:

> For a mother . . . [t]he other is inevitable, she seems to say, turn it into a God if you wish, it is nevertheless natural, for such an other has come out of myself. . . . The "just the same" of motherly peace of mind, more persistent than philosophical doubt, gnaws, on account of its basic disbelief, at the symbolic's allmightiness. It bypasses perverse negation ("I know, but just the same") and constitutes the basis of the social bond in its generality, in the sense of "resembling others and eventually the species. (1987c, 262)

The mother's other, rather than the unreachable other, the phallus, is a natural other. "Turn it into a God if you wish," but it is not transcendent; it is real. The mother has bodily proof of this. For the mother this relationship with the other is not a struggle for recognition—either me or you, subject or object. The child really is/was part of the mother's flesh. And her own flesh exists for the sake of the child, because at the limit, the child does not and cannot "exist for itself." This other is not yet autonomous; it depends on the subject. As such, it threatens the "almightiness" of the symbolic, which requires an autonomous and inaccessible other. Within Lacanian theory, it is this inaccessibility that opens the gap between signifier and signified and produces the symbolic. The mother, however, gains access to what is off-limits. She "knows" better. She knows that there is no transcendent other, no phallus. The other is the flesh of her flesh—natural, loved. She knows that the other is not transcendent, that it is within.

Whereas the perverse negation, the fetishism, necessary to maintain the symbolic—"I know that the word is not the thing, but just the same," "I know that the other is not me, but just the same"—constitutes the social bond through force, the mother's "just the same" is its reverse (see 1980b, 37). The mother negates the symbolic even while ensuring its generation. She realizes that the other is the same, that the gap is not absolute. In the face of the symbolic and its transcendental signifier, she says, "just the same, I know," and this "just the same" constitutes the social bond through love, not force. This "just the same" threatens to do away with difference: "It can crush everything the other (the child) has that is specifically irreducible" (1987c, 263). In other words, it threatens to do away with the symbolic. It threatens psychosis. Even if the symbolic denies the existence of the other, she cannot, for the sake of her child, deny the existence of the symbolic. She must wean the child. She must instigate the breakup of their primary symbiosis. She must be silent about what she "knows," because she knows better (260).[15]

The child must separate from its mother in order to be an autonomous being. It cannot remain dependent on her. And it is the mother's love and her love for her own mother, a narcissistic love from generation to generation, that supports the move into the symbolic, that fills language with meaning. It is possible that primary narcissism is repressed because it is a reunion with the mother's love, which is founded on yet mistaken for a union with the mother's body? In the traditional psychoanalytic story, primary identification with the mother is repressed because of the paternal law against incest. Could the father of the law be wrong? Perhaps primary identification is not with the mother's body but with the mother's love. Could this be some primordial transference from body to love which constitutes the first identity? This maternal love is not (yet) the *metonymic* desire for the phallus; rather, it is what Kristeva calls the *metaphor* of love. In terms of the phallocentric discourse, this love is narcissism without a properly alien other. Alterity is within. Yet without this narcissism, Kristeva's "primary narcissism," the other's "narcissism," discourse is empty, meaningless, mourning the loss of love.

A Politics of Difference: *Strangers to Ourselves*

Kristeva's fantasy of the imaginary father is a fantasy of identity that does not set up an absolute alterity imposed by a paternal threat. The primary identification with the imaginary father neither absorbs nor ostracizes the difference of the other. Rather, it is a fantasy that invites difference and thereby a new conception of identity. Kristeva maintains that throughout her writings she has concentrated on texts that break traditional notions of identity. Certainly this is true of the three types of "texts" that take priority in her writings: maternity, poetic language, and psychoanalysis. In each of these "texts" the identity of the unified subject is called into question: the subject is most explicitly "inprocess/on trial." Each of these three discourses points to the alterity within identity. After turning away from politics over a decade ago because she saw it as merely self-serving and theological, in her latest writing, Kristeva uses discourses of alterity in order to develop a new politics born out of a new ethics—"herethics."

In the case of maternity, as I explained earlier, identity is called into question. "It is an identity," says Kristeva, "that splits, turns in on itself and changes without becoming other" (1986, 297). According to

Kristeva, pregnancy is "the splitting of the subject," which translator Alice Jardine claims "refers directly to Kristeva's subject in process/on trial" (1982, 49). Pregnancy, then, is a case in which identity contains alterity as a heterogeneous other without completely losing its integrity, in which the very notions of identity and difference are called into question.

Like maternity, poetic language problematizes the notions of identity and difference, for Kristeva another case in which identity is full of difference and yet somehow maintains its integrity as language. In poetic language, the heterogeneity in language is at its most apparent; it is language that is also not language, language other to itself. Like maternity, it points to subject-in-process/on trial. While the alterity within poetic language is imaginary or symbolic, however, in maternity it is real. As Ewa Ziarek argues, the alterity within poetic language is less shocking than the alterity within maternity because while poetry may seem esoteric, maternity is a fact of everyday life (1992).

And psychoanalysis, of course, is a discourse of alterity within identity. The notion of the unconscious makes any stable or unified subject, truth, or meaning impossible. Even the individual is full of difference, other to itself. For Kristeva, psychoanalysis analyzes a series of splittings—birth, weaning, separation—as indispensable to an individual's identity (1987a, 132). It is a science of subjects-in-process/on trial; it records the evolutions and devolutions of these strangers. Kristeva argues that, like subjects undergoing psychoanalysis, pregnant Madonnas, and avant-guard poets, we are all subjects-in-process, strangers to ourselves. It is on the basis of this psychoanalytic insight that Kristeva begins to develop a politics of difference.

Her books *Strangers to Ourselves* (1991) and *Lettre ouverte à Harlem Désir* (1990) are about how we can live with difference. Kristeva suggests that psychoanalysis can provide a new way of thinking about difference, not to reify and exclude it but to welcome it. She argues that this was Freud's project (1991, 284). Freud tried to show that alterity is within us, and he created psychoanalysis as an invitation to live with it. Kristeva maintains that psychoanalysis sets up an ethics that respects the irreconcilable (1991, 269). Psychoanalysis accepts—even invites—difference, nonmeaning, otherness, and in turn, she argues, this ethics of psychoanalysis implies a politics.

So, after over a decade of denouncing politics, in the conclusion of *Strangers to Ourselves* Kristeva provides the foundation for a politics that she argues grows out of psychoanalysis: "The ethic of psychoanalysis implies a politics: it would be a question of a cosmopolitanism of a new type which, transversal to governments, to economies and to markets, works for a humanity whose solidarity is founded on the consciousness of its unconscious—desiring, destructive, fearful, void, impossible" (284). For Kristeva, psychoanalysis calls on us to work toward this humanity, whose solidarity is founded on a consciousness of its unconscious (284). She instructs us to recognize the difference in us as the condition of our being with others (1991, 285; 1990, 19). Recall Lacan's phrase: the unconscious is the discourse of the other. It is the unconscious that allows us to be with others. For the first time in history, says Kristeva, in the absence of any community bond other than economic, without either a community embracing our particularities or the power to transcend them, we must live with differences in moral codes (1991, 290). She imagines a "paradoxical community" "made of strangers who accept themselves insofar as they recognize themselves as strangers to themselves" (290).

In all of her writing, Kristeva has attempted to introduce us to the stranger in ourselves. Following Freud, she has developed the notion of alterity as inherent in identity. For Kristeva, this strangeness in identity can found a new ethics and politics. Maternity provides a fundamental metaphor for an ethics through which we can love the other in/as ourselves. Psychoanalysis provides a fundamental metaphor through which we can accept the stranger in/as ourselves. Both of these metaphors serve the same function. The ethics of psychoanalysis is born out of "herethics," and neither this ethics nor the politics it implies is enforced by an exterior paternal law. In her view, the crisis in the paternal function is a welcome crisis in the authoritarian reign of the stern father. She imagines that this crisis can and must open the possibility for a loving father, a fantasy of union through and because of difference. The loving father is neither an exterior support nor locked inside the subject(-to-be). Rather, the loving father is already implicated in the maternal function, and its logic can be found even in the maternal body, which is full of alterity. Only the loving imaginary father can make the trip from mother's body to mother's desire—from drives to language—a pleasant one. And, for Kristeva, it is pleasure that ensures that we will keep on talking and live together meaningfully.

5

Recognition, Witnessing, and Identity: Drucilla Cornell on Family Law

In one of her most recent books, *The Imaginary Domain* (1995), Drucilla Cornell develops a notion of legal equality that entails equal protection of minimum conditions of individuation. She uses this notion of legal equality to analyze the ways in which pornography, restrictions on abortion, and sexual harassment limit women's equal protection of the minimum conditions of individuation. Sensitive to the tension between legal circumscription of equality and the possibility of freedom, Cornell tries to develop a notion of equality that expands rather than restricts freedom and maintains the tension between equality and freedom in productive ways. In her recent work on family law, Cornell uses the framework she developed in *The Imaginary Domain* to analyze family law, specifically laws governing adoption.

In this chapter I want to explore a deeper conflict between legal equality and personal freedom implicit in Cornell's analysis, a conflict that turns on the freedom to self-identification heralded in her work. Both legal equality (and the legal recognition, entitlements, or restrictions that it entails) and personal freedom (with its social imbrications) involve identity. Legally circumscribed equality involves redeploying and redefining various categories of identifications, including those explicitly challenged by Cornell (citizen and parent) and those left unchallenged by Cornell (each one of us, persons, mothers, and fathers). Personal freedom requires the space for constantly renegotiating identity and those categories inscribed by social institutions, including legal institutions.

Through my engagement with Cornell, I try to further problematize theories of identity based on either abjection or recognition and further develop alternative notions of identity based on witnessing to what is beyond recognition. To this end, I take up four related questions, which I hope will advance the discussion of motherhood and citizenship, as well as the more general discussion of the relationships between recognition, witnessing, and identity: (1) What notion of identity is consistent with Cornell's theory of the equivalent chance to become a person? (2) What is the relationship between the concept *mother* and the concept *citizen*? (3) Is it important to discuss paternity in a feminist analysis of family law? (4) What is the relationship between feminist witnessing and recognition?

Identity and Citizenship

Cornell claims that we need to emphasize *the right* instead of *the good* because current family law defines the family strictly in terms of heterosexuality and sex role stereotypes and thereby gives priority to the good as proscribed by the church, which conflates, rather than separates, church and state. Rather than protect the conservative patriarchal values of the church, Cornell maintains that the state through its civil laws should protect the subjectivity of each citizen. She rearticulates the Hegelian insight that law is the guardian of subjectivity "to demand equal protection of the imaginary domain of each one of us, the psychic space in which we both struggle against, contend with, and playfully take on sexual and genderized personae" (11). She advocates "the equal protection of the imaginary domain in the name of citizens' equivalent chance to become a person, to interiorize and cohere the identifications that make us who we are into a self" (6).

In *The Imaginary Domain*, Cornell criticizes even liberal political theorists who assume that human beings are from the beginning persons with equal rights. Instead, she maintains that becoming a person is a project that requires basic conditions of individuation, conditions that include primary care while we are children, and self-respect, which is possible only if psychic space is free from social and legal restrictions on our identity and personhood. Theories that assume personhood from the beginning devalue the labor of mothers in raising children and ignore the difficulties involved in overcoming stereotypes that confine many of us in roles that define us as inferior, dependent, or incapable of the kind of individuation necessary to become a complete person. Degrading stereotypes of femininity, for example, affect our images of ourselves as women and undermine our self-respect, which is fundamental to the formation of personhood.

"We are degraded," says Cornell, "when our 'sex' is defined, symbolized and treated as antithetical to equal personhood and citizenship" (10). When this happens, other people's images of us, or stereotypical images of us, are forced on us in ways that rob us of respect for our own sexuate being (8). When our sex is treated as antithetical to personhood or citizenship, then we are in the impossible situation of choosing between being persons or citizens, *or* who we are as sexuate beings. Cornell concludes that public constraints on degradation, or downgrading on the basis of sex or sexuality, are legitimate and necessary to ensure the prerequisite minimum conditions of individuation for the equivalent chance to become a person. In her analysis, the protection of these minimum conditions of individuation does not undermine freedom but makes it possible (20).

This brings me to my first question: What notion of identity is consistent with Cornell's theory of the equivalent chance to become a person? More specifically, what notion of identity is consistent with Cornell's analysis of a productive tension between equality and freedom? I want to start by explaining why one currently popular theory of identity based on Mary Douglas's notion of defilement is not consistent with Cornell's theory of equality. My motivation in this analysis is that I reject any normative claims that Douglas's followers make for structures of identity based on abjection, and I believe that Cornell's theory can be used to argue against such notions of identity.

In *Purity and Danger,* Douglas describes defilement as the danger to identity constituted by filth, which is always defined in relation to the borders of that very identity (1969). Douglas's theory of defilement has been transformed by Julia Kristeva (1980b) into her neo-Hegelian theory of abjection, with which she purports to explain the dynamics of both group and individual identity as constituted through the rejection of otherness. Judith Butler expands the theory of abjection when she analyzes the dynamics of exclusion inherent in identification (1989, 1993). Many other feminists and theorists of marginalization have followed suit.

I agree with Cornell when she suggests in *The Imaginary Domain* that theories of abjection are useful in describing some of the oppressive logics of patriarchy, but abjection cannot be part of a theory of equality (26). Theories of abjection can diagnose the operations of oppression, but they do not in themselves suggest alternatives. In fact, if taken as standards for identification, theories of abjection *normalize* the most hateful and threatening kinds of discrimination, exclusion, and oppression. If our identities are necessarily formed by rejecting and excluding what is different, then discrimination is inherent in the process of identification. On the level of individual identification, if self-identity is formed by rejecting what is different, in the first instance, as the story goes, the infant rejects its mother. If abjection of the mother or maternal body is described as a normal or natural part of child development, then one consequence is that without some antidote to this abjection, all of our images of mothers and maternal bodies are at some level abject because we all necessarily rejected our own mothers to become individuals. I will say more about our images of mothers when I take up my second question about the relationship between our conception of *mother* and our conception of *citizen*. On the level of social identification, if group identity is formed by rejecting what is different, then war, hatred, and oppression are inevitable and unavoidable parts of social development.

Aside from my own squeamishness in the face of such pessimism, if we accept Cornell's notion of the necessity and possibility of the equivalent chance to become persons through the legal protection of the minimum conditions of individuation required to do so, we must reject normative notions of abjection. We can endorse theories of abjection as *descriptions* of the dynamics of oppression and exclusion without accepting that abjection is *necessary* to self-identity. If abjection is necessary to self-identity, then the equivalent chance to become persons becomes an impossible dream. If my ability to individuate *necessitates* that I hate and exclude you because you are different, then by protecting the minimum conditions for my individuation, the law must threaten the minimum conditions for your own individuation. My argument is that the notion of identity based on abjection describes individuals as inherently antagonistic in the essence of their individuality and self-identity. Theories that normalize abjection leave us stuck at the level of Hegel's master-slave dialectic in which a fight to the death is inevitable.

Cornell's theory of equality suggests an alternative notion of identity in which one individual's ability to become a person is not opposed to another's. If all sexuate beings can be guaranteed the minimum conditions of individuation to protect their equivalent chance to become a person, then every being's self-identity and self-respect can and must be consistent with another's self-identity and self-respect. Although the content of their individuality may vary greatly—how each acts and behaves—their chance at individuation must be equal. This suggests that in principle we can form individual and group identities in harmony, at least on the level of the fundamental structure of identity, if never on the level of the content of identity.

Part of my own project has been to suggest alternatives to the traditional philosophical and psychoanalytic views of individuation and self-identity that are built around the exclusion of otherness and difference. In particular, as an alternative to models of the mother-infant relationship that view the mother as an obstacle that must be overcome in order for the infant to become a social subject, in the last chapter of

Womanizing Nietzsche (1995) and the first two chapters of *Family Values* (1997), I present a model of the mother-infant relationship that views the mother as the first cooperative partner in a social relationship that makes subjectivity possible. The reason that so many traditional theories of the mother-child relationship see the mother as an obstacle to autonomy is that motherhood and maternity are conceived in opposition to everything social and everything fundamental to civil society. Mothers have been imagined as creatures motivated only by instinct and natural tendencies.

Mothers and Citizen

This brings me to my second question: What is the relationship between the concept *mother* and the concept *citizen?* On the one hand, in "Re-thinking Consciousness Raising: Citizenship and the Law and Politics of Adoption," Cornell argues that women should be entitled to the protections of citizenship apart from their roles and duties as mothers (1996). On the other hand, Cornell argues that we need to recognize as mothers both women who give birth to children and those who raise children. Specifically, she argues that birth-mothers who relinquish their children to adoption should be given legal access to their children, including custodial rights if all parties consent, and all the information on their children that might help them negotiate their identities as mothers. In other words, the state should protect the imaginary domain in which birth-mothers conceive of themselves as mothers. Cornell argues that current family law limits women's entitlements according to how well they perform their duties as mothers and that women should be entitled to protection apart from their status as mothers.

We might conclude, then, from Cornell's arguments that the law should protect birth-mothers as citizens apart from their roles as mothers, that birth-mothers should be entitled to relationships with children on the basis of *citizenship* and *not* on the basis of *maternity,* and that giving full citizenship to birth-mothers will ensure that they are recognized as mothers. In the history of political philosophy, however, mothers are not considered full citizens and citizens are not considered mothers. In fact, traditionally the power of mothers is perceived as a challenge to civil society. So, if citizens are to be mothers and mothers are to be citizens, we have to rethink not only what it means to be a citizen but also what it means to be a mother.

According to Hegel, for example, whose notion of citizenship Cornell invokes (not without qualification), men can become citizens, while women can become mothers. In *Philosophy of Right,* Hegel says that man has his "actual substantive live in the state" and woman has her "substantive destiny in the family" (1952, 114). Whereas men are capable of higher intellectual life, "women correspond to plants because their development is more placid and the principle that underlies it is the rather vague unity of feeling" (263). In Hegel's *Phenomenology of Spirit,* it becomes clear that man can enter culture *because* woman never leaves nature (1977). Women provide men with the physical and psychic support necessary to become self-conscious citizens. Women, on the other hand, do not receive the same support, which would be lost on them anyway since, according to Hegel, they are incapable of self-consciousness or reason.

We are all familiar with the ways in which mothers have been associated with unconscious, irrational, natural instincts that supposedly tie them to their bodies and limit their intellectual possibilities. Of course, these limitations apply to all women whether or not they are actually mothers since within this patriarchal imaginary women's function is to reproduce. Cornell suggests that women's entitlements and protections should be based in their citizenship and not in their motherhood. Yet, not just *any* citizen can claim an entitlement to a relationship with a particular child; the birth-mother's claim, for example, is undeniably bound to her pregnancy and childbirth. She can claim an entitlement to custody of her child because it is "her child"; and although several citizens may claim entitlement to relationships with this same child, not just any citizen is entitled. To imagine mothers as citizens and citizens as mothers, we need to reconceive of mothers as social subjects, not only capable of, but also foundational in the development of, subjectivity and individuation.

To better understand the relationship between birth-mothers and adoptive mothers, forced relinquishment and custody court battles, then, we need to analyze our images and stereotypes of mothers. While in the past mothers have been denied any agency even in the gestation or development of their children, now courts and medical institutions consider mothers active agents or subjects, but only when they are responsible for harming their children. Mothers are never praised for raising children or benefiting them; they are only blamed for neglecting children or harming them. Women are held responsible for prenatal fetal development and the harm that their behavior during pregnancy may cause their fetus. Children's psychological or developmental problems are attributed to their relationships with their mothers. And, recently in the media and political campaigns, single mothers have been blamed for the so-called decline in family values and the moral decay of whole neighborhoods. Within mainstream patriarchal culture, there is no such thing as a good mother, only varying degrees of bad and evil mothers.

Birth-mothers who relinquish their children to adoption are legally recognized as mothers who have given up their rights to their children. The birth-mother's decision to relinquish her child is seen as the result of her free will as a subject and a citizen in spite of the fact that, on the one hand, the legal system is still infested with the underlying belief that mothers are not subjects or citizens but animals responding to the call of nature and, on the other hand, she is enmeshed in a social circumstance that often forces her to give up her child against her best hopes. In the courts and the media, the birth-mother is seen as a mother, but a heartless and cruel mother for giving up her baby. The fact that she relinquishes her child is used as evidence that she is a bad mother who should not have custody of children. Insofar as she is responsible, she is bad.

The adopting mother, as Cornell points out, is also suspicious. She cannot be a good mother because either she cannot or will not give birth. Her reason for adopting, rather than giving birth to, a child is seen by the courts and the media as suspicious. In the first case mentioned by Cornell in her essay "Re-thinking Consciousness Raising: Citizenship and the Law and Politics of Adoption," the case of "baby Jessica," the media portrayed both mothers as guilty of wrongdoing; it was not a case of a good mother versus a bad mother but a case of two selfish bad mothers who would just as soon see a King Solomon split the baby in two as give her up to the other (109).

Cornell argues that adoption law pits one mother against another in a battle over the child. But, unlike the media, the court did *not* decide the case of baby Jessica on the basis of one mother versus another. The Iowa court would not even consider Clara Clausen's rights to custody of her daughter since she had signed them away, but it did consider Dan Schmidt's rights to custody of his daughter since he could not sign his rights away because he did not even know that the child was his. This court privileged the rights of the biological father over the rights of the birth-mother, adopting mother, or adopting father. This brings me to my third question: Is it important to discuss paternity in a feminist analysis of family law? A related question is, What is the discursive effect of avoiding paternity in a feminist analysis of family law?

Paternity and Family Law

To address Cornell's concern that "we need to have a deeper analysis of why [that] relinquishment has historically been enforced and felt by many to be necessary to the protection of 'family values' " (1996, 3), we must consider the role of paternity within patriarchy. It is not a coincidence that most of the mothers giving up their children to adoption are *unwed,* many of them young. It is not a coincidence that *unwed mother* and *teenage pregnancy* carry stigma and guilt, but there is not even a common term for *unwed father* or *teenage egg fertilizer,* evidenced by the fact that I cannot even think of what to call the male counterpart of the female's *teenage pregnancy.* Why are women blamed for the consequences of sexual activity and men are not? Why, in fact, are men often praised for their virility in these contexts?[1] Why do women alone face the consequences and take responsibility—that is, *blame?*

These are difficult questions that require complex answers. Obviously, in the case of pregnancy, while it is impossible for women, it is easier for men to avoid facing the consequences. Also, until relatively recently with the advent of high-tech paternity tests, men could successfully deny their paternity whenever they chose. But, there is more to the story. Our conception of masculinity is wrapped around an image of virility. Among other things, a man's manliness or virility is measured by his ability to reproduce. Infertility, however, compromises not only his manhood but also his legacy. Historically, our conception of paternity has been tied to property and property rights. In more concrete terms, historically, in the courts children have been seen as their fathers' property, and paternity has determined the transfer of property from one generation of men to another.[2]

The links among paternity, virility, and property cut across both sides of the adoption issue. The biological father may want to deny his paternity out of a fear of loss of his property through child support or inheritance. He seeks to deny financial responsibility. The adopting father, on the other hand, may want to deny his own infertility to protect his manliness. Both of these factors contribute to the secrecy involved in adoption procedures. Biological fathers may not want children to have access to their identity for fear of legal and financial responsibilities for the child. Adopting fathers may not want the adoption made public for fear of compromising their manliness or perceived virility.

Because the social status of both women and children has been dependent on relations with men for legitimation, children born without fathers are called *illegitimate* or worse. Without fathers children and their unwed mothers are considered illegitimate persons. In addition, in most cases the economy of patriarchy has made it impossible for women to gain the financial means necessary to raise a child without a man. So the shame involved in being illegitimate, without a man, is another reason that birth-mothers have been hidden.

As Cornell points out, adoption is also surrounded by shame. But it is not just the shame pressed on the imagined infertile woman that demands complete relinquishment by birth-mothers. Rather, it is the combination of virility and property at stake in our conceptions of masculinity and paternity that forces relinquishment for the sake of *family values.* After all, *as a general rule,* patriarchal institutions (such as the court system and state adoption agencies) promote women's shame to promote men's self-esteem. Within the patriarchal imaginary, adoption raises the more urgent question of *the man's infertility.* Take, for example, the debates in the press about Tom Cruise's sperm count. The centrality of virility to our conception of masculinity makes adoption with its images of infertility a threat to men. Moreover, the conception of children as their father's property, and the eventual transfer of his property to them, makes the denial of the child's biological parents necessary to sustain the traditional image of the patriarchal family. Historically, in adoption, the child's questionable paternity—that is, its illegitimacy—combined with the threats to the adopting father's virility and property, have been factors in enforced relinquishment and silence about genealogies. We cannot begin to understand the state's interest in forced silence about adoption until we consider the role of paternity.

In general, I have come to believe that we need to talk about paternity in feminist discussions of the family. For what is the *discursive effect* of avoiding paternity in a feminist analysis of family law? The absence of paternity or fathers is remarkable in Cornell's work on adoption. Yet, we must be careful when analyzing the ways in which categories of femininity, motherhood, and woman have been constructed and imagined within patriarchal institutions without also analyzing the ways in which categories of masculinity, fatherhood, and man have been constructed and imagined within patriarchal institutions. The danger in *not* doing so is that *man* continues to operate as a norm, standard, or natural category within even our own discourses that call into question the naturalization of categories that entomb women. That is, the *discursive effect* of a feminist analysis concerned only with the construction of the category woman or mother is to leave the natural category man or father intact; within this discourse women's sex and gender appear to be the only ones constructed.

Elsewhere, I argue that this absent father *is* the patriarchal father, the father who absents himself from the family scene to claim his place in the public sphere, the father whose authority is grounded in the strength of the body that he necessarily denies to claim his place as a citizen subject, the father who supposedly frees himself from his emotions and bodily passions so that, using his reason, he can better control his property, including his wife and children.[3] Insofar as the body with its passions has been opposed to rationality and has been relegated to the domestic sphere of women, to enter the public sphere of citizens, men disassociate themselves from the body.

If motherhood has been traditionally opposed to citizenship, it is because mothers are reduced to their bodies and reproductive functions but citizens do not have bodies. Citizenship, like subjectivity, is traditionally based on capacity for reason or other mental characteristics disassociated from the body. Traditionally, citizens do not have bodies because bodies interfere with the responsibilities and rationality of the citizen. Of course, in spite of the way that citizenship apparently operates as a category for which the body is irrelevant, *in fact* the color of your skin or what kind of body you have *has* historically determined whether you are a citizen. So, Cornell's notion of equality gives us the hope of the possibility of citizens who are mothers, and mothers who are citizens, the hope of embodied sexuate citizens whose equal chance to become persons is protected by law, only once we give up the patriarchal opposition between body and citizenship, the denigration of the body, the reduction of the mother to the body, and the elevation of paternity to disembodied citizenship at the expense of the mother.

Feminist Witnessing and Recognition

Given that the hope of the law recognizing embodied sexuate citizens, whose equal chance to become persons it protects, seems a distant future, Cornell addresses the question "What can we do now?" She concludes that we can, and must, engage in at least three types of feminist witnessing: (1) "witnessing to the injustice of any family law system that defines a woman's legal identity through her duties in the heterosexual family," (2) witnessing to the asymmetrical positioning of those legally defined as women within the family law system because of race, class, and sexual preferences, and (3) witnessing to the ethical call "to take responsibility for the address to us by the other woman without pretending that there is an experience that we share" (1996, 125–26). The first type of witnessing involves challenging the inequities of patriarchy. The second type of witnessing involves recognizing that, as women, we do not all share the same experiences. The third type of witnessing involves heeding the ethical call to responsibility from the other whose experience we do not, and cannot, know.

Cornell rejects Catherine MacKinnon's notion that consciousness raising is a "process in which grasping a 'shared reality of treatment becomes the basis for identification' " (1996, 109). Instead, she proposes that "consciousness raising faithful to what I have called ethical feminism proceeds through the labor of mourning. Solidarity is produced as often as not by witnessing what we have not shared, indeed cannot share given the way in which we are asymmetrically positioned and differentially judged by the normalized meanings that make up femininity and therefore some of us are condemned as unworthy of parenthood" (1996, 111). Because I am sympathetic to Cornell's project, I think that it will be worthwhile to unpack and analyze the different notions of witnessing and recognition presupposed in her essay "Rethinking Consciousness Raising." I hope this analysis will bring us closer to a theoretical understanding of the relationships between recognition, witnessing, and identity.

First, it might be instructive to consider why Cornell insists that the consciousness raising of ethical feminism proceeds through the labor of mourning. Although she does not mention mourning again in this particular essay, mourning is a central concept in the body of her work. Reading Derrida's *Glas,* Cornell sees an essential relationship between mourning and loving the other. She proposes mourning as an alternative to nostalgia, which suffers from the illusion that we can come home to the other (1993, 53). Instead, she maintains that "we know the Other as the other through the mourning for the absence that can never be overcome" and that "it is only once we have given up on the striving for reconciliation that we can love" (1993, 53).

So, although we cannot know the other, we can know the otherness of the other through the mourning of that absence that can never be overcome but that is a prerequisite for love. Love is possible only by acknowledging, or more precisely experiencing through mourning, the difference of the beloved. For this reason, Cornell calls love a kind of mourning. It is not just that mourning the absence inherent in any relation to the other is necessary for love but that love is a way of giving up the unethical and delusional hope of possessing the other. Feminist witnessing, then, which heeds the call to mourning necessary for love or solidarity, begins by acknowledging our differences, those absences that we experience as otherness.

In the first instance, feminist witnessing is a testimony to the injustices of patriarchy that does not treat women as equals. In the second instance, however, feminist witnessing is a testimony to the differences in women's various experiences that make equal treatment unjust. And, in the third instance, feminist witnessing is the recognition of an ethical responsibility to respond to the other's call for treatment as an equal. Cornell proposes that we should witness to the ways in which law and society need to be restructured such that every person is recognized as a free and equal citizen, which does not mean that each is treated equally since freedom demands that each can express her own differences.

Whereas in *The Imaginary Domain* Cornell is concerned to maintain a productive tension between equality and freedom, insisting that we can be free only when we are treated as equals, in "Re-thinking Consciousness Raising" this tension becomes less one between necessary legal restrictions for the sake of equality and personal freedom and more one between equality and difference. Cornell is trying to devise a theory of equality that accounts for differences. Following Ronald Dworkin and others, she calls for treatment as equals rather than equal treatment. The problem with this distinction, however, is that both treatment as equals and equal treatment employ the same types of identificatory classifications, which are determinant in both.

The distinction between equal treatment and treatment as equals turns on the question of identity. Our legal history shows that arguments for equal treatment are often unfair because they often come down to claims that if a man were in a woman's shoes, he would be treated the same. So, if men were mothers, then they would not be given pregnancy leave either (doubtful!), or if heterosexuals were gay, then they could not adopt children, either.[4] Of course, these arguments are absurd since they are based on counterfactuals. These arguments and legal decisions rely on definitions of what it means to be employed, or insured, or a parent, and so forth. But, if the definitions of these terms were changed to include those excluded, then equal treatment would become treatment as equals. So, if "parent" included heterosexuals and homosexuals, married and unmarried, then equal treatment in custody disputes or family law would amount to the same thing as treatment as equals.

The problem in both cases (equal treatment and treatment as equals) is to determine the identity of that, or those, person(s) treated equally or treated as equals. The question "Equal to whom?" raised by equal treatment becomes the question "Equals in what way?" raised by treatment as equals. The effect of these questions is the same. To either treat people equally or treat them as equals, you first must determine or classify some set of similar identifying characteristics.

In her discussion of feminist witnessing, Cornell imagines another type of identification and recognition, one based on differences rather than sameness. Recognizing another *as like us* and therefore part of our group (citizens, persons, parents, etc.) and as entitled as we are seems at odds with recognizing that another is *not like us* but as entitled as we are. In an important sense, the second necessitates suspending recognition as a prerequisite for entitlement. Whereas the first assigns the role of judge and master to the recognizers (the law or state, or those empowered thereby), the second assigns the responsibility to answer to those whose experience cannot be recognized to a subject who is not in a position to master or judge the other's experiences. The inability to recognize the other's experiences as being like mine prevents me from assuming the position of mastery that recognizing entails.

Recognition is never mutual or reciprocal if the "recognizer" is in the position of power in relation to the "recognizee," as is the case of the citizen to the law or state and those empowered by them. The "recognizee" is at the mercy of the "recognizer" who validates her through his recognition, which traditionally comes through either his rationality or his mercy. In this way, the notion of legal recognition of the other follows Hegel's master-slave dialectic in which recognition involves dominance and subordination.

Throughout "Re-thinking Consciousness Raising" Cornell talks about the need for legal *recognition* of each one of us as a free and equal person (1996, 113). To overcome the roles imposed on women by the ideal of the good family, we must "don the identity of citizens and demand that we be *recognized* as full persons before the law" (1996, 114, my emphasis). Cornell concludes that "if we are truly to free ourselves from patriarchy and allow each of us to have the equivalent chance to become a person, we must break completely with the state's definition of the proper family and from the state's excluding citizens who do not fit into that mode from legalizing their love if they choose to do so and from being allowed full legal *recognition* as parents" (1996, 121, my emphasis).

Cornell's first type of feminist witnessing to the injustices of patriarchy involves demanding this kind of legal recognition. The second and third types of feminist witnessing, however, require a different kind of recognition, the recognition of the impossibility of recognition. Witnessing our differences requires recognizing that the experience of the other is beyond our recognition. Legal recognition is recognition in the sense of acknowledging or validating entitlement, whereas the recognition of the impossibility of recognition involved in feminist witnessing is recognition in the sense of admission or confession. Moreover, whereas Cornell's notion of legal recognition seems to be heir to a Hegelian notion of recognition, the recognition of feminist witnessing takes us beyond recognition in subordination or mastery. While we demand that the law should recognize each person as equal and free, we also demand that each person's freedom necessitate an admission of the impossibility of recognition.

I would like to explore the tension between these types of recognition, a tension that complicates Cornell's discussion of the relationship between legal reform and feminist witnessing and between rights and the good, a tension that takes us back to Cornell's Derridian discussions of the necessity and impossibility of justice. What does it mean for the state or the law *to recognize* each one of us as a free and equal person or as a parent? What does it mean *to recognize* that we cannot share the other's experience? And, most important, how do we reconcile these two types of recognition?

Cornell's notion of legal recognition in "Re-thinking Consciousness Raising" cannot found the kind of treatment as equals based on differences that she imagines because all legal recognition is the identification of sameness. Cornell's shift from discussions of motherhood or parenthood to citizenship only transfers the problems with identification. Cornell argues that each one of *us* should be recognized as equal citizens, but that *us* is precisely what is at stake in legal recognition. That is, where the state or law is recognizing "each one of us," or citizens, or parents, or mothers, or persons, ultimately the *process* of identification is what is at stake in changing how *we* are defined. So, merely shifting the terms from *mother* to *citizen* or from *persons* to *each of us* does not address the problem at the heart of legal recognition.

The legal classification *person* is a good example of the problem. Although most of us might assume that we are all persons, until relatively recently many of us were not recognized as persons by the law. As late as 1971 states could use the U.S. Supreme Court ruling in the 1894 case of *In re Lockwood* (154 U.S. 116) to confine their definition of *person* to males only. This is precisely the problem that Cornell is trying to address when she challenges the state's definition of parents as partners in a heterosexual family. My point is that moving the locus of identity away from one identity classification to another, even if (maybe especially if) that classification is as vague as *each of us* or *each person,* does not address the problem of legal recognition.

Who is *each of us*? Who are *persons*? These are still identity classifications open to legal interpretations based on recognition. And the law is still created, interpreted, and enforced by men. I mean that in two senses: legal recognition is still the result of human beings' recognitions of each other, and our legal system is still dominated by men and patriarchal ideals. So, what does it mean for the law to recognize someone as a person, a citizen, a parent, or as one of us? If, as Cornell suggests it should, the law recognizes gays and lesbians as parents, isn't the law recognizing them as the same in their parental status, parental rights, or parental entitlements, as heterosexuals? If the law recognizes all mothers as citizens with the entitlements of citizens, isn't that recognition based on the equation of mothers and all other citizens? Even treatment as equals or legal recognition requires the identification of common characteristics or shared identities.

With her notion of feminist witnessing, however, Cornell imagines that rather than entitlement and solidarity following from a group formation based on recognition of others like me or us—the equation of differences—entitlement and solidarity follow from admitting that we are not alike, that we cannot be alike, that in important ways we are not a group. With her notion of feminist witnessing, she suggests an alternative to legal recognition. The type of recognition that is part of witnessing is the recognition of the impossibility of recognition, recognition as a confession or admission that we are not in a position to validate the other's experience. As Cornell maintains, this witnessing begins in the recognition of an ethical call from the other. Rather than the process of recognition starting from the rational autonomous subject of legal authority, the process of recognition begins with a call from the other. Yet, the call can only be answered, or perhaps even heard, if we give up the position of master-authorized-to-recognize-and-validate the other. We have to give up the assumption that if we cannot recognize the other's experience, then it does not exist. Also, we have to recognize, in the sense of witness, that the privilege to "give up" is ours because of our asymmetrical positions of power within a sexist, racist, and nationalist society.

Cornell echoes Derrida that answering the call from the other is the only possibility for justice (1991, 107–18; 1992, 133–44). In "Force of Law" Derrida maintains that justice is the impossible limit of law (1992a). With equal force he emphasizes the urgency of justice—justice will not wait—and the impossibility of justice. Derrida suggests that to open ourselves to the call of the other, to hear it, we must be vigilant in our quest for justice. This vigilance demands that we insist that justice is never done, it is never here but always in the future. That is, we can never content ourselves that we have been just or that we have obtained justice. To do so is to risk closing off the other, to turn a deaf ear to the other. Justice demands its own impossibility. Its possibility depends on our vigilant insistence that it is never here.

Justice depends on listening to the call from the other, but fixing justice by setting out the terms or procedures of its possibility closes off the possibility of hearing calls from the other, calls that proclaim our "justice" unjust. Justice relies on the open possibility of challenge from those who experience the system as unjust. This challenge, or call, can only be heard once we acknowledge that we cannot recognize the other's experience. More concretely, if we experience our legal system as just, then we cannot admit a challenge from others without acknowledging that there is something about their experience that we do not understand. As Cornell concludes, we must witness to our differential positions in relation to the system.

What is at stake in our witnessing to differences, and more profoundly in our search for justice, is this *we*—who is included and who is excluded from the categories of entitlement (citizen, person, parent, each one of us, etc.). The call from the other, the call to justice, transforms these categories. As Derrida says in "Psyche":

> Nor is it possible for us to say that *we* are searching: what is promised here is not, is no longer or not yet, the identifiable "we" of a community of human subjects, with all those familiar features we wrap up in the names of *society, contract, institution,* and so forth. . . . It is another "we" that is offered to this inventiveness . . . a "we" that does not find itself anywhere, does not invent itself: it can be invented only by the other who says "come" and to whom a response with another "come" seems to me to be the only invention that is desirable and worthy of interest. (1992b, 342)

In the face of these transformations, made in the name of justice, we must continually open ourselves to further challenges from those whom we do not yet, or cannot ever, recognize. We must recognize the impossibility of recognition. Just as justice requires its impossibility, so too does recognition. We can recognize the other only by admitting that recognition is impossible. Only then will our search for justice, our search for recognition of others, yield our own self-overcoming toward the other. As Derrida suggests, we are not the agents of the call; we are, and must be, the respondents. When others call us to responsibility, we must answer. More often than not, this call from those othered by the system will not be Derrida's "come" but demands for entitlement, for justice, which must be met with our own call for a justice that never sleeps, justice for all of us/those *othereds.*

6

Face to Face with the mOther: Alterity in Bergman's *Persona*

In this chapter, I use Ingmar Bergman's 1966 film *Persona* to explore the relationship between identity and abjection, particularly as they relate to the maternal body. Starting with the Hegelian model of self-recognition as antagonistic struggle, moving through psychoanalytic theory's reinvention of the Hegelian scenario, focusing on the alienating struggle to verbalize our basic bodily needs, I analyze the relationship between the two protagonists in Bergman's film. In conclusion, I suggest that by the end of the film the two come to terms with the ways in which the very antagonism that put them at odds with each other and themselves is the sustenance of their own lives.

The Struggle for Self-Recognition

In Hegel's famous master-slave model, self-recognition is the result of a life-and-death struggle with another self-consciousness. The self can only recognize itself when it is recognized by another self-consciousness. The recognition of the other, however, turns the self into an object of its own consciousness. Unable to take the position of an object and a subject for itself at the same time, the self must recuperate its subjectivity by first recognizing itself *in the other,* and thereby identify with the other's recognition of itself, and then *supersede the other.* This last moment is crucial. To return to itself from the place of the other, the self must supersede the otherness of its self-recognition. It must overcome its self-alienation in its relation to the other. This dialectic struggle between self and other is a violent battle in which the self must either kill the other or commit suicide to avoid the inevitable murder of the other.

The French Freudian psychoanalyst Jacques Lacan amends the Hegelian scenario. He claims that the self-alienation inherent to self-recognition continues throughout self-conscious life. Lacan describes what he calls the "mirror stage" as a developmental process that takes place between six and eighteen months of age. The subject can only see itself as the image reflected in the mirror or in the body of another; the self is reflected in the Other. This recognition becomes the model for subsequent relations and self-definition. For Lacan as for Hegel, self-consciousness comes only through an encounter with another. As Lacan puts it, the subject must split into its reflection and itself to become one subject. In the mirror model this is the splitting between the mirror image through which the child recognizes itself and the child's body itself. Without this splitting, the child would not have the recognition of itself as a unified self. This is the paradox of self-consciousness: to become one, you must become two.

This self-alienation results in a primary frustration that becomes the ultimate driving force behind human life. The real body that stands on this side of the mirror experiences a fragmented body and fragmented desires. It does not experience a mastery over its body—it is just a little baby. The image of the body in the mirror, on the other hand, is whole and perfect. The child imagines that it can master that perfect body; after all, it is its own body. When the child realizes that this other is alien and beyond its control and yet constitutive of its own identity, a struggle begins. Lacan's diagnosis of this phenomenon is that the child's desire is the "desire of the Other."

> The subject originally locates and recognizes desire through the intermediary, not only of his own image, but of the body of his fellow being. . . . [I]t is in so far as he recognizes his desire in the body of the other that the exchange takes place. It is in so far as his desire has gone over to the other side that he assimilates himself to the body of the other and recognizes himself as a body. (1988a, 147)

On this level of images the subject is in a precarious position in relation to the other. The tension that Lacan describes is the tension between Hegel's master and slave. Ultimately, it is a dialectical struggle for recognition. This specular relation, where the subject can only see itself through the other, leads to an absolute rivalry with the other. The subject wants to annihilate the other so that it might exist (1988a, 170–73).

Once the subject sees its image in the mirror or in the body of another, it realizes that it is separated from the rest of the world and from its mother to whom it had an intimate and satisfying attachment, until now. Following the mirror stage, the mother takes the place of the mirror image as other. In other words, the child is beginning to see her as another being. Now the child becomes dependent on her to fulfill the child's needs in a new way. If the mother is another being, then the child is alienated from her in a way in which the child was not before in the child's imaginary unity with her. The child recognizes that the mother can go away and that it has no control over her. At this point, since the child cannot communicate its needs and does not yet have access to symbolic substitutes, its only options for satisfaction are either to extinguish its desire or to annihilate the object who controls the satisfaction of its desire.

Before the subject enters language and a symbol can stand in for its desire, "desire is seen solely in the other" (1988a, 170). After the subject can express itself in language, the imaginary struggle with the other is no longer life-threatening. Language mediates between the two subjects, and their interdependent existence, which appeared on the imaginary level as mutually exclusive, is reconciled. Through language one subject can recognize and acknowledge another subject qua subject. Desire is given a voice, however inadequate.

French psychoanalyst and cultural theorist Julia Kristeva reconceives of the Hegelian-Lacanian model so that self-recognition becomes a question not of killing the other but of embracing the other. We can imagine that if self-recognition necessitates the alienation of this mediate other, then rather than killing off the intermediate, we could embrace it. Rather than denying our alienation, we could accept it. For Kristeva this is the project of psychoanalysis. This was Freud's project; showing us how to live with, even embrace, the return of the repressed. Kristeva maintains that the other is repressed both in the individual psyche and in the society. The individual and the society need to learn to embrace the return of the repressed rather than trying to kill the other. What we try to exclude from our identity as individuals and societies is that within ourselves which we project onto the other in order to repress it. As Kristeva describes it, this repressed other can safely make its way back into our psyches and society through language (in the broadest possible sense). Something of this repressed other, what Kristeva calls the "semiotic," is discharged into language. The semiotic is the affective tonal rhythmic element of language, the element that means without referring. It is the linguistic trace of repressed material drive force.

If we return to the Lacanian model, only through representation, through the image in the mirror, has the subject any recognition of self. Only through representation does self-recognition take place. By the very nature of representation, however, that self-recognition is always other, always split, always alienated. Because we can never adequately or completely represent ourselves, we keep trying, we keep talking.

Ingmar Bergman's *Persona* (1972) is a study in the psychic dynamic of self-recognition through an encounter with an other. It is a study in the inability of representation to represent semiotic drive force. It is a study in the breakdown of identity inherent in the very process of becoming self-identical. *Persona* begins with a visual poem full of images of sacrifice, crucifixion, vampires, and death. Next we meet Sister Alma, a nurse who has been assigned to care for an actress, Elisabet Vogler. Elisabet, we are told by her doctor, stopped during the second act of a performance of *Electra,* fell silent for a minute, then continued as usual, went home as usual, but refused to get out of bed the next morning, and has refused to speak for three months. Immediately after the performance, Elisabet claims to have had a fit of laughter during that second act. Elisabet's doctor sends her and Sister Alma to the doctor's beach house for a therapeutic summer rest. At first Elisabet and Alma enjoy each other's company and the restful life at the beach. They pick mushrooms, read, and walk on the beach. Alma opens up to Elisabet and tells her things that she has told no one else. Although Elisabet still refuses to talk, she occasionally writes a letter. One day she sends Alma to town with a letter addressed to Elisabet's doctor. In the car on the way to town Alma notices that the envelope is not sealed. She yields to her temptation to read Elisabet's letter. This is a turning point in the film when Alma discovers that Elisabet claims to be studying and using her, and Alma feels betrayed.

The Sacrifice

Elisabet gives up speaking because her words seem empty and false. She realizes that all representation is just acting and all self-representations are just so many persona, so many masks. In a long monologue in the first part of the movie, her doctor suggests that she no longer talks so that she will no longer lie:

> I do understand, you know. The hopeless dream of *being.* Not doing, just being. Aware and watchful every second. And at the same time the abyss between what you are for others and what you are for yourself. The feeling of dizziness and the continual burning need to be unmasked. At last to be seen through, reduced, perhaps extinguished. Every tone of voice a lie, an act of treason. Every gesture false. Every smile a grimace. The role of wife, the role of friend, the roles of mother and mistress, which is worse? Which has tortured you most? Playing the actress with the interesting face? Keeping all the pieces together with an iron hand and getting them to fit? Where did it break? Where did you fail? Was it the role of mother that finally did it? (Bergman 1972, 41)

While Elisabet futilely resorts to silence to try to shed her masks, her persona, Alma encourages her to accept the lies. She suggests that all we have are lies; in fact, lies might be the truth of human communication:

> Is it so important not to lie, always to tell the truth, always to have the right tone of voice? Can you even live without talking as it comes? Talking nonsense, excusing yourself, lying, evading things? I know you have stopped talking because you're tired of all your parts, all the parts you could play perfectly. But isn't it better to let yourself be silly and sloppy and lying and just babble on? Don't you think you'd be a bit better really, if you let yourself be what you are? (1972, 80)

Alma accepts that communication necessarily breaks down, that every representation is a false image. She encourages Elisabet to accept that all forms of communication are surface attempts to represent the unrepresentable semiotic. In *Persona,* however, this failure of language to represent semiotic drive force and affect leads to violence. Like the monk who early in the film appeared on Elisabet's television burning himself in Vietnam as a protest, Alma resorts to violence to be heard. Late in the film, after Alma has read the fateful letter that makes her feel betrayed, she breaks a glass on the porch. She sweeps up the glass except for one piece. She decides to leave this one piece when she hears Elisabet coming out from inside the house. She leaves the glass for Elisabet to step on. Eventually Elisabet steps on the glass while Alma is watching through the window from inside the house. They exchange hostile glances, and at that moment the film appears to dissolve Alma's image and burn up. All forms of representation, including the film, cannot adequately represent human affect. *Persona* makes allusions to the shortcomings of various forms of representation and communication, including radio, television, photographs, music, letters, and speech. In all of these cases something exceeds the medium, something that cannot be communicated. What motivates representation itself cannot be represented.

This excess of language bursts out in moments of violence, it is spoken by the movements of the body, but it is sacrificed to the symbolic order, the social order. The force of affect is cut off from language because the material bodily drives that give rise to affect are repressed in symbolic representation. For Kristeva, the original seat of these drives is the maternal body. In relation to the maternal body human beings first experience the excitation of drives. In its first years of life, typically, a maternal figure regulates the child's bodily processes so that these processes and the drives connected to them become associated with the maternal body. The repression of drives, then, is the repression of the maternal body, especially the autonomous subject's relation to, dependence on, that body. What Kristeva calls the semiotic element in representation, which is repressed within and yet motivates signifying systems, is associated with the maternal body. Both Elisabet and Alma feel the inadequacy of language and all forms of representation. Both of them feel frustrated because they cannot represent what seems closest and most important to them. And for both of them this frustration is deeply associated with maternity. Whereas Elisabet protests her frustration through silence, Alma expresses her frustration through talking continually; silence and empty speech are both reactions to the inability of language to express affects connected to bodily drive force.

During the course of their stay at the doctor's beach house, because Elisabet will not talk and Alma does all of the talking, they begin to exchange roles. Alma takes the place of the patient while Elisabet takes on the role of the listening therapist. Alma begins to hear herself through Elisabet's ears. She begins to see herself in Elisabet. In the first half of the film when the two women have separate identities, Bergman usually shows them together in the same frame, while in the second half of the film as the boundaries of their individual identities blur and it becomes impossible to separate them—as if depicting the Lacanian mirror stage in which identity is always set up on a splitting—Bergman shows the two women almost exclusively in separate frames.

In their exchange, Alma is figured as the sacrificial lamb of the opening visual poem, while Elisabet, the therapist-actress, is figured as the vampire. In two scenes Elisabet's association with a vampire is striking. In one scene Elisabet sucks the blood from a cut on Alma's wrist. In another Elisabet appears in the night like a shadow, creeps into Alma's room, and bends over to kiss her neck. Like a vampire or parasite, Elisabet, the artist-therapist sucks the life out of Alma. Elisabet is using Alma, studying Alma for her own purposes, and gives her nothing in return except alienated images of herself. Elisabet is a mirror that reflects Alma's words, and Elisabet's silence eventually makes Alma's words seem empty and false.

Just as the monk shown on television protesting the Vietnam War sacrifices himself to warn us that we have reached the limit of the social, so does Alma. She is willing to sacrifice herself and be sacrificed so that Elisabet will talk and reenter society. Free-floating violence, violence that cannot be represented, threatens the social order. Kristeva argues in *Revolution in Poetic Language* that ritual sacrifice is foundational to the onset of society because it channels violence and makes it representable:

> [F]ar from unleashing violence, sacrifice shows how representing that violence is enough to stop it and to concatenate an order. Conversely, it indicates that all order is based on representation: what is violent is the irruption of the symbol, killing substance to make it signify. . . . [S]acrifice reminds us that the symbolic emerges out of material continuity through a violent unmotivated leap. (1974, 75, 78)

Sacrifice makes violence representable and indicates that society cannot exist without representation even while it indicates that something always exceeds representation. For Kristeva, sacrifice and prohibitions, especially dietary prohibitions, in the Bible are associated with, analogous to, the maternal:

> Dietary abomination has thus a parallel—unless it be a foundation—in the abomination provoked by the fertilizable or fertile feminine body (menses, childbirth). Might it be that dietary prohibitions are a screen in a still more radical separation process? Would the dispositions . . . be an attempt to keep a being who speaks to his God separated from the fecund mother? In that case, it would be a matter of separating oneself from the phantasmatic power of the mother, that archaic Mother Goddess who actually haunted the imagination of a nation at war with the surrounding polytheism. (1980b, 100)

As Kristeva describes it, even sacrifice is an attempt to come to terms with the mother. If both sacrifice and representation in general are forms of separation, then they are associated with a separation from the maternal body. This separation, the primary separation, within the Hegelian and Lacanian scenarios anyway, is a violent struggle with the mother for recognition as an autonomous subject.

Matricide

In *Persona* the struggle between self and other for recognition becomes focused on maternity and the relationship between mother and child. Near the end of the film is a scene that is replayed from two angles. We see Elisabet and Alma sitting across the table from each other; it is unclear whether this is Alma's fantasy or whether it is real. The first part of the scene is shot from Alma's point of view, and we see Elisabet's reactions while Alma is talking. Then the scene is replayed from Elisabet's point of view and we see Alma's face as she is talking. Alma is describing Elisabet's experience of motherhood as if it were her own, by switching between the pronouns *you* and *I*. She describes a pregnancy that is the result of pressure from others, a pregnancy that operates as a threat to her bodily integrity. She describes a desire to terminate the pregnancy. Even after the child is born it is threatening, and Alma and/or Elisabet wish that it would die:

> —So Elisabet Vogler the actress got pregnant. When I realized I couldn't change my mind, I got frightened. Didn't I?—frightened of the responsibility, of being tied down, frightened of drifting away from the theatre, frightened of the pain, frightened of dying, frightened of my body swelling up. But the whole time I played the part . . .—In the meantime you tried several times by yourself to abort. And you failed. In the end you went to a doctor. He realized it was no longer possible. When I saw there was no way out, I became ill and began to hate the baby and wished for it to be still-born.—It was a long and difficult delivery, I was in agony for days. In the end, the baby was pulled out with forceps. Elisabet Vogler looked with disgust and terror at her crippled, piping baby. Left alone with her first-born, she kept hoping and muttering:—Can't you die now, can't you die.—and I thought what it would be like to kill the baby, smother it under the pillow as if by accident, or crack its head against the radiator. But he survived. (Bergman, 1972, 96)

Alma could be describing her own experience of pregnancy that ended in abortion that she described earlier in the film. Elisabet's doctor suggests that her role as mother led Elisabet to silence: "Where did it break? Where did you fail? Was it the role of mother that finally did it?" Even the radio play that Alma turns on to soothe Elisabet in the hospital reminds her of the pain of motherhood. A woman's voice from the radio says, "Forgive me so that I can breathe again—and live again. What do you know of mercy, what do you know of a mother's suffering, the bleeding pain of a woman?" (29).

Persona presents us with a mother who wants to kill her child, a mother whose identity is threatened by her child. Maternity becomes the emblem of the subject's struggle with otherness. In the case of the maternal body, the other is within the self. The maternal body presents the quintessential undecidability of the subject—is it one or two subjects? Within the dialectical dance of subjectivity described by Hegel we do not see a moment of such questionable identity. Because with maternity alterity is within, in this case, Hegel's struggle to the death with the other becomes a struggle within the self. In Hegel's scenario we are involved here with infanticide and possibly matricide.

Is it an accident that Elisabet stops, falls silent, laughs to herself, not to speak again during the second act of *Electra?* We do not know which character Elisabet plays in the drama. Does she play the vengeful, childless daughter Electra or the murdered and murdering mother Clytemnestra? One of the subtexts of Sophocles' *Electra* is that words are worthless compared with actions; actions speak louder than words

(1967). What would be the second act of the drama is an argument between Electra and her mother Clytemnestra in which Electra derides her mother for the murder of her father Agamemnon and Clytemnestra defends her action. This exchange becomes an argument over speech and the right to speech:

> **Clytemnestra:** You brazen one! Truly I and my sayings and my deeds give you too much matter for words.
> **Electra:** The words are yours, not mine; for yours is the action, and the acts find utterance.
> **Clytemnestra:** Now by our lady Artemis, you shall not fail to pay for this boldness, as soon as Aegisthus returns.
> **Electra:** Look, you are transported by anger, after granting me free speech, and have no patience to listen.
> **Clytemnestra:** Now will you not hush your clamor or even suffer me to sacrifice when I have permitted *you* to speak unchecked?
> **Electra:** I am not hindering; pray begin your rites. Do not blame my voice, for I shall say no more. (52)

Their argument is interrupted by a messenger who delivers the news that Orestes, Clytemnestra's son and Electra's brother, is dead. This news should be good news to the mother and bad news to the daughter because Orestes was Electra's ally in her vengeful plots against the mother. What is at stake in Orestes' death is also silence:

> **Clytemnestra:** Then will not Orestes and you silence me?
> **Electra:** We are silenced, much less should we silence you. (55)

Through the son the mother is silenced. In the end she is silenced for good when Orestes, who is still alive, kills her. Perhaps this is what makes Elisabet laugh in the middle of act 2 when upon discovering that Orestes her son and enemy is dead, Clytemnestra says, "There is a strange power in motherhood; a mother may be wronged but she never learns to hate her child." Elisabet laughs because she never learns to love her child. She laughs at the way in which in *Electra* infanticide begets matricide.

Using Kristeva's theory of feminine sexuality, Alma and Elisabet's infanticidal desires can be read as matricidal desires. In *Black Sun* (1987a) Kristeva describes something akin to what she calls the abjection of the maternal body in *Powers of Horror.* Abjection

> is an extremely strong feeling which is at once somatic and symbolic, and which is above all a revolt of the person against an external menace from which one wants to keep oneself at a distance, but of which one has the

> impression that it is not only an external meance but that it may menace us from inside. So it is a desire for separation, for becoming autonomous and also the feeling of an impossibility of doing so. (1980b, 135–36).

The child at the stage of weaning needs to experience its mother as abject, as something both repellent and fascinating. Alma and Elisabet have an abject relationship to each other: they are both fascinated and yet repulsed by the other. In the end, Alma especially wants separation from Elisabet, and she insists, "I'm not you, I'm only trying to help you, I'm Sister Alma. I'm not Elisabet Vogler. It's you who are Elisabet Vogler. I would very much like to have—I love—I haven't" (Bergman 1972, 97). And yet Alma cannot separate; she desires separation and feels separation impossible. This is the experience of abjection.

In *Black Sun* Kristeva's notion of abjection becomes more extreme. It is not merely the case that the maternal body must be abjected so that the child will not abject itself. Now, on the imaginary level, the maternal body must be "killed" so that the child will not "kill" itself. "Matricide," says Kristeva, "is our vital necessity" (1987a, 27). The child must leave the maternal body. The child must agree to lose the mother to imagine her or name her. Kristeva suggests that the speaking being seems to be saying, " 'I have lost an essential object that happens to be, in the final analysis my mother' . . . 'But no, I have found her again in signs, or rather since I consent to lose her I have not lost her (that is the negation), I can recover her in language' " (1987a, 43).

Kristeva argues that female sexuality is more likely to be a depressive sexuality because it is more difficult for females to commit the necessary matricide (1987a, 28–29). Because of the female's bodily identification with the maternal body, it is difficult for her to kill the maternal body without also killing herself. In the case of the female, matricide does not ward off suicide; instead, matricide is a form of suicide. Kristeva suggests that female sexuality is melancholy partly because within our heterosexist culture a woman canot have a mother substitute as an object of desire in the way that a man can. In other words, female sexuality is melancholy because it is fundamentally homosexual and must be kept a secret within a heterosexist culture. It is possible, however, that if the dependence on the maternal body can be separated from the dependence on the mother, then the necessary "matricide" can take place, and a woman can lose the maternal body and still love her mother. This means that she can lose the maternal body as maternal container and love her mother's body, her own body, as the body of a woman. Unlike Freud, who maintains that to develop normally, females must change their love objects and erogenous zones by *denying* their original love objects and erogenous zones, Kristeva suggests that females must admit, even (re)*embrace,* those original loves and pleasures.

For Kristeva, one way that a woman identifies with her mother on this semiotic level of bodily drives is through childbirth. This reunion is bittersweet because it reminds the new mother what she has lost. Kristeva argues that through the experience of maternity and birth a woman identifies with her own mother. Both Elisabet and Alma find this identification with the mother difficult to bear. Their recognition of themselves in the mother is both terrifying and fascinating. Perhaps their infanticidal desires are really matricidal desires, desires to separate from the mother whose identity has become overbearing and claustrophobic. In *Persona,* feminine sexuality winds around these matricidal desires.

One of the strangest scenes in *Persona* is near the end of the film when Elisabet's husband, Mr. Vogler, visits the beach house. In a hallucinatory scene, Alma greets Mr. Vogler, who speaks to her as if she is Elisabet. At first Alma insists that she is not Mrs. Vogler. When Elisabet comes out of the house to watch, Alma begins to respond as Elisabet. Mr. Vogler says, "The most difficult thing is to explain to—your little boy. But I'm doing what I can. There's something deeper there, that it's difficult to see" (Bergman 1972, 84). Alma responds with tender words for "our little boy." After her expression of love for "our little boy," Mr. Vogler is overcome with passion and begins to kiss Alma. Alma passively admits Mr. Vogler's caresses while Elisabet watches from the side. Alma looks at Elisabet the whole time that she is speaking to Mr. Vogler. Alma's identification with Elisabet and specifically Elisabet's motherhood is consummated in this scene with Mr. Vogler. Alma's is a sacrificial sexuality. Alma displaces her desire for Elisabet by identifying with Elisabet so that Alma is able to have sex with Mr. Vogler. Only because Elisabet is there, and for the sake of Elisabet's son, can Alma go through with it.

Midway through the film Alma describes another voyeuristic sex scene involving two women. Slightly drunk one evening, Alma tells Elisabet about one summer afternoon on a beach sunbathing with a woman from next door whom she did not know. They were sunbathing nude and noticed two young boys watching them from the rocks above. The neighbor invited them down, and the two women took turns having sex with the boys. Alma describes how excited she was by this voyeuristic scene. Alma watches her neighbor Katarina both while Katarina is having sex with the boy and while she, Alma, is having sex with the boy. Alma affectionately describes Katarina's naked body. All the while Elisabet listens intently, nodding her head.

Within the film this scene is overdetermined. The film begins with a young boy, of the same age that Alma describes on the beach, watching and caressing the face of a woman, Alma/Elisabet, on a big screen. Also in one of their first encounters, Alma reads a letter to Elisabet in which is enclosed a picture of Elisabet's son. Elisabet tears the picture in half and hands it back to Alma in disgust. The recurrence of these young boys—the young boy in the beginning of the film, Elisabet's son, and the young boy on the beach—is charged with both sexual and maternal desire. The recurrence of these scenes also marks Alma's identification with Elisabet. Like Elisabet, Alma had been pregnant, as the result of the afternoon on the beach with the boy. And through the experience of pregnancy Alma takes over Elisabet's discourse in that scene shot twice from both of their perspectives in which Alma refers to herself as "I" when telling the story of Elisabet's unwanted pregnancy. Alma knows about unwanted pregnancy from her own experience. Only unlike Elisabet, she has had an abortion. Now, in this twice-shot scene, Alma wants to have a child. She wants to be Elisabet, the mother, even while she tortures Elisabet with her account of Elisabet's unwanted pregnancy.

Even Alma's name is an allusion to the mother. Alma, Latin for "bounteous," is an allusion to the Alma Mater, the bountiful mother, the Virgin Mary. Kristeva suggests that like sacrifice, the myth of the Virgin contains the violence of semiotic drives by turning violence against them. And like sacrifice, the violence of the semiotic returns within the very ritual that attempts to repress it. Through the myth of the Virgin Mary the mother's power is brought under paternal control. It is domesticated:

> It is as if paternity were necessary in order to relive the archaic impact of the maternal body on man; in order to complete the investigation of a ravishing maternal *jouissance* [ecstasy, total joy] but also of its terrorizing aggressivity; in order somehow to admit the threat that the male feels as much from the possessive maternal body as from his separation from it—a threat that he immediately returns to that body. (1975, 263)

Man returns the threat to the maternal body through the myth of the Virgin. The maternal body is allowed only joy in pain. Her body has only ear, milk, and tears (Kristeva 1987c, 248–49). The sexed body is replaced by the "ear of understanding," the Virgin Mary of the Catholic Church (257). Kristeva suggests, however, that the silent ear, milk, and tears "are metaphors of nonspeech, of a 'semiotics' that linguistic communication does not account for" (249). The Virgin mother becomes the representative of a "return of the repressed" semiotic (249).

Although the myth of the Virgin can *control* the maternal semiotic, it cannot *contain* the semiotic.

Like the Virgin Mary, Sister Alma, bountiful mother, a mother without boundaries, gives herself over for the sake of the social. The boundaries of her self dissolve. She is lost so that the social relationship might be restored and Elisabet will talk again. By the end of the film, although no final resolution occurs, both women realize that in some ways they need each other in order to be whole. This realization, which was in the beginning the source of self-alienation and violence, may in the end be a consolation as they each go back to their respective lives to take up their duties, their persona, as they did before.

III

SUBJECTIVITY WITHOUT SUBJECTS

7

Fractal Politics: How to Use the Subject

By now the strange predicament of the subject in contemporary continental philosophy is quite familiar. Traditionally, "the subject" is the epistemological corollary of phenomenology's intentional object. Something like this subject, of course, predates phenomenology, with Descartes, Locke, Kant, and Hegel. In its variety of formulations, from Descartes's *cogito* through Husserl's transcendental ego, the subject has been the home of consciousness. It stands in relation to the world of objects as their source, or their product, or their dialectical partner. Through its permutations and complex operations, the subject remains unified.

It is this unified subject that often becomes the object of Nietzsche's critique. As we know, since Nietzsche, Marx, and Freud, the unified "subject" hangs perilously between quotation marks that both protect and threaten it. Nietzsche suggests that "the subject" is a fiction of grammar. Marx suggests that it is a historical product. And Freud suggests that it is a construct set up against the unconscious. The subject, then, loses both its connection to consciousness and its unity. The well-defined equation between "subjects" and "objects" becomes intractable.

Some poststructuralist theorists have taken advantage of the precariousness of the subject. Derrida and Foucault, in particular, have carried out, and perhaps completed, Nietzsche's attack on the unified transcendent subject. In their wake, there have been attempts to resuscitate, or at least remodel, the subject of political action. Marxists, feminists, and those generally concerned with an emancipatory politics have tried to rescue some notion of political agency from poststructuralists' attempts to explode "the subject."

Power, Resistance, and Agency

Derrida has said that any concept of a subject "necessarily refers to the concept of substance—and thus of presence—out of which it is born"

(1978, 229). As we well know by now, Derrida's project is to deconstruct this presence. Derrida displaces the metaphysics of presence's star witness, "the subject," by reducing it to the "play of linguistic or semiological differànce" (1973, 146). Derrida maintains that even he has no agency. He claims that he does not select interpretations. Rather, "the interpretations select themselves" (1980, 21). Thus, people do not act. Rather, they are acted by language. For Derrida, the project of resuscitating the political agent is hopelessly tied to substance. Not only that, notions of agency tied to substance or "subject" in its traditional usage fix and confine agency in ways that undermine its political efficacy. Derrida's displacement of "the subject" frustrates any notion of an individual agent—even Derrida does not, and perhaps should not, choose.[1]

While in Derrida's earliest writings he is concerned with the epistemological conundrums involved in the philosophical notion of the subject, in his subsequent writings, following Levinas, he has become more concerned with the ethical and political dangers of subject-centered philosophy. His latest work signals a turn to justice and its necessary openness to the other of a future that cannot be addressed through the negative deconstruction of presence in his early work.

Already in *Spurs,* Derrida talks of the need for an affirmative deconstruction, a deconstruction that not only challenges traditional binary logics but also opens up new concepts and fields of conceptualization. In "Psyche: Inventions of the Other," he continues this call for affirmative deconstruction. There, he insists that "deconstruction is inventive or it is nothing at all" (1992b, 337). Deconstruction is inventive, productive, and its process involves affirmations of an open future. How does it do this? Through performative iteration and what I will call vigilance.

In "Psyche," Derrida once again deconstructs the speech act theorists' distinction between the performative and the constantive aspects of language. All language both shows and tells, performs and describes. Through its performance the very structures of language that make performance possible can be changed. In fact, Derrida maintains that deconstruction is inventive only insofar as its performance changes the rules for performance:

> The very movement of this fabulous repetition can, through a merging of chance and necessity, produce the new of an event. Not only with the singular invention of a performative, since every performative presupposes conventions and institutional rules—but by bending these rules with respect for the rules themselves in order to allow the other to come or to announce its coming in the opening of this dehiscence. That is perhaps what we call deconstruction. (1992b, 340)

Although the performance can exhibit the precarious structure of the rules even while following them, that is not enough unless it is accompanied by a kind of vigilance that suggests itself in Derrida's discussion of justice and the other:

> Performativity is necessary but not sufficient. . . . The deconstruction I am invoking only invents or affirms, lets the other come insofar as, while a performative, it is not only performative but also continues to unsettle the conditions of the performative and of whatever distinguished it comfortably from the constative. This writing is liable to the other, opened to and by the other, to the work of the other; it is writing working at not letting itself be enclosed or dominated by that economy of the same in its totality. (1992b, 342–43)

Liable to the other, this project must work at not letting itself be content with the same. This work involves a vigilance, which entails a constant process of self-examination and self-criticism, or what Derrida calls deconstruction, perhaps similar to what Nietzsche calls self-overcoming. It is a process that allows the impossible to become possible and yet never settles for the possible by always demanding the impossible. It is, then, a process that never ends, not because human limitations keep us from our goal or time is infinite but because justice is never within the realm of the possible.

With affirmative deconstruction Derrida is writing for a future yet to come, always deferred, in which the impossible becomes possible. This happens, however, only when we deconstruct the past in order to open up possibilities previously closed; that is, to reinvent the future, we need to reinvent the past. Affirmative deconstruction implies a reverse causality whereby the future creates the past. The future creates a past that makes it (the future) possible. In a sense, we reread the past for the sake of a different future. And, only by reading the conditions of possibility of that future into the past can we open up alternatives to the present.

Yet, in Derrida's analysis, we are not the agents of this future. We cannot make an alternative future. We cannot make or invent the other who will save us from the fatigue of sameness. We can only prepare to welcome the other when it calls to us. In response to the call from the other, the call from the future, "we" will become something other; our response to the other will reinvent "us" (1992b, 342). Ours is a passive activity, the activity of waiting, of letting, of preparing—the activity of vigilance. But how do we engage in these passive activities? What is the agency of a letting or preparing that opens onto alternative futures and change?

At this point, I would like to shift my focus from Derrida to Foucault in order to approach this question from a different angle. Foucault is concerned with resistance and change, yet his critics often come up against the same question of agency. What is or who are the possible agent(s) of change in Foucault's analysis? Some theorists maintain that he allows for no agency and that his theory of power does not allow for any real resistance.[2] Some of the problems that are relevant to my discussion are best articulated by Linda Alcoff.[3]

Alcoff argues that Foucault's critique of liberal individualism leads him to reject all forms of subjectivity and thereby erase agency (1988). She states that Foucault eliminates agency because he eliminates the "causal story" of who resists. She argues that his account of the subject is negative and that he holds a one-sided pessimistic view that all humanist-inspired conceptions of the subject will be recuperated. She suggests that Foucault believes that there is one totalizing, monolithic conception of the subject and that he believes that political programs invoking any conception of the subject will lead to domination.

It can be argued, however, that Foucault does not eliminate agency. Strategically, he drives a wedge between agency and the transcendent subject. His genealogies recall resistance that has been recuperated by a certain view of history that makes it the discourse of the continuous, driven by the original subject of all historical development and all action, human consciousness. Foucault charts resistance that the humanist discourses of a unified subject disqualify. One of the primary objectives of Foucault's political agency is to resist the unified transcendent subject.

For Foucault, resistance does not require a unified transcendent subject. Resistance does not have to originate from *outside* the system of dominance. In fact, it can not. Feminists have been making this argument for decades. "Women" are constituted by social practices, yet they can resist. So, there is an immanent resistance. There is no external ontological cause of the sort that some theorists nostalgically seek behind Foucault's agency. There is only immanent causality that is realized in effects. Politically, argues Foucault, it does no good to look for external causes. These are always causes that stand outside history. These are always in the past; we are in the present. We need to look for positive functions, says Foucault, not causes (1980b, 135–36). And, it does no good to separate off a subject from resistant practices. The subject, says Foucault, "is constituted in *real practices*" (1983a, 250). But this conception of the subject does not eliminate agency. It does not foreclose resistance. Rather, it opens a space for resistance where there was no space.

Alcoff (1988) articulates another concern for theorists trying to use

Foucault's work for emancipatory politics. She argues that Foucault cannot theorize resistance since there is no resistant agent, no differential categories in relation to domination, and the identification of subjugated knowledge as resistant is problematic. But, just as Foucault does not deny the possibility of agency or any emancipatory subjectivity, he does not deny the possibility of differential categories. Foucault argues that differential categories exist but they do not *cause* domination. Rather, relations of power are internal conditions of differential relations: economic, sexual, and so forth (1980a, 93–94). And "/m/ajor dominations are the hegemomic effects that are sustained by all of these confrontations" (Deleuze 1988, 29). So there is domination. There are oppressed and oppressors. But, as Alcoff points out, the oppressors do not possess power. Power is immanent in the relationship. Or as Deleuze suggests: "Foucault does not in any way ignore repression and ideology; but as Nietzsche has already seen, they do not constitute the struggle between forces but are only the *dust thrown up* by such a contest" (1988, 29).

For Foucault, to say that one cannot get outside power is not to say that it is necessary to accept an inescapable form of domination (1980b, 141). Moreover, to say that everyone is caught in the machine of power is not to say that there aren't those who benefit and those who suffer. According to Foucault, "everyone does not occupy the same position; certain positions preponderate and permit an effect of supremacy to be produced" (1980b, 156; 1983b, 223). "Every relationship of power puts into operation differentiations which are at the same time its conditions and results" (1983b, 223). The oppressive effects of power relations are very real. And, although resistance is part of this power relation, it too is very real:

> [T]here is a plurality of resistances, each of them a special case: resistances that are possible, necessary, improbable; others that are spontaneous, savage, solitary, concerted, rampant, or violent; still others that are quick to compromise, interested, or sacrificial; by definition, they can only exist in the strategic field of power relations. But this does not mean that they are only a reaction or rebound, forming with respect to the basic domination an underside that is in the end always passive, doomed to perpetual defeat. (1980a, 96)

In fact, Foucault's analysis points to the fragility of systems of domination. They do not have one central power and therefore do not have only one central weak spot. Rather, they have weakness everywhere. There is potential for resistance on every level. Because power is not possessed and because it does not just emanate from the top down, even those disenfranchised by the dominate system are empowered. Power is not something that belongs exclusively to the oppressors. The "victims" are empowered. They are not blamed. They can resist. And their resistance can affect change.

In his own work, Foucault attempts to strategically recall points of resistance in the form of subjugated knowledges. "Subjugated knowledges," he says, are those "blocs of historical knowledge which were present but disguised within the body of functionalist and systematizing theory." Subjugated knowledge is by definition differential knowledge. It is oppositional knowledge. It is knowledge that is concerned with historical struggles (1980b, 82–83). It is not, as Alcoff suggests, a knowledge that could not be at odds with the dominate discourse. Foucault suggests that the genealogist uses subjugated discourses in order to effect a resistance to domination. Genealogy, says Foucault, is the "union of erudite knowledge and local memories which allow us to establish a historical knowledge of struggles and then make use of this knowledge tactically today" (1980b, 84). This, in fact, seems to be the project of feminists who are reclaiming women's history.

Are there "great radical ruptures, massive binary divisions, then?" asks Foucault in *The History of Sexuality.* And he answers:

> [O]ccasionally, *yes.* But more often one is dealing with mobile and transitory points of resistance, producing cleaves in a society that shift about, fracturing unities and effecting regroupings, furrowing across individuals themselves, cutting them up and remolding them, marking off irreducible regions in them, in their bodies and minds. (1980a, 96)

The ideal of taking the state and thereby overthrowing the "whole society" is, however, for Foucault, imposing an impossible condition which prohibits the actualization, success, and perpetuation of resistance projects (1977, 223). Foucault's emphasis on local strategies, which should not be interpreted literally in terms of space, provides individuals and groups with the hope of successful resistance. It seems to me that placing our hopes on an overthrow of state power is more hopelessly utopian than encouraging individual resistance on all levels.

Foucault suggests that "local" resistance on all levels can affect global change. If the state is the effect of a multiplicity of institutions, it can be changed by changing those institutions. Yes, changes can ripple through the system. In the language of contemporary chaos theory in physics, small perturbations create fractal patterns that cascade upward through the system. In other words, as Foucault suggests, disciplinary patterns are repeated on different levels. In some sense, they cascade upward through the system. So, then, could changes in those patterns. In this frustrating era of conservative politics, Foucault's local strategies provide the hope that individuals can make a difference.

Moreover, Foucault does not eliminate the possibility of challenging existing dominate parties through posing alternatives that involve seizing state power. He suggests that even global theories can be useful tools when their theoretical unity is overthrown (1980b, 81, 145). Conversely, it seems to me that local, nontotalizing strategies could, at least in principle, be used to overthrow the state. Foucault suggests that overthrowing, or taking, state power may be a valuable means in resisting dominate forms of power. However, those institutions would have to change along with their ideology (1980b, 81, 145).

When asked whether there is any point to the prisoners taking over the central tower of the Panopticon, Foucault replies, "Oh *yes*, provided that isn't the final purpose of the operation. Do you think that it would be much better to have the prisoners operating the Panoptic apparatus and sitting in the central tower, instead of the guards?" (1980b, 164–65). From the prisoners' point of view, of course the answer to Foucault's question might be yes. His point, however, is that the structure and effects of power must be changed, not just who is on top. We need to reevaluate our totalizing practices that serve to dominate and exclude people.

Agency without Subjects

Foucault suggests that his work has dealt with the "modes by which, in our culture, human beings are made subjects" (1983a, 208). Foucault's investigations into the modes used in the human sciences that turn human beings into subjects become criticisms of the disciplinary power that the experts in these sciences exercise over human subjects. Human beings are made individual subjects at the same time that they are made objects at the mercy of the experts. The experts know more about their "objects" than the "objects" know themselves. This "knowledge" becomes a means through which to discipline, to dominate, to turn human beings into "docile bodies." This same power dynamic is found in prisons (1979, 305). Foucault's second investigation has been into modes of objectivizing the subject that he calls "dividing practices" (1983b, 208). "The subject," says Foucault, "is either divided inside himself or divided from others. This process objectivizes him. Examples are the mad and the sane, the sick and the healthy, the criminals and the 'good boys' " (1983b, 208). In some sense, these "dividing practices" are founded on, justified by, our traditional notion of the subject. Normative conceptions of how consciousness ought to manifest itself become strategies for excluding, dividing, those who are not "normal individuals"—the mad, the sick, the "bad boys and girls."

Some feminists have argued that the traditional conception of "the subject" (autonomous and rational) excludes women. Certainly the notion of "normal individual," "healthy person," and "person" itself have been used to exclude women.[4] The U.S. Supreme Court in the 1894 case of *In re Lockwood* (154 U.S. 116) ruled that states could confine their definition of a "person" to males only. Until 1971 states could use this decision to exclude women from "personhood."

Certainly, we can benefit from Foucault's analysis of the dangers of notions of "the subject," "individual," "person," which are used as dividing practices. The effectiveness of these dividing practices is based on a *naturalization* of the notion of "subject." The categories of "subject," "individual," "person," it is maintained, refer to *natural* divisions. Nature divides "subjects" and "nonsubjects," "persons" and "nonpersons," and so forth. And nature is taken to be something fixed, static, and permanent.[5] In this traditional conception of the "subject," since exclusion is ordained by nature, or the *truth* about the nature of the subject, and nature is seen as something static and permanent, then resistance becomes problematic. In fact, as Foucault points out, resistance itself becomes more evidence of insanity, sickness, or criminality.

Foucault's last investigation is into "the way a human being turns him- or herself into a subject" (1983b, 208). Foucault analyzes how men have learned to recognize themselves as subjects of "sexuality." In connection with this, Foucault describes what he calls "pastoral power." Pastoral power, which originated in the Christian church, attends to the individual rather than the community. It "cannot be exercised without knowing the inside of people's minds, without exploring their souls, without making them reveal their innermost secrets. It implies a knowledge of the conscience and an ability to direct it" (1983b, 214). This type of power, which is dependent on the confessional, has expanded to the family, medicine, psychiatry, education and employers (1980a, 59).

This technique calls on individuals to search themselves, expose themselves, and ultimately discipline themselves. Just the gaze of Bentham's guard in the Panopticon is internalized, so is confessional surveillance, which, as Foucault points out, is not without its pleasures (1980b, 155). So, the psychiatrist takes over for the priest diagnosing sexual "abnormalities." The intervention of these experts expands through out society and is internalized so that we can all participate in self-surveillance in order to prevent any "abnormalities" (1977, 229). Thus, the modes through which we make ourselves, and are made, into "subjects" become modes of domination and surveillance; and the modes of domination and surveillance become the modes through which we make ourselves, and are made, into "subjects."

In an interview, Foucault summarizes his critique of "the subject":

> Humanism invented a whole series of subjected sovereignties: The soul (ruling the body, but subjected to God), consciousness (sovereign in a context of judgment, but subjected to the necessities of truth), the individual (a titular control of personal rights subjected to the laws of nature and society), basic freedom (sovereign within, but accepting the demands of an outside world and "aligned with destiny"). . . . The theory of the subject (in the double sense of the word) is at the heart of humanism and this is why our culture has tenaciously rejected anything that could weaken its hold upon us. (1977, 221–22)

Resistance, for Foucault, is resistance to this form of power (1983b, 212). It is not just the struggle of one group against another to gain the position of power. As Foucault asks, would we rather have the prisoners in the tower than the guards? He maintains that what we need to resist is this form of power:

> This form of power applies itself to immediate everyday life which categorizes the individual, marks him by his own individuality, attaches him to his own identity, imposes a law of truth on him which he must recognize and which others have to recognize in him. It is a form of power which makes individuals subjects. (1983b, 212)

Foucault claims that the problem is not to liberate the individual from the state but to liberate human beings from "both the state and the type of individuation which is linked to the state." He proposes that "we have to promote new forms of subjectivity" (1983b, 216).

Strategies for Practicing Theory

What we need, then, is a theory of the subject that does not eliminate the possibility of oppressed people organizing their emancipation and, at the same time, does not naturalize "the subject." This project does not simply involve creating a new theory that better describes the status of the subject than other theories. It is not a matter of formulating the *true* "metaphysics of the subject." It does not answer the question "What is the subject?" This project must involve a *new kind* of theory altogether. It must call into question, by its very formulation, the power structure and naturalizing tendencies of traditional theory making. In Derridian terms, we need a theory that can perform a challenge to the rules governing its performance.

The oppressive character of the naturalization of the subject does not come solely from the contents of the definition of "the subject." In other words, it is not just the belief that the subject refers to a unified consciousness, or anything else. Rather, the very structure in which definitions of the subject are developed are themselves oppressive. The structure of traditional theory making insists that one theory is better than another because it more accurately describes, predicts, explains reality. Any theory, then, in a sense, is naturalized because, in its essence, it purports to describe some fixed nature. My point here is that naturalization is part of the very process of assigning truth or falsity to any theory. The confirmation and falsification of any theory revolve around our conception of what nature is. The upshot for political theory is that any theory about the subject, in this traditional theoretical framework, necessarily naturalizes "the subject."

To escape from this trap, we must propose a revolutionary notion of theory. We must go beyond the politicalization of *theories,* to the politicization of *Theory.* It is not just that theories reveal political interests; in addition, they can be used as political tools. If theories are the result of political motives, then we can use theories to change theoretical politics. We can use theories strategically against oppressive structures.

In terms of the subject, there seems to be a contradiction between deconstructing the subject in theory (to avoid naturalization) and acting as subjects in practice (to liberate ourselves from oppression). But, this gap between theory and practice does not mean that *either* deconstructive theories of the subject accurately describe reality *or* presumptions of subjective agency in practice accurately describe reality, but not both.

Take, for example, the relationship between theory and practice in science. Scientific theories, especially with the onset of computer simulations, are formulated that cannot be put into practice, given current technology. A particular chemical or nuclear reaction, for example, can be simulated on a computer even though, because of current physical limitations, it cannot be performed in the laboratory. In theory, for example, we can talk about drugs that we do not yet have the materials to make or particles that we do not yet have the instrumentation to detect.

These speculative theories are not false because we cannot yet put them into practice. In some sense, in these cases, practice has to catch up with theory. In many cases, the only way practice can inscribe a particular theoretical innovation is by experimenting within older theoretical frameworks. In other words, practice inscribed by now questionable or outdated theoretical frameworks can be used to usher in the new framework. In addition, older theoretical frameworks may still be the best strategies for dealing with some systems, whereas the new framework may work best for others.

This is especially true in physics. For example, different equations of motion may work better to describe different systems than others. In spite of any romantic notions about unifying all theory and practice—which would put an end to all theorizing—it seems completely acceptable for science to proceed in this fragmented way (even though some scientists may disagree).

What insight might this example offer into our problem with subjectivity? This example provides at least one instance in which it is perfectly acceptable to formulate theories that cannot yet be inscribed in practice. We can imagine that although our innovative theory that deconstructs the subject may eventually be put into political practice, the "technology" does not yet exist to do that. We can also imagine that to put this new framework into action, we may have to continue our "experiments" within the old framework that posits some kind of semiunified subject.

In addition, we can imagine that different theoretical frameworks may work better in different situations. For example, perhaps whereas a politicized poststructuralist framework may be good strategy for overcoming oppressive categories within academic theories and theory making, traditional frameworks may be better strategies for overcoming oppresive categories within the U.S. legal system.

This brings us back to theory as strategy. We will need different strategies for changing, or even describing, different practices. For example, the strategies for changing the practice of theory making—the practice that most philosophers engage in—may be different than the strategies for changing the practices of welfare distribution or day care facilities. Therefore, while models that undermine the subject may be useful in the classroom, for example, they may not be useful in arguments before Congress.

We have learned from Foucault that we need to develop local strategies for dealing with particular sites of oppression. Theory does not have to be global to be effective. In fact, strategies developed to promote specific social changes within specific institutions can be more effective than global theories that do not come with instructions for use. Once a particular change has been made, the strategy with which it was made may be outdated or even destructive. Then, a new strategy will need to be developed. Thus, strategies change with our changing historical situation. What is "good" strategy now may not be "good" strategy later.

Oppressed peoples may need to insist on their individuality and a unified subject position in one instance and deny it in another. For example, even essentialist theories may be "good" strategies. Gayatri Spivak suggests a strategic reading of "the retrieval of subaltern consciousness" (1987, 204). She argues that this attempt to retrieve consciousness, or a subject position (what she calls "subject-effect"), can be read as "a *strategic* use of positivist essentialism in a scrupulously visible political interest" (205). Spivak argues that reading this move *strategically* allows us to see a move that falls prey to the antihumanist critique of the subject "within a historiographic practice that draws many of its strengths from that very critique" (207).

Struggles for emancipation are struggles that question the status of the subject. As Foucault says, "on the one hand, people struggling for emancipation assert the right to be different and underline everything that makes individuals truly individual. On the other hand, they attack everything that separates the individual, breaks his links with others, splits up community life, forces the individual back onto himself, and ties him to his own identity in a constraining way" (1983b, 211–12).

Analogously, as Spivak points out, class consciousness "seeks to destroy the mechanics which come to construct the outlines of the very class of which a collective consciousness has been situationally developed" (1987, 205). The upshot is that the subject can be used strategically as part of a project to liberate us from the dividing practices that result from the naturalization of the subject itself. Thus, the use of an identity, even an essentialist identity, can be used to organize against oppression that operates through the logic of identity. Eventually, however, even this strategic identity must be questioned, or we have yet another oppressive identity.

Chaos

In the rest of this chapter, I will try to sketch a reconceived politial agency modeled on chaos theory in contemporary physics. This model provides a way of looking at the subject that allows us to walk the line between the subject and agency. It gives a way to imagine how we can talk about agency without presupposing a transcendent unified subject as its cause. First, I will briefly describe some of the useful features of chaos theory for my project here.

Chaos theory is a way of describing freedom within a deterministic system. It is a way of describing infinite variety within finite space

(space/time, "phase space"). It is the study of dynamic, unpredictable, systems. The weather is such a system. That is why we all listen to forecasters, but no one trusts them. Long-range weather prediction seems impossible. In the 1960s Edward Lorenz programmed his Royal McBee to simulate weather patterns. His patterns were governed by Newton's laws of motion and therefore, with enough calculation, should have been completely predictable. Lorenz's machine would plot its simulated weather continuously. Early on, Lorenz decided to study one segment of his printout. Rather than start the whole simulation over, he defined his initial conditions in the middle of his calculations by assigning values read directly off a point on his printout. He rounded his numbers off to the nearest thousandth and assumed, quite legitimately within Newtonian mechanics, that this small difference would be inconsequential.

In regular classical mechanics, a small change in initial conditions, or a small perturbation, results in a small change overall. What Lorenz discovered was that this inconsequential change in the initial conditions had significant consequences for his simulated weather. His weather system was extremely sensitive to initial conditions.

Lorenz proposed what is now called the "butterfly effect." He suggests that it could be possible that a butterfly's wings in Brazil may, by changing the geometry of the situation, set off a tornado in Texas.[6] This idea points to a sensitive dependence on initial conditions that allows small changes to cascade upward through a system. This concept has revolutionary implications.

First, a simple deterministic system can be unpredictable and "creative." The effects of the amplification of a small change cannot be predicted. Simple systems, through disorderly behavior, can generate complexity (Gleick 1987, 43, 314). Whereas a periodic system merely repeats the same thing over and over again, a chaotic system is nonperiodic. It can create something new (Crutchfield et al. 1984, 56–57).

In some systems, there is a particular point, given certain conditions, where periodicity gives way to chaos. The system can go through regular, predictable changes and then suddenly break off into fluctuations that, in principle, cannot be predicted—apparent randomness (Crutchfield et al. 1984, 46, 53, 56). The system can take on a completely different characteristic.

Unlike integrable classical systems, which can be simulated by solving certain equations, chaotic systems can only be simulated by reiterating equations—or relationships, really—in a continual feedback loop. The equation signifies a relationship, and when it is iterated rather than solved, it becomes a proess rather than a description, dynamic rather than static (Gleick 1987, 227).

Although chaotic systems are unpredictable, they do exhibit recurrent patterns. Patterns, relationships, recur, on different scales but never exactly the same. For example, a slight change is amplified on larger and larger scales throughout a system. This is how small changes can cascade upward. They are patterns that repeat, with slight differences, on different levels. This type of behavior is found in systems analyzed from fractional dimensions. Patterns that repeat in this way are called fractals (Crutchfield et al. 1984, 51).

A fractal is a pattern that can be repeated to infinity. The strange thing is that this infinite iteration takes place in finite space. The Koch curve is an example of such a pattern. If you take a triangle and then add a triangle onto each of the three sides of that triangle and then add another triangle onto each of the twelve sides of your resulting star, and so on to infinity, you have an infinite line that always remains within a finite area: the area of the circle drawn around your original triangle (Gleick 1987, 99). We might say roughly that the space within which the infinite, unpredictable, iterations take place is what chaos physicists call strange attractors. These attractors appear to pull systems into patterns—they attract (Crutchfield et al. 1984, 50). Yet they are strange because they are both finite and infinite, determined and unpredictable. They are both disorder and a new order.

Lorenz's strange attractor is the map of the first chaotic system, which he discovered (Crutchfield et al. 1984, 51). No point on the map recurred, which appears to signal pure disorder, yet a pattern appeared that suggests order. The map had boundaries in spite of its infinite complexity (Gleick 1987, 30). "Chaos provides a mechanism that allows for free will within a world governed by deterministic laws" (Crutchfield et al. 1984, 57). Doyne Farmer, a physicist at Los Alamos National Laboratory, says of chaos:

> On a philosophical level, it struck me as an operational way to define free will, in a way that allowed you to reconcile free will with determinism. The system is deterministic, but you can't say what it's going to do next. . . . I always felt that the spontaneous emergence of self-organization ought to be part of physics. Here was one coin with two sides. Here was order, with randomness emerging, and then one step further away was randomness with its own underlying order. (in Gleick 1987, 252)

How can this deterministic, yet unpredictable, system help us model a new subjectivity? What can we do with chaos theory and "the subject"? And what of the title of this chapter: fractal politics?

Fractal Politics

In sum, I propose that although a move away from traditional notions of the subject is politically necessary to avoid "dividing practices" used to marginalize and oppress groups of people, emancipatory politics needs some notion of agency. Also, although a strategic use of traditional notions of the subject as the source of agency may work in some contexts, we need a new model of agency to displace those postmodern discourses that, in effect, do away with the possibility of agency and recuperate any possibility of resistance. In the end, I will not argue that the subject *is* part of a chaotic system. Rather, as a strategy for displacing contemporary conceptions of subjectivity that effectively prohibit political resistance, I am proposing a new model of subjectivity that allows for the possibility of agency without resuscitating a naturalized or transcendental subject.

With this model imported from contemporary physics, we can strategically construct a new model of the "subject." Let's imagine the subject effect as a strange attractor and agency as the infinite, unpredictable movement that creates fractal patterns cascading upward through the system. Also, although our subject is the effect of infinite unpredictable movement, it is part of a determined cultural and linguistic system.

We can imagine, for example, that a conscious animal is part of a periodic system that may be both determined and predictable. A limited number of patterns may recur in the same way over and over. A self-conscious, or social, animal, howver, is part of a nonperiodic system, which may be determined yet not predictable. Patterns may recur but never in exactly the same way and on different levels. Metaphorically, we can say that whereas consciousness can be described as a functional relationship in which the instantiation of variables yields a description of the event, self-consciousness must be conceived of as a process of iteration in which consciousness, in some sense, is folded over onto itself. That is, self-consciousness is more like the feedback loops used by physicists to generate chaos. We can imagine that the transition from consciousness to self-consciousness is a transition from a periodic system to a nonperiodic system. It is the onset of chaos.

The subject may be merely the pattern that results from agency. It is the effect or outline of movement. It may also appear to operate as a boundary or attractor. Within any system there may be more than one attractor, more than one "subject." It is merely the boundary of unpredictable relationships between the infinite movements of agency. It is, in some sense, defined by the system. It operates according to predetermined rules, the rules of grammar and propriety.

We can, then, talk about subjects as social constructions without undermining the infinite possibilities for agency. Establishing this balance is politically motivated. On the one hand, conceiving of subjects as social constructions allows us both to explain our complicity with our own oppression and to avoid the naturalization of the subject. On the other hand, it makes it difficult to imagine how we can escape this structure that has constructed us. That is, if we are socially constructed, then how can there be room for any political intervention? What we need, then, is a notion of subjectivity that can account for the deterministic relationship between the subject and structure of society and yet allow for innovative political intervention.

Conceiving of the subject as a strange attractor within a deterministic yet chaotic system may help us walk the line between the subject and agency. We can imagine that the social construction of the subject operates analogously to Newton's laws of motion with respect to chaotic systems. The laws still apply, the system is still deterministic, yet its movements are completely unpredictable. In addition, insofar as the strange attractor is a boundary of sorts and not the movement itself, it suggests that the attractor is the effect of the movement and not its cause.

In this model, the subject is not a resuscitated transcendental ego that stands behind agency as its cause. This subject is more akin to what Foucault and Deleuze call the "subject-effect." It is the lines drawn when we trace the movement of agency. When we talk about agency, we can be talking about one person's movements, a nation's, a culture's. Our talk is limited by our take on the system. An agency's locale will depend on the level at which it operates. But, if the system is chaotic, it should create a fractal geometry. Patterns on one level should repeat themselves, in slightly different ways, on others. Also, small perturbations on one level will cascade upward throughout the system.

The sensitive dependence on initial conditions ensures that small changes on one level will be amplified through the system. Chaotic phenomena is based on the concept of local instability (Chernikov et al. 1988, 27). Local instability allows small interventions that in turn are amplified exponentially on level after level until the very character of the system is changed. Changes on local levels, changes in the movements of agents, can be amplified exponentially throughout the system. Political action on a local level can affect the structure of the system. This is fractal politics.

This, it seems to me, is analogous to what Foucault meant by local resistance. The patterns of prisons cascade upward through the system, through the schools, through the government, until the model of surveillance and discipline recurs on several levels. Although some people are disturbed by the seeming hopelessness of this model in which disciplinary techniques spread like an epidemic, at the same time it provides the possibility that we can change the prisons, but not only the prisons, the schools, but not only the schools, the state, but not only the state, possibly even our way of thinking. A small change can have a big effect.

In this model of agency, there is no enlightenment notion of freedom. There is no freedom as Kantian self-legislation. There is not even Sartrian freedom as creation and projection. Perhaps there is something more akin to Beauvoir's notion of freedom that operates within social constraints.[7] But, social constraints and patterns of domination also open up patterns for resistance. For Beauvoir, we are made but not completely determined. We are made of contradictions that become the catalyst for change. The agency of change can act on an individual level, or it can be collective. As Foucault says, we must resist domination on every level. But there are no guarantees. There are no guarantees that our own hopes and strategies will not turn, or be turned, against us in our struggles to resist domination. But this is why we must continue to be self-critical and to defer the very identity on which our resistance seems to depend. As Derrida says, we must continually reinvent ourselves, or open ourselves to reinvention, by preparing to affirm chance encounters with others. We must continually ask, "Who is this we?"[8]

8

Between Soma and Psyche: Kristeva and the Crisis in Meaning

Meaning has become a central problem in the human sciences. I am thinking of two general senses in which this is true. Contemporary theorists ask, "What does our language mean—to what does it refer?" And this question stands upon another, larger question that has been the subject of philosophy since its inception: "What is the meaning of life?" Traditionally, theorists have tried to describe human experience by abstracting from their own experience, generalizing, and articulating the essential characteristics of that experience. As theory has become more aware of itself and its methodologies, it has become concerned with the relation between experience and its articulation of experience. This kind of reflection leads to the question "What might get lost in the translation from experience as it is lived to our articulation of it?"

The advent of psychoanalysis further complicates these questions. The psychoanalyst is concerned to diagnose displaced meanings that lurk behind the apparent meaning of our articulation of experience. The concern is no longer whether language can adequately capture, reflect, or copy experience but how we can interpret the meaning of this language as it points to that which necessarily escapes it. Now we are concerned with the hidden, veiled, or unconscious meanings of our language use; we are concerned precisely with the way in which our language does *not* re-present our conscious experience. Language and signification become signs that point to, rather than represent, our unconscious motivations. Language provides clues to discovering the key to the mystery of all of our questions of "Why?"—including the question "Why do we speak?"

I rehearse these questions of meaning here because I think that Julia Kristeva addresses them in a unique way. Where others have seen an impasse, Kristeva has imagined an adventurous journey, though certainly not without its dangers and pitfalls. In an age of theoretical pessimism on all sides, Kristeva brings together the two questions of meaning, the meaning of language and the meaning of life, to provide hopeful answers that are more than mere theoretical exercises. Taking up the question of "Why do we speak?" in all of its ambiguities, Kristeva addresses the issues of the relationship of meaning to language, the relationship of meaning to life, and the relationship of language to life. In fact, Kristeva's most famous contribution to language theory, the distinction between the symbolic and the semiotic elements of signification, speaks to these questions in a revolutionary way, opening pathways rather than resigning us to an impasse.

Kristeva maintains that all signification is composed to two elements, the symbolic and the semiotic. The symbolic element is what philosophers and linguists might think of as meaning proper. That is, the symbolic is the element of signification that sets up the structures by which symbols operate. The symbolic is the structure or grammar that governs the ways in which symbols can refer. The semiotic element, on the other hand, is the organization of drives in language. It is associated with rhythms and tones that are meaningful parts of language and yet do not represent or signify something. In *Revolution in Poetic Language* (1974), Kristeva maintains that rhythms and tones do not *represent* bodily drives; rather, bodily drives are *discharged* through rhythms and tones. In one of her most recent books, *New Maladies of the Soul* (1995), she discusses different ways of representing that are not linguistic in a traditional sense. There, Kristeva says that the meaning of the semiotic element of language is "translinguistic" or "nonlinguistic" (32–33, 31); she explains this by describing these semiotic elements as irreducible to language because they "turn toward language even though they are irreducible to its grammatical and logical structures" (35). That is, they are irreducible to the *symbolic element* of language. The symbolic element of language is the domain of position and judgment. It is associated with the grammar or structure of language that enables it to signify something.

The dialectical oscillation between the semiotic and the symbolic is what makes signification possible. Without the symbolic element of signification, we have only sounds or delirious babble. But without the semiotic element of signification, signification would be empty and we would not speak; for the semiotic provides the motivation for engaging in signifying processes. We have a bodily need to communicate, and the symbolic provides the structure necessary to communicate. Both elements are essential to signification. It is the tension between them that makes signification dynamic. The interdependence of the symbolic and semiotic elements of signification guarantees a relationship between language and life, signification and experience, and between body (soma) and soul (psyche).[1]

One of Kristeva's most important contributions to contemporary theory is her attempt to bring the speaking body back into the discourses of the human sciences. She attempts to bring the speaking body back into discourse by arguing both that the logic of language is already operating at the material level of bodily processes and that bodily drives make their way into language. She postulates that signifying practices are the result of material bodily processes. Drives make their way into language through the semiotic element of signification, which does not represent bodily drives but discharges them. In this way, all signification has material motivation. Drives move between soma and psyche, and the evidence of this movement is manifest in signification.

Kristeva takes up Freud's theory of drives as instinctual energies that operate between biology and culture. Drives have their source in organic tissue and aim at psychological satisfaction. Drives are heterogeneous; that is, there are several different drives that can conflict with each other. In *Revolution,* Kristeva describes drives as "material, but they are not solely biological since they both connect and differentiate the biological and symbolic within the dialectic of the signifying body invested in practice" (1974, 167). Nearly two decades later, Kristeva emphasizes the same dialectical relationship between the two spheres—biological and social—across which the drives operate. In *New Maladies of the Soul,* she describes the drives as "a pivot between 'soma' and 'psyche', between biology and representation" (1995, 30).[2] Drives can be reduced neither to the biological nor to the social; they operate in between these two realms and bring one realm into the other. Drives are energies or forces that move between the body and representation. This notion of drives challenges the traditional dualism between the biological and the social, the body and the mind. Kristeva's attempts to bring the body back to theory also challenge traditional notions of the body; for her, the body is more than material.[3]

By insisting that language expresses bodily drives through its semiotic element, Kristeva's articulation of the relationship between language and the body circumvents some of the traditional problems of representation. Traditional theories postulating that language represents bodily experience fall into an impossible situation by presupposing that the body and language are distinct, even opposites. Some traditional theories purport that language is an instrument that captures, mirrors, or copies, bodily experience. The problem, then, becomes how to explain the connection between these two distinct realms of language, on the one hand, and material, on the other.[4]

Instead of lamenting what is lost, absent, or impossible in language,

Kristeva marvels at this other realm that makes its way into language. The force of language is living drive force transferred into language. The tones and rhythms of language, the materiality of language, is bodily. Signification is like a transfusion of the living body into language. This is why psychoanalysis can be effective; the analyst can diagnose the active drive force as it is manifest in the analysand's language. In *Time and Sense* (1996) Kristeva suggests that transference in the psychoanalytic session inscribes flesh in words. Psychoanalysts "transform the patient's flesh, which [they] have shared with [their] own, into word-presentations." In this way, psychoanalysis can treat somatic symptoms by transforming the body through words. The connection between flesh and words conjured and refigured in analytic transference opens up the space for idealization that Kristeva associates with love and psychic space. This space for idealization gives the analysand a renewed image of him- or herself. Language is not cut off from the body. Also, although for Kristeva, bodily drives involve a type of violence, negation, or force, this process does not merely necessitate sacrifice and loss. The drives are not sacrificed to signification; rather, bodily drives are an essential semiotic element of signification.

In addition to proposing that bodily drives make their way into language, Kristeva maintains that the logic of signification is already present in the material of the body. In *Revolution in Poetic Language,* she proposes that the process of identification or incorporation, and differentiation or rejection, that make language use possible are operating within the material of the body. She maintains that before the infant passes through either what Freud calls the Oedipal situation, which accomplishes self-identity, or what Lacan calls the mirror stage, which inaugurates self-identity, the patterns and logic of language are already operating in a pre-Oedipal situation. In *Revolution,* she focuses on differentiation or rejection and the oscillation between identification and differentiation. She analyzes how material rejection (e.g., the expulsion of waste from the body) is part of the process that sets up the possibility of signification.

She calls the bodily structures of separation the "logic of rejection." For Kristeva, the body, like signification, operates according to an oscillation between instability and stability, or negativity and stasis. For example, the process of metabolization is a process that oscillates between instability and stability: food is taken into the body and metabolized and expelled from the body. Because the structure of separation is bodily, these bodily operations prepare us for our entrance into language. From the time of birth, the infant's body is engaging in processes of separation; anality is the prime example. Birth itself is also an experience of separation, one body separated from another. For Kristeva, these physical separations prefigure psychical separation; patterns of separation move from soma to psyche.

Part of Kristeva's motivation for emphasizing these bodily separations and privations is to provide an alternative to the Lacanian model of language acquisition. Lacan's account of signification and self-consciousness begins with the mirror stage and the paternal metaphor's substitution of the law of the father for the desire of the mother. In the traditional psychoanalytic model of both Freud and Lacan, the child enters the social or language out of fear of castration. The child experiences its separation from the maternal body as a tragic loss and consoles itself with words instead. Paternal threats make words the only, if inadequate, alternative to psychosis. Kristeva insists, however, that separation begins prior to the mirror stage or Oedipal situation and that this separation is not only painful but also pleasurable. She insists that the child enters the social and language not just because of paternal threats but also because of paternal love in the figure of the imaginary father.

At bottom, Kristeva criticizes the traditional account because it cannot adequately explain the child's move to signification. If what motivates the move to signification are threats and the pain of separation, then why would anyone make this move? Why not remain in the safe haven of the maternal body and refuse the social and signification with its threats? Kristeva suggests that if the accounts of Freud and Lacan were correct, then more people would be psychotic (see 1974, 132; 1987c, 30, 31, 125). The logic of signification is already operating in the body, and therefore the transition to language is not as dramatic and mysterious as traditional psychoanalytic theory makes it out to be.

Reconnecting bodily drives to language is the project not only of her theoretical work but also of her clinical psychoanalytic practice and one aspect of her fiction. Since *Tales of Love* (1987c), Kristeva has been regularly including notes from analytic sessions in most all of her theory and fiction. In her theory, she uses these notes to further substantiate her diagnosis of literary texts and culture. Her strategy of including her notes from analytic sessions, enriched with the words of her analysands, brings the speaking body into theoretical discourse. These speaking bodies are articulating the pain of living in worlds where symbols have been detached from affect, where the meaning of words has been detached from the meaning of life, from what matters.

As Kristeva says in *Tales of Love,* we are extraterrestrials wandering and lost without meaning owing to an abolition of psychic space: "What analysands are henceforth suffering from is *the abolition of psychic space.* Narcissus in want of light as much as of a spring allowing him to capture his true image, Narcissus drowning in a cascade of false images (from social roles to the *media*), hence deprived of substance or place'' (1987c, 373). We experience somatic symptoms cut off from their psychic or affective meaning. It is within this psychic space that affects materialize between bodily organs and social customs. Our emotional lives depend on this space. Meaning is constituted in this space between the body and culture. Our words and our lives have meaning by virtue of their connection to affect. The meaning of words (in the narrow sense of the symbolic element of language) is charged with affective meaning (in the broader sense of the semiotic element of language) through the movement of drive energy within psychic space.

The goal of the analyst, then, is to reconnect soma and psyche, body and soul. The ''talking cure'' involves giving meaning to language by reconnecting words and affects, and thereby giving meaning to life. Psychoanalysis is unique in that it tries to open up psychic space and provide various interpretations with which to give meaning to both language and life.

In *Tales of Love,* Kristeva identifies meaning—the meaning of words and the meaning of life—with love. Love provides the support for fragmented meanings and fragmented subjectivities. Love provides the support to reconnect words and affects. Kristeva says that ''*love is something spoken, and it is only that*'' (1987c, 277). Our lives have meaning for us, we have a sense of ourselves, through the narratives that we prepare to tell others about our experience. Even if we do not tell our stories, we live our experience through the stories that we construct to ''tell ourselves'' to another, a loved one. As we wander through our days, an event takes on its significance in the narrative that we construct for an imaginary conversation with a loved one as we are living it. The living body is a loving body, and the loving body is a speaking body. Without love we are nothing but walking corpses. Love is essential to the living body, and it is essential in bringing the living body to life in language.

The contemporary crisis in meaning is a crisis in love. The popularity of self-help programs, various forms of therapy and counseling, antidepressant drugs, and New Age religions suggests a widespread search for meaning, acceptance, self-esteem, and, ultimately, love.[5] Bookstores across the Western world have self-help sections filled with books discussing how to find love, how to maintain love, how to rekindle love, how to feel lovable, how to love yourself.[6] Why are we haunted with feelings that we are unloved or unlovable?

Kristeva diagnoses feelings of lack of love and lack of meaning in *Tales of Love*: ''Today Narcissus is an exile, deprived of his psychic space, an extraterrestrial with a prehistory bearing, wanting for love.

An uneasy child, all scratched up, somewhat disgusting, an alien in a world of desire and power, he longs only to reinvent love" (1987c, 382–83). She suggests that the analysand is a child with no adequate images of a loving mother or a loving father. Without images of loving mothers and fathers, how can we love ourselves?

Fundamental to psychoanalytic theory is the belief that our primary relationships become models for our subsequent relations. This belief is why in their sessions analysts return their clients to childhood relations to diagnose current relations. The idea is that by examining how early relationships developed the analyst can diagnose problems in current relationships. Equally fundamental to psychoanalytic theory is the notion that to become social, children must separate from their mothers; they must be weaned from the antisocial dependence on their mothers' bodies. Psychoanalytic theory revolves around these issues of primary identification and separation.

These two issues come into conflict, however, in such a way that the impossibility of maintaining both identification and separation sets up the impossibility of love.[7] Cultural norms for primary relationships, norms manifest in psychoanalytic theory, normalize the *impossibility* of love. In other words, our conceptions and images of our primary relationships exclude the possibility of being loved or lovable. Western images of conception, birth, and parental relationships leave us with a father who is not embodied, who cannot love but only legislates from some abstract position, and a mother who is nothing but body, who can fulfill animal needs but cannot love as a social human being. We have absent fathers and animal mothers, neither of whom can provide an adequate image of love.

Given the thesis that all of our relations are modeled on our primary relations, our relations should be modeled on our first relation, the relation to the maternal body. Yet, the way in which the maternal body is conceived within psychoanalytic theory, philosophy, and Western culture in general prevents this relation from serving as a model for any subsequent social relation. The relation with the maternal body is imagined as antisocial, a nonrelation, which, if anything, threatens the social. If infants do not separate from their mothers' bodies, then there can be no society. The first relationship with the maternal body, then, is in the contradictory position of both providing the prototype for all subsequent relations and threatening the very possibility of any social relation.

The paradoxical position of the mother is the result of the imagined opposition between nature and culture. Western philosophy as we know it began with the birth of the soul. Plato proposed a dramatic and antagonistic relationship between body and soul. Aristotle followed by insisting that it is humans' capacity for reason that separates them from the animals. Bodies and animals are governed by the laws of the natural world, but the mind and human beings are governed by the higher principles of reason. With its emphasis on reason against body, philosophy has insisted on a sharp distinction between nature and culture. Only human beings are properly social; only human beings have culture; only human beings love. The legacy of this mind/body dualism has been fraught with problems, not the least of which is the paradox of love.

When the bodily activities of procreation and sex are opposed to sociality, the infant is conceived in an antisocial space where love is reduced to biology, and there is no love in nature; animals are incapable of love. Yet, only if our animality is *opposed* to our sociality are the bodily activities of sex and procreation relegated to an antisocial sphere. The reduction of procreation to nonsocial biology ensures that the mother and child are trapped below the social until some cultural force ruptures that natural unity. If the mother-child relationship is natural and not social, then it is determined by animal instinct and not love.

The reduction of sex to nonsocial biology is another aspect of the opposition between body and culture. The identification of sex and nature leads to the philosophical notion of Eros as disembodied reason rather than embodied passion. Eros is opposed to sex just as mind is opposed to body. Recall Plato's gory description of the near death of bodily passion for true Eros in the *Phaedrus.* This abstract disembodied love is associated with the father as the representative of culture. But the infant, with its undeveloped reason, cannot *feel* this distant love. Our images of procreation and sex, and of maternal and paternal relations, leave us with an absent no-body father and an animal body mother, neither of which are capable of allowing the infant/child to feel loved.

If the mother's love is made paradoxical by the identification of mother and antisocial body, the father's love is made abstract or impossible by the identification of father and antibody culture. Within Freud's account, the relationship between father and son is one of rivalry and guilt, while the relationship between father and daughter is one of envy and frustration; the father is the representative of threats and power. Within Lacan's account, the father is associated with the Name or No; that is, the father brings language and law to break up the primary dyad. The father's body does not matter: "For, if the symbolic context requires it, paternity will nonetheless be attributed to the fact that the woman met a spirit at some fountain or some rock in which he is supposed to live. . . . It is certainly this that demonstrates that the attribution of procreation to the father can only be the effect of a pure signifier" (Lacan 1977, 199). Why is the father's body irrelevant to procreation? How can paternity just as well be attributed to a spirit? What does this tell us about our cultural images of paternity in an age when so many fathers are absent from their children's lives?

Traditional images of fatherhood and paternity rely on an absent father. In important ways the necessity of the father's absence is embedded in recent rhetoric of family values and manly responsibility. The association between the father and the law, name, or authority makes the father an abstract disembodied principle. Patriarchy is founded on the father's authority. Paternal authority is associated with culture against maternal nature. In both philosophy and psychoanalytic theory, however, it turns out that the paternal authority that legitimates culture and breaks with antisocial nature is founded on the father's *natural* authority because of his *natural* strength or aggressive impulses. The paternal authority of culture is founded on the father's *naturally* stronger body; might makes right. After grounding the father's authority in nature, our philosophers and psychoanalytic theorists have disassociated the father from nature by disembodying him. The father is physically absent from the family scene because he is part of culture. Just as our stereotype of the mother-infant relationship as an antisocial natural relationship does not permit love because love is social, our stereotype of the disembodied abstract father who represents the authority of culture cannot provide love because love is concrete and embodied.

Kristeva attempts to provide us with images of a social mother and a loving father. She tries to rescue the mother from the crypt of nature by separating the maternal body as a container that meets the infant's needs from the maternal function that sets up the possibility of language and law. The maternal body as the satisfier of needs must be abjected; "matricide," says Kristeva, is "our vital necessity" (1987a, 27). But the mother is more than a container; she is a desiring subject, and as such she is social. Moreover, in her relations with her infant she provides regulation, what Kristeva calls the maternal law before the law, that sets up paternal law. So, although Kristeva insists that the maternal body must be abjected, she describes the maternal body as protosocial. Materniity is between nature and culture, and the maternal body can never be left behind by culture. In Kristeva's texts, the maternal body challenges the opposition between nature and culture. If the mother is not reducible to her body and if her body encourages rather than threatens the social, then we might go one step further than Kristeva and imagine a loving mother. If the maternal body cannot be reduced to antisocial nature, we might go two steps further than Kristeva and suggest that matricide is necessary only to maintain patriarchy.

Kristeva, however, prefers to talk about a loving father. She identifies the cause of the loss of meaning and lack of love as an erosion of the loving father:

> There has been too much stress on the crisis in paternity as cause of psychotic discontent. Beyond the often fierce but artificial and incredible tyranny of the Law and the Superego, the crisis in the paternal function that led to a deficiency of psychic space is in fact an erosion of the loving father. It is for want of paternal love that Narcissi, burdened with emptiness, are suffering; eager to be others, or women, they want to be loved. (1987c, 378)

In *Tales of Love,* Kristeva attempts to curb this erosion with her notion of an *imaginary father,* which she proposes as the counterbalance to the abject mother. In *Family Values,* I argue that the imaginary father is really an attempt to counterbalance a more threatening fantasy than the abject mother, that of the abject father. In Kristeva's account, the child has a fantasy of an imaginary father, which is really the fantasy of a "mother-father conglomerate." This fantasy of the mother-father conglomerate allows the child to feel loved even while it is separating from its mother's body. The imaginary father provides as necessary support for the child to be weaned. The idea is that the child must disassociate itself from its mother and her love, but it can still feel loved because of this fantasy of the imaginary father.

Although Kristeva's notion of the imaginary father may go some distance to supplement the Lacanian symbolic father of the law, it still does not provide us with a notion of embodied paternal Eros. Against Lacan, Kristeva maintains that we can give up the stern father of the law without risking psychosis:

> Maintaining against the winds and high tides of our modern civilization the requirement of a stern father who, through his Name, brings about separation, judgment, and identity, constitutes a necessity, a more or less pious wish. But we can only note that jarring such sterness, far from leaving us orphaned or inexorable psychotics, reveals multiple and varied destinies for paternity . . . one that can also be playful and sublimational. (1987c, 46)

In fact, she suggests that if paternity is reduced to law and threats, then we would have no reason to leave the safe haven of the maternal body. The paternal function that introduces the child to language and culture must have some rewards and pleasures, or else more of us would refuse to leave the maternal body and become psychotic. The father must promise love.

Although Kristeva's imaginary father is designed to move the child away from the maternal body and into culture, this paternal image is channeled through the maternal body and the imaginary union between maternal and paternal bodies; Kristeva's imaginary father defines the father only in relation to the mother. It is as if the contingency of paternity can only be counteracted by the imagined determinacy of the maternal contribution to procreation. The imaginary father is a fantasy of conception that allows the child to feel loved and chosen by its father and mother: if it imagines that it was conceived out of love between its parents, then it too can be loved.[8]

Ultimately, however, Kristeva's imaginary father collapses into the Lacanian symbolic father. She develops her notion of the imaginary father from Freud's notion of the father of individual prehistory. She finds in Freud the suggestion of a pre-Oedipal father who parallels the pre-Oedipal, or imaginary, mother. Yet, this pre-Oedipal father, as it turns out, is produced by the mother:

> Nevertheless, clinical experience has led us to ascertain that the advent of the *Vater der persönlichen Vorzeit* [father of individual prehistory] takes place thanks to the assistance of the so-called pre-Oedipal mother, to the extent that she can indicate to her child that her desire is not limited to responding to her offspring's request (or simply turning it down). This assistance is none other than maternal desire for the Father's Phallus. (1987c, 40)

The identification with the mother-father conglomerate turns out to be an identification with the mother's desire for the father's phallus. At the level of the pre-Oedipal, the mother's desire for the father's phallus is the mark of the symbolic father of the law on her body. The fantasy that provides the guarantee that the child can be weaned is none other than the father's law in the place of the mother's desire. We have not moved far from the Lacanian scenario after all.

Where is the father's body in all of this? The mother's desire for the father's phallus is not a desire for the father's body except insofar as it represents that power. For Lacan, and Kristeva follows, the phallus is not the penis. The phallus is the fraudulent representative of the possibility of all representation; it is the fraudulent representative of the power of culture and discourse. Fraud or not, the phallus covers over once again the father's body. If, as Lacan says, the phallus can only be effective when veiled, behind the veil is the paternal body in all of its contingency and uncertainty. Just as within ancient medical discourse the paternal body provided the seed or form that grows in the maternal soil or matter, within Kristeva's discourse the imaginary father provides the "seed of the Ego Ideal" (1987c, 374).

What is abjected in our images of conception is not the maternal body but the paternal body. Maternal bodies are easy to identify, but what are the marks of a paternal body? Kristeva argues that the child must abject the maternal body so that the child itself does not become abject by identifying with the maternal body. The maternal body, she says, calls into question the borders of the self, and ultimately the child may imagine itself a waste product expelled from the maternal body—in Kristeva's analysis in *Powers of Horror,* excrement and menstrual blood are connected through the maternal body. Yet, insofar as, unlike the female organ, the male organ for reproduction is the same as the organ for urination (a problem that even Hegel identified), it is the paternal issue that can be confused with a waste product expelled from the body. In spite of the association of the maternal body and menstrual blood with chaos and lack of control or containment, the maternal contribution to procreation, the egg, is imagined as determinant and solid. The paternal contribution, on the other hand, is erased or solidified because it is fluid and cannot be contained. It is indeterminate, and the infant produced by the accident of one sperm cell penetrating that egg is a product of chance.

Kristeva's notion of an imaginary father is necessary to counter not the abject mother, as she suggests, but the fantasy that is too much to bear, the fantasy that the child is merely a waste product of the paternal body. Behind the abject projections onto the maternal body is the leaking paternal body not in control of its own production.

In *Powers of Horror,* Kristeva develops a notion of abjection based on Mary Douglas's notion of defilement. In *Purity and Danger,* Douglas describes defilement as the danger to identity constituted by filth, which is always defined in relation to the borders of that very identity. The identity of the subject is tied to the identity of the borders of the body that are threatened by bodily secretions:

> Matter issuing from them [the orifices of the body] is marginal stuff of the most obvious kind. Spittle, blood, milk, urine, feces or tears by simply issuing forth have traversed the boundary of the body. . . . It follows from this that pollution is a type of danger which is not likely to occur except where the lines of structure, cosmic or social, are clearly defined. (Doublas 1969, 113)

Notice that Douglas does not mention semen, which for Kristeva becomes a special case.

Kristeva describes those things, which are not quite objects, that threaten the boundaries of our identities, both individual and social, as abject. Following Douglas, she maintains that the abject corresponds to the attempt to clearly delineate borders. To delineate borders, a line must be drawn between the inside and the outside, between the clean and proper self and the abject other. That which threatens identity must be jettisoned from the borders and placed outside. In this sense, identity is constituted through a process of abjection. As Kristeva describes it, both individual and social identity are constituted by abjecting *maternal* elements. The maternal body threatens the borders of the individual and social subject. It threatens the individual subject who was born out of another body and must deny this to establish its own proper identity. It threatens social identity insofar as the maternal body is associated with nature, and the social must distinguish itself from the forces of nature. So, those bodily secretions—blood and milk—associated with the maternal body are the most strictly regulated by cultural and religious rituals. Kristeva discusses food prohibitions that revolve around blood and milk, always associated with the maternal.

Although she does not explain why, Kristeva exempts semen from the types of dangerous fluids that call into question the boundaries of identity. Perhaps the exemption of semen stems from Kristeva's premise that it is the fluids associated with the maternal body that are the most dangerous for identity. In any case, she identifies two types of polluting objects, excremental and menstrual, both of which she associates with the maternal body:

> [T]hose two defilements stem from the *maternal* and/or feminine, of which the maternal is the real support. That goes without saying where menstrual blood signifies sexual difference. But what about excrement? It will be remembered that the anal penis is also the phallus with which infantile imagination provides the feminine sex and that, on the other hand, maternal authority is experienced first and above all, after the first essentially oral frustrations, as sphincteral training. (1980b, 71)

In the infant's imagination the phallic mother has an anal penis and maternal authority governs excrement, so, like blood, excrement is associated with the mother.

Language and culture are born out of this presymbolic maternal authority but only after this authority is repressed. "If language, like culture, sets up as separation, and, starting with discrete elements, concatenates an order, it does so precisely by repressing maternal authority and the corporeal mapping that abuts against them" (1980b, 72). Bodily fluids associated with maternal law and maternal power are repressed so that paternal symbolic culture can legitimate its own authority by denying maternal authority. As Kristeva asks, "what happens to such a repressed item when the legal, phallic, linguistic symbolic establishment does not carry out the separation in radical fashion" (1980b, 72) or, we might add, cannot carry out the separation in radical fashion? After all, the maternal and feminine, though repressed and denigrated, abjected and defiled, cannot be completely eliminated, or even culture and its reproduction would be sacrificed. And it is precisely at this point, where culture is dependent on that which it denies, that it begins to employ Freud's kettle logic. Freud tells the story of a man who borrows a kettle and tries to deny that he broke it by telling its owner first that he did not break it and next that it was not broken and finally that he did not borrow the kettle.[9] These zealous denials produce inconsistencies that betray the culprit.

Well, we might say that semen is a broken kettle. How can semen be exempt from the category of dangerous fluids?[10] According to a story in the *New York Times,* research has in fact *determined* that the seminal fluids of fruit flies is toxic to female fruit flies; and although the scientists use their studies to try to convince us that human beings are analogous to fruit flies, they draw the line at toxic semen. Even the journalist ends the article by reassuring us that human semen has not been found toxic to human females. Given their arguments about the similarities between reproduction and evolution in fruit flies, their conclusion should be that semen is also toxic to human females; but like Kristeva, they make an exception for human semen.[11] Semen (and its danger) is invisible within our cultural imaginary in which the virile male body is a purifying force.[12] The invisibility and purification of semen in our culture are both covers for and indications of its imagined threat.

The earliest theories in Western biology and medicine, those of Aristotle and Galen, proposed that male semen is purified by the heat of the male body while female semen (menstrual blood) is cooler and less pure. They took the difference in color as evidence; male semen, once as impure as female semen, is translucent because of the purification process.[13] This physical purification process corresponds to the male's cathartic purification of passions and lusts from his clean and proper self. The separation of the male body from the mess of reproduction, the separation of masculine identity from the male body's role in reproduction, allows masculine identity to be constituted by abjecting everything messy about reproduction and associating it with the female body. In this way, males maintain their own clean and proper selves. But a broken kettle leaks regardless of the anxious stories one tells in order to cover one's mess.

As Elizabeth Grosz argues in *Volatile Bodies,* anxieties about male bodies are projected onto female bodies: Female bodies leak, male bodies do not (1994).[14] The male body absents itself in favor of solid objects that do not flow, on one level, and mind that is eternal and without corporeality, on another. Fatherhood is defined not in terms of the paternal body or its contribution to procreation but in terms of the father's name or law, contracts (or physical surveillance) that guarantee that the child is his. Fatherhood is made determinant by denying the body. The paternal body is absent from discourses about fatherhood because the paternal body necessarily leaks and brings with it indeterminacy and chance.

Behind the Oedipal story and the struggle for mastery is the fear of the father's body, not because its omnipotence threatens to kill the son but because its lack of determinacy threatens the son's very existence; the contingency and chance of its contribution to procreation is a threat to the son. The son becomes an accident of chance, a contingency as precarious as any individual sperm cell once it leaves the father's body. Even more disturbing, in this fantasy the child may become merely a waste product expelled from the father's body. The fantasy of the father's omnipotence protects the child from a more terrifying fantasy, the fantasy of the father's impotence, which threatens not just the child's death but the child's coming to be. The threat of an *abject father* is more terrifying than the threat of an omnipotent father. At least the omnipotent father promises omnipotence for the son who one day can take his place. An identification with an abject father, on the other hand, promises indeterminacy and contingency with regard to even life and death. In the end, both the fear of the omnipotent fathers and the terror of the impotent father operate within the same economy of virility, which trades on the fear of a male body.

Images of disembodied symbolic fathers and imaginary father are attempts to contain the abject paternal body with its flows and contingency. These images, however, cannot counterbalance the threat of the abject father. The repressed paternal body returns to haunt discourses of fatherhood. Fantasies of virile controlling fathers of the law leave us feeling alienated and unloved. Kristeva's imaginary father, who turns out to be another face of the father of the law, cannot replace the real or embodied father. An identification with a desire for a father is an identification with the longing for love, which in itself cannot provide the necessary guarantee for feeling loved by a father. Why is the paternal body replaced by the fantasy of an imaginary father who turns out to be the mother's desire for a father? What is the threat of the paternal body? Of bodies in general?

In *New Maladies of the Soul,* Kristeva describes a threatening body that has completely colonized the soul. There, she asks "do you have a soul? . . . In the wake of psychiatric medicines, aerobics, and media zapping, does the soul still exist?" Her question is motivated by what she identifies as the lack of psychic life, which she defines as the representation and interpretation of experiences. She describes a "modern man" who is "losing his soul" and becoming merely "a body that acts" (1995, 7). "We have neither the time nor the space needed to create a soul for ourselves, and the mere hint of such activity seems frivolous and ill-advised. Held back by his aloofness, modern man is a narcissist—a narcissist who may suffer, but who feels no remorse. He manifests his suffering in his body and he is afflicted with somatic symptoms" (7). Kristeva describes a modern man for whom the collapse of time and space has collapsed the psyche, a modern man who has a body but no soul. "The body conquers the invisible territory of the soul"(8).

The life of the psyche, and thus the soul, is inhibited by drugs and media images. These have become the weapons used in the body's takeover of the soul. Kristeva diagnoses the body's takeover of psychic space that leaves modern man without a place of his own. In *Tales of Love,* she calls modern man "an exile, deprived of his psychic space, an extraterrestrial with a prehistory bearing, wanting for love" (1987c, 382). Kristeva's discussion suggests that drugs and media images have flattened the psyche. The psyche and soul have become two-dimensional, worn on the skin of a body that suffers from their thinness. The body suffers, and the modern Narcissus turns to more drugs and more images to ease the pain. Drugs, however, only regulate the oscillation between pain and relief, and media images reflect false selves that ultimately only exacerbate our feelings of out-of-placeness. Neither can compensate for the "erosion of the loving father."

Kristeva suggests that each individual has his or her own malady of the soul that requires an individual discourse to articulate it. What analysts should do is help their analysand find his or her own discourses in which his or her own emptiness and his or her own out-of-placeness "become essential elements . . . of a *work in progress*" (1987c, 380). Discourse has become normalized and standardized and thus meaningless; it cannot speak *my own* experience (see 1995, 8). So the analyst is in the business of providing a space of ownness that allows the psyche to reinflate, to be filled with individual meaning. The problem with *modern man* is his inability to represent himself, which "hinders sensory, sexual, and intellectual life" and "the psychoanalyst is then asked to restore psychic life and to enable the speaking entity to live life to its fullest" (1995, 9).

The problem, it seems, comes down to emptiness or fullness. To be full is to be content; to be empty is to be hungry for something else.

Our psyches are hungry and need nourishment, but from drugs and the media they receive only artificial nutrients and junk food. For Kristeva, only the loving father can feed and fill the psyche; the mother's body has already nourished the body and been disposed. The same mouth that fed on the mother's milk now feeds on the father's words. It turns out, however, that those words are abstract; they are used by everyone; they are normalized and standardized. They are all used up and they do not speak to the son's individuality. They do not elect *him* as the chosen one, the only one. They are given equally to everyone and so do not fit him. As a result, as Kristeva says, *he* wants to become other, "to become woman," in the hopes of being loved, of being chosen, of having his own discourse, his own space, a womb of his own. But his womb is always experienced as *empty* or *artificial* and therefore never satisfying.

Yet, isn't the desire for one's own discourse, and providing individual spaces for each psyche, itself a narcissistic desire? Does the attempt to create an individual discourse address modern narcissism? Or, like drugs and media images, does it merely perpetuate its frustration? If Narcissus suffers when he realizes that he sees only *his own* image reflected back to him, that he is alone, then doesn't he need companionship and communion, communication and a shared discourse, instead of *his own* individual discourse? Are modern men and contemporary analysands looking for their own space or a shared space? Are they looking for their own individual language or someone else who understands their language? Are they looking for ownership or the gift of love?

Perhaps if words are cut off from their affective meaning and we cannot represent our experiences, it is not because the body has conquered the soul or because we do not have our own individual languages. Rather, perhaps words are cut off from their affective meanings because our psyches have been colonized by the soul and we are alienated from our own individual bodies. As Nietzsche might say, we are no longer bodies that act but souls that react in ways that are increasingly cut off from the force, drives, and affects of the body. Rather than ask Kristeva's question "Do you have a soul?" we might ask, "Do you have a body? In the wake of psychiatric medicines, aerobics, and media zapping, does the body still exist?" In the end, maybe these come down to the same question.

What is it that psychiatry, aerobics, and media images have in common? They all objectify the body. Media images present two-dimensional idealized bodies, often as commodities to be purchased. Aerobics and body building are attempts to control the body and realize the ideals of those media images. And psychiatry turns the body into an object for scientific study. The body with its pains and secretions becomes a laboratory experiment that can be controlled with chemicals. These attempts to objectify and control the body do not signal the conquest of the soul by the body but the emptying of the body. The body becomes a two-dimensional surface, a container for discrete and removable organs, on which the symptoms of its own forced silence appear as illness.

Our experiences do not find language because we cannot speak (of) the body except in terms of these discourses that turn it into a dead object. Since we cannot speak the life of our bodies, we become hysterics whose bodies speak for themselves in the painful codes of somatic symptoms. The only discourse that does not shy away from the body, espcially the paternal body, is the medical discourse that renders the body safe by dissecting it. The medical discourse contains the body within the realm of nature. As long as the body is contained and nature and culture are properly opposed, the body cannot threaten culture with a fall back into nature. But if the body that represents culture and law, the paternal body, turns out to be natural and uncontrollable, this becomes a dangerous threat.

This is why aside from the gym, the medical discourse is where we find men's bodies, and it is the only place that we find the paternal body. The contingency of the paternal body is contained by medical discourse, not only because the paternal body and its fluids are measured and calculated but also because high-tech tests make it possible to determine paternity. As a result, the medicalized paternal body shows up in the courtroom as evidence for rights and responsibilities. The medical discourse translates the flows and secretions of the paternal body into objects. It controls those uncontrollable elements by framing them in terms of productions. It rarely addresses the flows in themselves or as secretions of a body whose pleasures are out of control. The pleasures of the paternal body are measured in terms of the motility of sperm to determine the chances of producing offspring. Or, they are identified to assign rights to, or responsibility as a sort of punishment for, those offspring.

It seems that whereas the female body is reduced to the maternal body and relegated to nature, the male body is a ghostly absent paternal body that safeguards culture. Whereas the female/maternal is reduced to body, the male/paternal is dissociated from body. He is not his body; rather, his body and its products are his possessions. In this virile imaginary, his body is a thing to be controlled and an instrument for control and for reproducing himself. In this image, the father does not love—he possesses. The disassociation of the father from the body ensures that all fathers are absent fathers. In order for the child to feel loved, the symbolic or imaginary father can never replace a real embodied father. Whether or not there is a father physically present, our images of fatherhood should include an embodied loving father rather than just the stern symbolic father of the law or an imaginary father who collapses into either the symbolic father or the maternal body.

If we can re-create meaning, both the meaning of words and the meaning of life, then we have to re-create love. And to re-create love, we have to re-create ourselves out of the possibility of loving mothers and loving fathers, mothers who are social and fathers who are embodied. Only then can we feel loved and love. Only then can soma and psyche, body and soul, fill each other with meaning.

9

Subjectivity without Subjects: Circulation from Vision to Visions

In this chapter, I would like to extend and develop the model for intersubjectivity that I suggested at the end of *Womanizing Nietzsche: Philosophy's Relation to the "Feminine"* (Oliver 1995). There, taking up biologist Hélène Rouch's remarks in an interview with Luce Irigaray, I proposed the fetus-placenta-maternal body as a system of exchange that prefigures and sets up intersubjective exchange. Here, I want to complicate that model by focusing on the transitions from placental systems to sensory systems and from sensory systems to linguistic systems of intersubjective exchange. While much of modern and "postmodern" philosophy and psychoanalysis have seen these transitions as abrupt and alienating, I focus on the continuity of primary patterns of circulation whose rates of exchange vary with the change in material elements through the transitions from one register to another. By questioning prevalent notions of vision presupposed by (neo-Hegelian) theories of recognition, I suggest this alternative account of intersubjectivity as a crucial supplement to contemporary feminist theories of identity based on recognition and abjection.

I will begin to flesh out the placental model by engaging with the two most frequent criticisms of it. First, some feminists have been concerned about taking the maternal body as a model for intersubjectivity or an ethical relationship. Variously they believe that a reduction of women to maternity has worked to oppress women and that maternity requires sacrifices from the mother for the sake of her child that make this relationship unfit as a model of cooperative or reciprocal intersubjective exchange. Second, feminists and others are troubled about the role of violence in the placental model and in intersubjective relations themselves. Obviously violence is possible in human relationships, but we disagree about its necessity. So, two related questions with which I start to develop a model of subjectivity without subjects are, Why the model of the maternal body? and, Is violence necessary?

First, why the model of the maternal body? Note that this is a model of the maternal body and not the mother-child relationship. My emphasis is on the placenta as the medium of exchange between the maternal body and the fetus. I am not suggesting a phenomenology of motherhood or maternity, nor am I suggesting an ethics of care. Rather, in a Nietzschean vein, I am using a provocative biological model as an image for subjectivity that calls into question the autonomous subject in an attempt to remodel our notion of subjectivity. The implicit principle of one body, one soul or subject that motivates most of traditional philosophy is radically challenged by the maternal body. The maternal body is a powerful image because it gives us two bodies in one.

This, however, is precisely why it is also so easy to slip from using a model to explain the pattern of subjectivity, on the one hand, to thinking of these two bodies as two subjects or potential subjects, on the other, a problem that has significant political implications for abortion debates in which the supposed rights of one subject are pitted against the supposed rights of another potential subject. We may avoid many philosophical problems if we think of subjectivity without a subject. On the level of my biological model, there is no subject. And, while the fetus is dependent on the maternal body in a physical way that the maternal body is not dependent on the fetus, the maternal body also becomes what it is only through the process of conception and fetal formation.

More than this, both fetus and maternal body are dependent on the placenta, which operates as a circulatory system between two bodies that share the same fluids but not the same DNA. What could be experienced by the body as the hostile invasion of an alien that triggers the production of antibodies with which the body protects itself is not experienced this way because of the function of the placenta. The placenta sets up the circulatory communication between (and within) the maternal body and the fetus so that rather than destroy each other, through the mediation of the placenta, they engage in mutually beneficial fluid exchange. On the phenomenological level, of course, the woman whose body is undergoing these changes may experience them as either (or both) pleasant or unpleasant, gift or sacrifice.

This model is meant as a corrective to the Hegelian lordship-bondsman scenario, which contemporary philosophy has inherited (1977). Of course, what is attractive about Hegel's model is that he gives us for the first time a full-blown account of subjectivity as intersubjective, as relational. It seems that in spite of the dialectic of subjectivity, however, Hegel's two self-consciousnesses are already autonomous subjects. The metaphor of master and slave smuggles in with it the very subject whose onset Hegel is trying to describe. Clandestine subjects or not, they are certainly two virile wills who must be eager to engage in a fight to the death. But, because both quickly realize that death defeats the purpose of risking their lives in the first place, they settle for domination and enslavement. This servitude is necessary for a self-consciousness that recognizes itself through its labor and fear; ultimately it recognizes its freedom only through the limitation of its freedom.

In Hegel's model, subjectivity requires hostility, alienation, dominance, servitude, a clash of wills, for the sake of a recognition of myself in/from the other that makes me a self-conscious subject. In this formative stage, there is no free exchange, no communication, no cooperation, no fundamental connection between the two self-consciousnesses. The placental model, on the other hand, offers exchange, communication, connection, negotiation, which are not driven by a desire or need for recognition. A circulatory system takes the place of recognition that is based on visual cues. And, more important, channels of embodied connection or contact replace recognition that presupposes some internal core of the self forever haunting and haunted by the outside always so close and yet so far away.

Subjectivity is not the result of a dialectic jerking back and forth from self to other. Rather, if anything, self and other are the illusory by-products of subjectivity, perhaps even the refuse of the continual process of intersubjective exchanges that nourish and sometimes threaten. Identity is not necessarily bought through the abjection, exclusion, or domination of others.

Hegel and his willing (and unwilling) followers are right in thinking that the subject is desire (which is to say that it is no subject at all). But desire is not as they describe it. Desire is not the urge to overcome the otherness in the self and to recuperate oneself from the other. Subjectivity does not attempt to close in on itself and fortify itself against the other. Rather, subjectivity opens itself onto the other, multiplies itself but not in the sense of reproducing itself. Desire is the urge to move out into otherness. I do not define myself in relation to a hostile external world against which I am me by virtue of denying everything that I am not. The self and the other, the I and the I am not, are never fixed; and they are certainly never polar opposites.

Our experience of ourselves is not as a fortress defending itself against the outside world. Instead, we experience ourselves as flux and flows of moods, sensations, and thoughts that are changing. In fact, it is difficult, maybe impossible, to take some metaperspective on one's own changing persona. We cannot step out of the circulation of ourselves and our relations to others. And in this circulation we are just as much moving toward others as we are withdrawing and recuperating ourselves.

While continuing to address the question "Why the maternal body?" I want to shift my focus to the second question, "Is violence necessary?" by suggesting a genealogy of theories of subjectivity based on recognition and violence. By thinking of subjectivity as fluid, as the circulation of sensation and language that echoes the circulation of placental blood, I hope to navigate between two extremes that plague contemporary attempts to theorize difference: at the one pole, the position that I can understand anyone just by taking up their perspective, which makes communication unencumbered; and at the other pole, the position that I can understand no one because of radical alterity that prevents me from taking up their perspective, which makes communication impossible. The first assumes that we are absolutely identical, which erases our differences, and the second assumes that we are absolutely different, which erases our communion.

What, however, both views presuppose is that the space between us puts identity and difference into an oppositional relation. Both the presumed ability or inability to take up the position or perspective of another relies on an image of subjects as at least semifixed things whose borders are defined by the space between them and other things or subjects. Identity and communication are presumed possible only when the space between us can be closed and I inhabit your position or perspective. And if it is impossible for me to take up your position or perspective, then the space between us is an impassable gulf and communication is ultimately impossible. In this view, identity and difference are opposites, or at least mutually exclusive: you can have one but not the other. After all, two different things cannot be in the same place at the same time.

Perhaps the polar nature of this discussion is inflamed by philosophers' attempts to talk about identity and difference without shedding their metaphysical and logical inheritance. Psychological identification or identity does not operate like logical identity or metaphysical identity (at least as they have been traditionally conceived). Identity as it plays within the realm of subjectivity is not the A = A of logical identity. Neither is it the mutually exclusive identity of physics or metaphysics that might insist that two things cannot be in the same place at the same time unless they are identical. Although subjectivity is the result of bodies interacting in space, these are porous bodies whose fluids, energies, and affects circulate between them. In Deleuzian parlance, they are bodies that can couple in multitudes of ways. Also, the space within which bodies couple is not made up of discrete units separated by an impassable gulf. In fact, it is only in crossing over apparently impassable gulfs that the sparks of subjectivity fly.

The circulatory system that is set up within the maternal body among maternal body, placenta, and fetus, then, continues after birth when sensory perception is mediated by air and elements instead of by blood and veins. After birth, the tissues that connect us are still a shared material environment that very much affects how we feel, think, and act. Although like any model, the model of the placental system has its limitations, it also has a genetic power lacking in the Hegelian model. As Teresa Brennan explains it, birth opens up space and time that are absent in the womb, and this space and time slow down the circulation of affects and sensations and give rise to the perception-consciousness system (1993). It is not, however, as Brennan suggests, that space and time open up after birth; rather, the elements change, and thus the rate of circulation through those elements changes as well. Another way to describe the transition from placental circulation to the circulations of the perception-consciousness system is to attend to the shift in sensual development after birth.

At the level of the placental system there is sensation, but it is sensation of flow and rhythm or vibration and movement—what, in terms of the classic five senses, we would associate with touch. But already this model calls into question touch and the distinction between touch and sound, for example. What is sound but vibration and rhythm? What are vibrations and rhythm when they are experienced in tissues and capillaries? Are they touch or sound? The one sense most obviously absent from this primordial relationship is sight. Vision requires light, not to mention eyes.

But, the very technologies that give us visual access to the darkest recesses of the living body engaged in its various physiological processes also suggest a relationship between the mediums of sight, sound, and touch. The sonogram and ultrasound technologies that enable us to "see" inside the body also react to vibrations and not illumination. Just as one sensory register translates into others after birth, recent technology allows us to translate from the registers of vibration and movements into the register of vision. After all, the eye and its object are connected by the air or elements through which light travels and is reflected. And it is the circulation of light that makes vision possible.

Since models of identity that rely on notions of recognition seem to be linked somehow to vision, what notion of vision do they presuppose? And, what are the implications of this particular notion of vision for a theory of subjectivity? The link between vision and recognition is explicit in Lacan's influential account of ego formation in "The Mirror Stage" (1977). There, Lacan suggests that humans differ from other animals in that as infants we compensate ourselves for lack of real motor coordination with images that anticipate motor coordination. While Lacan makes a point of telling us that visual images are central to the development of other species—pigeons and locusts, for example—humans are especially reliant on visual images because of our "premature birth," "anatomical incompleteness," and "residual humors from the maternal organism" (1977, 4).

Lacan calls the mirror image the threshold of the visible world (3). It is the infant's entrance into the outside world in which things are visibly distinct from each other. But, more important, we find out, the mirror image is the threshold between the inner world and the outside world (1977, 4). The mirror image is not just any other visible image available to the sense of sight. No, for Lacan, the mirror image initiates a psychic image or imago that is not sensible but mental. The mirror image is the threshold of the visible world and the psychic world, the outside world and the inner world, the body's eye and the mind's eye. It is the threshold between *vision and visions.* It is in fact the threshold of the I (the agency of the ego). At the threshold of the visible world we slip from physical to psychic, from material to immaterial, from sensible to mental, from body to mind.

But why does this visible physical image in the mirror give rise to an invisible psychic image? How does the visual image trigger the process of identification wherein the subject assimilates an aspect, property, or attribute of that image that becomes an unconscious representation or imago? Why this connection between vision and recognition (or its flip side in Lacan's scenario, misrecognition—which already presupposes something that could be recognized but is not)? Doesn't Lacan's analysis create the very split between the inner and outer worlds that his theory attempts to reconnect through the mirror stage? This brings me back to my earlier question: What notion of vision is presupposed in theories of identity based on recognition, or in this case misrecognition?

Reminiscent of Hegel's account of alienation in the master-slave relationship, Lacan's analysis of the misrecognition in the mirror stage is dependent on the gap or empty space between the body and its image. This gap or empty space is seen as a void or abyss that permanently separates "us" from our "object," even if this object is our own image or another self-consciousness. Bridging this gap, or filling that empty space, is the motivation for Hegel's *Phenomenology of Spirit* and much of modern philosophy (1977). The dilemma of modern philosophy is, In order to know the object, we must be separate from the object, but if we are separate from the object, how can we know it? The contemporary version of this dilemma has become, How can I know or understand the other if I am separated from the other? But hasn't the notion of vision as a distancing force that brings with it the illusion of control over the visible world led us astray?

Why is it that for Hegel, Freud, Lacan, and their followers, vision and its accompanying recognition (the body's eye becoming the mind's eye) involve violence? For Hegel it is the sight of the other self-conscious body mimicking your actions that makes you want to kill it. For Freud, the sight of the castrated sex initiates all of the rage, jealousy, and murderous impulses of the Oedipal situation. For Lacan, the alienating function of the I as it is misrecognized in the mirror releases aggressivity in relation to any other (1977, 6). Psychoanalysis postulates a violence and hostility at the root of all interpersonal relations, even the most loving.

In all of these cases doesn't vision involve a sense of lack and castration? Being essentially cut off from the world and the other? Being fundamentally alienated and alone? Don't they seem to suppose that what we see when we recognize ourselves or the other is the distance between us? And the rest of our lives are spent futilely and violently trying to fill that gap? Our sense of frustration at this alienating distance makes us violent. We blame the other for the distance that separates us; we think that we can overcome the alienation and destroy the gap by overcoming or destroying the other. We confuse distance with the other. But perhaps the distance presupposed by these theories of recognition, supposedly produced through vision, is our real enemy.

Isn't it precisely because our vision fails us that we see the object or other as distant? That we see the other separated by space that the eyes by themselves can never mediate or close without losing sight of it altogether? We are like Narcissus longing to close the gap between ourselves and our image, destroying the image in our attempts to get close. What our eyes cannot see are the elements that fill the space between ourselves and our objects and link us in the circulation of light and air that makes vision possible. Our vision fails to see the light and air and elements that mediate our seeing and what we see. But, if the physical gap between seer and seen does not exist, then how can it trigger the psychological gap between self and other or between subject and ego or Ideal-I? What is it about the sense of sight that makes us feel cut off and thereby opens psychic space?

Our other senses—smell, hearing, taste, touch—all seem to bring us closer to their objects, to the point that with taste, for example, it is difficult to distinguish between the sensation and its object. But, it is not just physical proximity that distinguishes sight from other senses. We can smell something at a distance, and we can hear sounds at even greater distances. Perhaps it is the illusion that smells travel *into* our noses, sounds *into* our ears, tastes *into* our mouths, but that sight somehow radiates *out of* our eyes. Yet, we see only because light travels into our eyes and meets our optic nerves. Our eyes *appear* to be solid, mirrors reflecting images on their pupils, windows onto the soul, but they are porous and fluid. Like the other senses, vision is the result of pressures, vibrations, particles, and waves affecting the nerves. Moreover, visual images are surrounded and informed by tastes, smells, sounds, and palpitations.

Merleau-Ponty presents a phenomenology of vision in which he describes palpitations of the eyes as a variant of tactile palpitations in a vision-touch system. "Vision is a palpitation with the look" (1968, 134), and the world is visible because it is tactile, because it is corporeal. Merleau-Ponty describes the corporeality of the visible world as the connective tissues that nourish and sustain the possibility of seeing. He describes vision in terms of thickness, corpuscles, tissues, grains, waves, channels, circuits, currents, embryos, and pregnancy, the very corporeality out of which sensation, thought, and language are born. Ultimately he concludes that the delimitation of the senses is crude. First, all of the senses are interconnected in one body. Second, each sense is really a complex of sensations that fundamentally implicates the others. Third, sensation operates in the reversible world of sensible and sentient that fold the senses back onto themselves in a way that produces new levels of sensation and consciousness.

Because of the interconnection between the senses and the elements that make vision possible, the distance necessary for vision is not alienating but enabling. Vision does not necessarily put the world or others or our own image at an unreachable distance. If vision is part of a sensory system that includes what we take to be more proximal senses like touch, taste, or smell, vision becomes a sort of touching, a palpitation with the eyes. If the eyes are porous membranes and not solid mirrors or windows, then vision like the other senses necessitates a type of interpolation of elements that challenges any neat distinctions between inside and outside, or self and other.

Moreover, if, as I suggested earlier, vision is possible because of various interconnected elements—air, light, waves, particles, nerves, tissues—interacting, then distance is never empty space, an unbridgable gap, or an abyssal void; rather, the distance between us is the connective tissues of earthly elements. As Merleau-Ponty says, "this distance is not the contrary of this proximity, it is deeply consonant with it, it is synonymous with it. It is that the thickness of the flesh between the seer and the thing is constitutive for the thing of its visibility as for the seer of his corporiety; it is not an obstacle between them, it is their means of communication" (1968, 135).

In *Womanizing Nietzsche,* I suggest the placental model as a prototype of communication. Just as sensation operates through a kind of circulatory system of elements, so do language and communication (1995). Language is the circulation of bodily affect and meaning through systems of sounds, voice, breath, gestures, words, symbols, alphabets, always inflused with sensation. Language is not a representation of our embodiment; it is part of it. To echo Merleau-Ponty once again: "if we were to make completely explicit the architectonics of the human body, its ontological framework, and how it sees itself and hears itself, we would see that the structure of its mute world is such that all the possibilities of language are already given in it" (1968, 155). Language has its source in the body and not just because it takes a mouth to speak and a hand to write. Language speaks and writes bodily affects and bodily drives, without which there would be no motivation for language. We use language not only to communicate information but also to make psychophysical connections to others. Communication is also a form of communion.

Lacan might be right that every demand is a demand for love, but he is wrong that these demands are forever cut off from the needs that they speak. We need to speak, we need to make demands, just as we need food and warmth. Demands, then, are not cut off from our basic need for satisfaction that Lacan associates with love. As we have learned from Kristeva, drives and bodily needs are discharged in language, and the law and regulation necessary to set up language are already operating within the body. So, our first contact with the regulating rhythms, sonorous vibrations, and circulatory exchanges that set up the possibility of language are within the maternal body. Moreover, the apparent distance or gap between the body and language, between needs and demands, that replicates the visual distance or gap between the infant and the mirror in Lacan's mirror stage is a symptom of the pathology of the theory itself.

The placental model is intended as a corrective to the antagonistic pathos of alienation inherent in some philosophical accounts of otherness, but it can also work as an orthopedic measure in relation to contemporary feminist theories of identity. I want to address not just the devaluing of motherhood shared by traditional philosophy and some post-Beauvoirian feminisms. After all, rather than throw out the mother with the bathwater, why not reclaim and revalue maternity, even motherhood, for feminism? But, in addition to "saving the mother," there is another way in which the placental model of subjectivity attempts to provide a supplement to contemporary feminism.

Heirs of Nietzsche, Lacan, and Derrida, continental feminists seem to have inherited a neo-Hegelian notion of identity as recognition of self through abjection of other. The use of theories of identity as constructed through the exclusion or abjection of the other is widespread—and not just among feminist theorists. Following anthropologist Mary Douglas, Teresa Brennan, Judith Butler, and Julia Kristeva, for example, all propose such theories. In various ways, they all maintain that identity is possible only by abjecting the other.

Mary Douglas describes defilement as the danger to identity constituted by filth, which is always defined in relation to the borders of that very identity (1969). Julia Kristeva has transformed Douglas's theory of defilement into her neo-Hegelian theory of abjection, with which she purports to explain the dynamics of both group and individual identity as constituted through the rejection of otherness (1980b). Judith Butler expands the theory of abjection when she analyzes the dynamics of exclusion inherent in identification. Butler maintains, "The construction of the 'not-me' as abject establishes the boundaries of the body which are also the first contours of the subject" (1990, 133). She extends her analysis of the exclusion inherent in identification when she describes materiality as delimited through a violent and normative procedure that "marks a boundary that includes and excludes, that decides, as it were, what will and will not be the stuff of the object to which we refer" (1993, 11). The theory of abjection is also in the background of Teresa Brennan's notion of a foundational fantasy through which the masculine ego re-creates the world in its own image by annihilating heterogeneity in favor of more of itself to control its environment (1993, 11).

Although theories of abjection can diagnose the operations of oppression, they do not in themselves suggest alternatives. In fact, if taken as standards for identification, theories of abjection normalize the most hateful and threatening kinds of discrimination, exclusion, and oppression. If our identities are necessarily formed by rejecting and excluding what is different, then differentiation or discrimination is always oppressive or violent. The best we can do is to acknowledge our own violence, which itself must necessarily be another form of violence. Theories that propose that identity is dependent on the exclusion of difference, however, presuppose that one's sense of oneself needs to be contained, or is containable, that we can set up the borders of ourselves because we are discrete entities or cites of performance. Our experiences of ourselves, however, are not as contained or containable discrete units. Rather, they are fluid movements in a circulation of sensation, affect, thought, and language that put us into contact with others.

Although wars, oppression, subjugation, hatred, and discrimination exist, these are not *necessary* to identification. We need new explanations of our relations with others that can account for both oppression and communion, without reducing one to the other. We need a way to describe the negotiations between ourselves and others that can lead to paranoia and war *or* to a sense of adventure and love. To develop such a theory we cannot begin with the notion that our own identity is formed through hostile relations with others.

I suggest that these theories are based on a faulty notion of space that views difference as distance and distance as void. This view of space as empty seems to come out of a notion of vision as the distancing sense. I am not challenging, as others have, the priority of vision over other senses in the history of thought. Rather, I am challenging the prevalent notion of vision that postulates it as a unitary force that spans the very gap between us and the outside world that it creates. This view of space and vision leaves us forever cut off from the world outside ourselves unless we can incorporate it and make it our own. In this view, difference and identity are opposites because space is discrete and not fluid; two things cannot be in the same place at the same time unless they are identical. But, if we replace this model with one of circulation that links vision to the other more proximal senses, we see that there is no inherent gap between us and the world outside. We are, by virtue of the distance that separates us from others, a distance that is filled with the elements that sustain us and make relationships possible.

10

Beyond Recognition: Witnessing the Other Otherwise in Varda's *Vagabond*

In this chapter I use Agnes Varda's 1985 film *Vagabond* to begin to develop a theory of subjectivity based on witnessing rather than recognition. In *Vagabond,* Varda presents various reactions to Mona, the vagabond character, that allow us to imagine many different relations to otherness, from compassion to abjection. The film's presentation of relations to otherness and the incomprehensibility of the other opens up possibilities for imagining relations of difference besides abjection on the one hand or idealization on the other. In the last chapter, I suggested that while Kristeva's theory of abjection can be useful in diagnosing the exclusion or murder of others, it should not be taken as a norm for self-identity or self-other relations. There are other ways of relating to others besides abjection and exclusion. Of course, Kristeva's notion of abjection is complex in that it describes both fascination and repulsion with another. So, her theory can be used to explain both idealization and exclusion of others and otherness. As we have seen in previous chapters, Kristeva describes abjection as both a stage in the development of the self and a constant threat to individual identity. Without a proper counterbalance, abjection can lead either to fragmentation and self-abuse or the exclusion of the other and otherness, either suicide or murder.

The expression of abjection in signification—language, poetry, art—however, can also lead to a rebirth of the subject in process. Taking up a neo-Aristotelian view of catharsis in *Powers of Horror,* Kristeva suggests that rather than lead to purification—the concern of philosophers—the repetition of abjection in analytic discourse can lead to a "rebirth with and against abjection" (1980b, 31). It is as if abjection gives the fragile subject in process something (i.e., precisely not a thing) to hold onto long enough to do away with the need for such flimsy safeguards. The abject—not-yet object for a not-yet subject—serves as a type of transitional *object* for a fledgling subject. In this way, it helps give birth to a new and improved self, with and against abjection.

Interestingly, in "From One Identity to the Other" Kristeva suggests that the position of elaboration of semiotic drive force (and therefore abjection) may be reserved for a woman. She says:

> [I]t is probably necessary to be a woman . . . not to renounce theoretical reason but to compel it to increase its power by giving it an object beyond its limits. . . . [T]his expanded theory of signification cannot give itself new objects except by positing itself as nonuniversal: that is, by presupposing that a questionable subject-in-process exists in an economy of discourse other than that of thetic consciousness. And this requires that subjects of the theory must be themselves subjects in infinite analysis; this is what Husserl could not imagine, what Céline could not know, but what a woman, among others, can finally admit, aware as she is of the inanity of Being. (1975, 146)

While men may play the dangerous game with incestuous poetic language, taking signification back to its maternal origins, women, always too close to the maternal to go back, can take up the position of analyst, the position of symbolic mastery, with therapeutic effect precisely because they can never take it, or themselves, too seriously.

Always threatened by abjection, subjects in infinite analysis are not limited to it. Objects beyond the limits of reason are not always or necessarily abject. And, relations to self or other are not always phobic. One of the implications of Kristeva's theory is that law-abiding analyses by those on the margins, by those already abjected by the law, can put into motion a return of the repressed other that uses the force of the law itself to expand its horizons. There is the hope that, against the phobic, the marginal figure who refuses to identify with the abject in favor of the law, reason, or, more precisely, the elaboration of the way in which law and reason depend on her abjection can renegotiate her identity and her social status. While her male revolutionary poets challenge the law by transgressing it, Kristeva imagines herself as woman and analyst transforming the law by playing it in another register.

While, as an artist, in her film Agnes Varda does not elaborate her relation to the law or her main character's relation to the law—she leaves that to us—she does play it in another register. If we may not discern anything else from the enigmatic and reticent main character, Mona, it is hard to avoid a certain sense of the inanity of Being. Mona's many relationships create a spectrum of possibilities that break out of the restrictive confines of the theory of abjection. As if undergoing infinite analysis itself, the notion of abjection, so vividly portrayed in Varda's *Vagabond,* declares its nonuniversality. Through my elaboration of the relationships in *Vagabond,* I hope to continue an analysis that expands the horizons of the notion of abjection, refusing to let abjection itself become law and thereby rethinking recognition and what it means to be recognizable.

Outlaw Love?

Sans toit ni loi (Without roof or law), as *Vagabond* was originally titled in France, uses Varda's trademark documentary style to give it the effect and authority of social science. After the opening shot through a desolate field, a farmhand finds a dead woman in a ditch. In the next scene a voice-over of a woman (the only voice-over used in the film) tells us that "no one claimed the body, so it went from a ditch to potter's field. She had died a natural death without leaving a trace. I wonder, do those who knew her as a child still think about her? But people she had met recently remembered her. Those witnesses helped me tell the last weeks of her last winter. She left her mark on them. They spoke of her not knowing she had died. I didn't tell them. Nor that her name was Mona Bergeron. I know little about her myself, but it seems to me she came from the sea." The rest of the film is a mixture of those witnesses' responses to our invisible and voiceless interviewer directed at the audience and action sequences showing Mona's last weeks of her last winter.

Oscillating between action and testimony, the film itself has a certain analytic quality. As the audience, we are put into the position of the analyst silently listening to the "witnesses" confess themselves and their desires. The interviewer, our documentarian, that social scientist, has disappeared and we are put in her place, the place of authority. And, of course, we learn more about our witnesses than about Mona in their descriptions of her. Mona operates like a mirror in which we see them. But, the juxtaposition of action and testimony allows us to glimpse just how much Mona is distorted to serve as their mirror. It is not that *we* see the *real* Mona but rather that we see too many different Monas through the eyes of our witnesses. Which raises these questions: To whom do they bear witness? What does it mean to witness? How can we bear witness to the other? What is the audience's role as witness?

I will return to these questions about bearing witness to the other when I turn my attention to the problem of recognition at the end of this chapter. For now, I want to analyze, even catalogue, the types of relationships represented in Varda's *Vagabond.* In many ways each of the various relationships that we witness in the film is unique and defies my attempts at typology. Still, there are some general types that share certain characteristics: There are those who idealize Mona and her lifestyle, those who despise her, those who exploit her as a sex object, those who identify with her, those who fear her, those who wonder at her, those who enjoy her company, those who feel compassion toward her, perhaps even those who love her. Of course, some people represent a combination of these. All of these different representations can give us insight into our complex relations with others.

Idealization

Several of the characters whom she meets seem to idealize Mona. Not knowing what her life is like or who she is, they imagine her life as perfect. Their idealized projections onto Mona are responses to the failures and disappointments of their own lives. For them, Mona provides the dream of an alternative life, a better life, one that is not their own. They envy Mona and wish that they were in her shoes. The three most telling examples of this type of idealization are three women of different ages, a girl, a thirty-something woman, and an older woman.

The girl meets Mona when Mona stops at her house asking for water. After their brief encounter, the girl tells her parents that she wants to leave so that she can be free like the girl who stopped by asking for water. Her mother tells her that that girl does not have a mother feeding her at home, and her daughter responds that sometimes it is better not to eat and to be free. This girl imagines that Mona is free. Without any conception of what Mona's life is like or its hardships, she wants to be like her. What the film shows us of Mona's life, however, hardly seems enviable. In fact, from the viewer's perspective, it seems hard to idealize Mona's life—and her eventual death, all alone freezing in a ditch.

The second character who seems to idealize Mona's life is Yolanda, the live-in caretaker for an old woman named Lydie. Yolanda first sees Mona when she is visiting her uncle at the estate where he works as a caretaker. Yolanda is taking a walk while her boyfriend Paulo is drinking with her uncle. On her walk, she peeks into a little abandoned château where she sees Mona asleep in a man's arms. When she returns, she tells the camera, "I wish Paulo would dream with me like the lovers in the château in each other's arms." Later she tells Paulo that she wishes that they could be like the couple that she saw, so good to each other, so loving. Finally, when she actually meets Mona when she picks up Mona hitchhiking, she tells Mona that when she saw her in the château in the arms of that man, she thought it was eternal love. Without knowing anything about the couple in the château, Yolanda imagined that they had true love, eternal love, the love for which she longed. The viewer knows that Mona just met this guy on the road and that she left at the first sign of trouble, which makes it hard not to see Yolanda's image of the relationship as her own fantasy.

The third case of idealization is an old woman who is telling her husband that she "liked that hippie" because "she's got character. She knows what she wants. . . . If I'd sent you packing at her age, I'd be better off. Marry the wrong man and you're stuck for life." This woman imagines Mona as self-possessed and self-determined. Yet, as we see Mona wandering from place to place going wherever she ends up, we are led to wonder whether being without roof or law is freedom, whether freedom can be random, or whether it requires more self-determination. It is especially ironic that this scene with the old woman complaining to her husband comes after a scene in which a goat-herding philosopher tells the camera that Mona's problem is that she does not know what she wants, that she does not want anything. Whereas the goatherder insists that she does not know what she wants, the old woman imagines that Mona knows exactly what she wants. *Vagabond* continually gives us different and conflicting perspectives on the same character.

In each of these cases it is disappointment in one's own life that causes the idealized projection onto an other. The other becomes the representative of one's own unfulfilled desires. She becomes the object of envy and admiration because she is imagined as more successful at meeting one's own aspirations. Is it a coincidence that all three of these cases are women dissatisfied with their relationships? A girl who feels the restrictive authority of her parents? A woman who feels unloved by her boyfriend? A woman who regrets getting married?

These women feel trapped by their lives and the roles that they are expected to play. To them, Mona represents the freedom from those roles. They see her as a woman who does not have to answer to a man who is insensitive to her needs, as someone who knows what she wants and gets it, the agent of her own life. The old woman and the girl, especially, idealize Mona's agency. They feel that they are not the agents of their own lives, so they project the possibility of their agency onto Mona and envy the possibility of their own agency in her. For them, even while Mona reminds them of their own failures and limitations, she also represents the possibility of their choosing otherwise. She represents the possibility of choosing an alternative life, which confirms their own agency and freedom even as it reminds them of their plights. Their encounters with Mona inspire them to imagine themselves otherwise, to dream of alternative lives for themselves. Mona gives them hope that "it doesn't have to be this way."

Identification

Another form of idealization shown in the film is identification with Mona. One of the most memorable characters in *Vagabond* is a philosopher-goatherder who idealizes his own life through an identification with Mona's life on the road. He tells Mona that he used to be on the road, suggesting that he knows what it is like for her. She reminds him that with a wife and a herd it was different for him. He responds that he spent one Christmas alone, as if that meant that he experienced the same kind of isolation and solitude that she does alone on the road. Mona is not impressed, so he says, "Maybe you are freer than I am. Good for you. I choose a middle road between loneliness and freedom. You chose total freedom, but you get total loneliness. The time comes when if you go on you destroy yourself. You head for destruction. If you want to live, you stop. My friends who stayed on the road are dead or alcoholics or junkies. The loneliness ate them up in the end." Mona appears unaffected by his sermon, which seems to be more for his own sake than hers, anyway.

The philosopher-goatherder tries to help Mona by giving her a trailer to stay in and a little plot of land on which to grow potatoes, but she prefers laying around smoking and reading to working the land. At one point the goatherder confronts Mona and demands that she start working because it is unfair that he and his wife work all day and she does not. Mona responds, "What do you want?" And he answers, "You don't *want* anything! You have an empty head." To which she replies, "You gotta have something in it? Gotta be a shepherd like you?" She explains that she quit being a secretary because she did not like having a boss, and now she does not need to have a boss on the road. He concludes that she is a dreamer. And later in an interview, he claims that what she did was not wandering but withering, without goals or plans.

The goatherder idealizes life on the road, his version of it. He is supportive of Mona as long as he imagines that she shares his ideals and goals. She realizes, however, that he wants her to be just like him, that he expects her to have the same aspirations as he does. He identifies with Mona to idealize his own life. In the end, he uses Mona to justify the compromises that he has made as necessary to life.

In his testimony he maintains that Mona merely proved the system that she rejected by refusing any goals or plans, "by being worthless." If Mona proves the law by refusing it, the goatherder reinscribes the law by valorizing its margins and making his own law. He rejects the system, but in the name of another system, his own system of law and ideals. Once Mona rejects them, he rejects her. The goatherder idealizes the outlaw as long as the outlaw is made law, but he cannot imagine a life without any law, a life without structure, goals, or plans. His way of fighting his marginalization by the system is to make those margins the center of his own system.

Another possible example of idealization as identification is the character with whom Mona spends some time in the abandoned château. We see Mona and Dave happily eating, drinking, and smoking together. At one point Mona writes their names in the steam on a pane of glass with her finger. But when Dave is beat up during a robbery at the estate (staged by Yolanda's boyfriend Paulo), Mona escapes. Later, in an interview Dave says that he thought that she was a homebody, the staying kind. He imagined that Mona wanted the same things that he did; perhaps he imagined her as the girl of his dreams. He projected his own desires onto her and then was disappointed to find out that he did not really know her.

Objectification

There are many ways in which Mona is made into an object by various characters in the film, perhaps by the film itself (and by my commentary on it). But the most brutal cases are those in which she is treated as a sex object and an exploitable resource for sexual experimentation. The first testimony in the film is by a young man who talks about seeing Mona swimming in the ocean. He says that he tried to convince his friend that this was their chance to have her, a girl all alone like that was easy prey. But his friend was too chicken. Later, Mona washes a few cars at a gas station to make some money, and we see the gas station attendant go into her tent with his pants unzipped. In his testimony he tells the camera that he had her wash a few cars to get her hands clean, that all female drifters were alike—they are loafers who chase men—and that she told him that he had a dirty mind (presumably when he went to her tent), to which he exclaimed, "What nerve!" Perhaps one of the most exploitative characters is a guy whom Mona meets in the train station, a grifter, who laments losing Mona because she "was a good fuck . . . a good piece of ass," and he planned to make money off of her by putting her in porn films. Finally, the most violent is the unknown man who rapes Mona in the woods.

These men see Mona there for the taking. She belongs to them in the way that any other natural resource does. Like any other object, she is there for their exploitation. Either they do not concern themselves with her desires (objects do not have desires), or, in the case of the gas station attendant, they imagine that she "wants it" because all female drifters chase men. What is more horrifying than the attitudes of these men is how normal it all seems. This sort of thing happens everyday. If upon reflection we find it offensive, even appalling, what is truly appalling is that it is also mundane and ordinary.

Perhaps if this sexual objectification of women really involved taking them as objects, then there would be some surprise when the object objected. It seems, however, that men who objectify women in this way do not hear their objections for what they are; rather, they seem to hear the sounds of some abject, not-yet object and not-yet subject, that enrages them all the more (as the gas station attendant exclaims, "What nerve!"). In the conclusion of *Tales of Love,* Kristeva suggests that in a culture that does not have sufficient positive images of motherhood to counterbalance what she sees as the necessary abjection of the maternal body, all women become abjected (1987c, 374). The female body becomes conflated with the maternal body and abjected or excluded so that the subject can set up its own clean and proper borders.

Abjection

Two particularly interesting relationships to Mona in *Vagabond* can be interpreted as examples of the two sides of abjection. The borderline or ambiguous state of the abject can evoke fascination, horror, or both. Mona's position on the border of society and law seems to evoke these two reactions in Professor Landier, a biologist who studies a cancerlike fungus killing planetrees, and her assistant Jean-Pierre. Unlike most of the other characters in the film, neither of these two characters are shown talking directly to the camera in interview fashion. Rather, when they speak about Mona, both of them are shown on the phone talking to some unknown and unheard interlocutor on the other end. Perhaps to call attention to the fact that in spite of the profound affect Mona has had on them, neither of these characters can bear witness to her since they are caught up in protecting their own self-identity; neither of them are shown testifying to the camera.

We first meet Professor Landier in her bathtub talking on the phone to some friend about her encounter with the vagabond. She describes how Mona stunk and says that the thing that upset her the most is that "I soon got used to her stink, her poverty." Professor Landier is kind to Mona. She picks her up hitchhiking, lets her stay overnight in her car, buys her beers and food, and lets her listen to the radio. When she eventually drops her off, she gives her a bag of food, some money, and a kiss on the cheek. Later after a near-death experience with electricity, Professor Landier describes seeing images from her life pass before her and the vagabond's image coming back over again. She asks her assistant Jean-Pierre to go find the hitchhiker. She is worried and feels bad about just dropping her off.

In addition to caring about Mona—or feeling guilty for not caring more—Professor Landier is fascinated by her. She talks about Mona as if she were one of the trees that she studies. Mona is an interesting specimen, one that she has not encountered before. Mona seems to sense that she might be like a specimen in a dish when Professor Landier tells her that she can spend the night in her car but she cannot leave the keys, and Mona exclaims, "You are going to lock me in!" In addition to her kindness, the professor is also observing Mona; she seems especially fascinated by Mona's relationship to her car.

Professor Landier feels a certain irresistible attraction to this stinky vagabond. But what upsets her is how soon she got used to Mona's stench. She is both fascinated and upset about how close she herself could be to the abject, how soon she could get used to it. She protects her own clean and proper boundaries by studying the abject using the distance provided by the scientific method. Although she is not a tree and does not have to worry about contamination from the tree fungus, her remark about what upsets her most suggests that she might be worrying about contamination from this more fascinating and dangerous specimen.

Jean-Pierre admits that he fears Mona. For him, she represents the other side of abjection, which evokes in him disgust and repulsion. He first meets Mona when she is hanging out in Professor Landier's car. The professor tells him that she has a weird girl in her car and asks him to go meet her on the pretext of fetching her red folder from the backseat. He is repulsed as soon as he opens the car door and is overwhelmed by the smell of smoke in the car. He tells Mona that she will suffocate in there. Mona gets out of the car to ask him for some cigarettes and asks whether he is afraid of her. Later that evening when Jean-Pierre goes home to his financée, he tells her about the encounter that is still haunting him. He tells her how Mona's hair reminded him of her, except whereas Mona's hair was witchlike, Elaine's is soft and silky. Whereas Mona is a "toad," Elaine is beautiful. Elaine tells him to quit feeling sorry for the runaway girl who is probably a criminal or a drug addict, anyway (as the film progresses, it becomes obvious that Elaine is the real witch).

Jean-Pierre is obsessed with the boundaries between Mona and himself. He insists that Elaine is nothing like her, that they are nothing like her. Later in the film Jean-Pierre sees Mona again at the train station. She is drunk and stumbling around, her boots torn apart. He calls a friend from a phone booth and says, "She is revolting. She makes me sick. Yeah, she scares me, because she revolts me. This confusion I can understand. Even me, I am lost sometimes. But to sink this low . . . she is crazy." As he says "She makes me sick," in the background we see *Mona* getting sick.

Precisely that he could be like her is what scares him. He is afraid of his own identification with the abject. He makes it clear that although he can be lost or confused, he is not crazy like Mona. He would never sink that low. What scares him is what he sees of himself in her, that part of himself that he finds revolting. He reassures himself that he is not like her to protect the boundaries of his clean and proper self against the threat of abjection.

The village grape festival near the end of the film is another example of the abjection of strangers or others. Mona wanders into the village to find some bread, but when she arrives, everyone closes their doors, and she is attacked by men soaked in wine with branches on their heads. These bizarre costumed men chase Mona and smear her with wine juice reminiscent of blood. Mona is terrified and runs away. This traditional French village festival celebrates the village grape harvest by chasing away any strangers or dipping them in troughs of grape juice. Much like a religious purification ritual, the strangers are washed in blood-red wine. The village identity is maintained through this festival in which the abjected strangers are either purified or chased away.

Compassion

At least two relationships portrayed in *Vagabond* cannot be explained merely in the terms of abjection or idealization. The first is Mona's relationship with a Tunisian vine picker, Assoun. Assoun lives in communal quarters with the other vine pickers, who are all Moroccan and have gone home for a holiday, leaving him there alone. The foreman agrees to let Assoun take Mona in until the others return. Mona goes to work with Assoun, who shows her how to cut the vines. He tells her to keep up with him to keep him company even if she does not clip all the vines since he can go back and do it over again if she misses some. He tells her that they can work together, like partners, because he gets paid a flat rate and can work however he pleases.

There is a touching scene when Assoun has prepared dinner for both of them and they are eating together. Mona strokes his hair and he caresses her hand, noticing that she has hurt herself cutting vines. She proudly says, "Yes, learning my trade." They laugh together when Mona tells him that the foreman's wife told her that vine cutting was not a job for a woman, but she told Mona that her daughter works in a jockey short factory. The foreman's wife also told Mona that Assoun was dirty, but Mona responded that she likes him because he has gentle eyes.

When the other workers return and refuse to let Mona stay, she is hurt and angry. She acts like she feels betrayed by Assoun, who had promised her a partnership. But, since he is outnumbered, there is nothing Assoun can do. Later in the film when he is being interviewed, he sits smelling the scarf that Mona had been wearing when she was with him, saying nothing. Even though Assoun does not testify, his testimony is the most compassionate in the film. He does not attempt to describe, understand, or judge Mona; rather, he mournfully enjoys her traces.

The relationship between Mona and Assoun is one of the only compassionate relations in the film. Mona does not judge him (until he tells her that she must leave), and he does not judge Mona. They treat each other with respect and care, not as curiosities or as sex objects but as partners caring for each other and working together. One of the only other compassionate encounters in the film shares some features with this one, laughter, respect, and marginalization.

After Yolanda picks up Mona hitchhiking, she takes her back to the house where she works for the old woman, Lydie. Yolanda is so lonely she hopes that Mona will be her companion. While Yolanda is running an errand, Mona puts on Yolanda's housecoat and begins to look around pretending to dust. Lydie talks to her as if she is Yolanda until Mona gets close to her and she realizes that she is not Yolanda and asks who she is. Mona sees some old photos on the table and asks Lydie about them. Mona takes a brandy decanter from the table and brings it over so that they can share a drink. The next scenes show Lydie and Mona drinking and laughing together. Tipsy, they amuse themselves laughing about how Lydie's nephew (Professor Landier's assistant, Jean-Pierre) is nice to his aunt Lydie only because he wants her house. When Yolanda returns and sees what is going on, she insists that Mona leave at once. Lydie wants her to stay, but Yolanda chases her off. Mona yells back that she does not have to worry, she will not take Yolanda's job.

Mona's encounter with Lydie and her encounter with Assoun have some common characteristics that might provide some insight into how these relationships work. One striking similarity is that Mona is shown laughing with each of them about the social norms and structures that work to marginalize them. Mona laughs with Assoun because the foreman's wife thinks that vine cutting is not a job for women but working in a jockey short factory is. She laughs with Lydie because the nephew flatters Lydie so that he can inherit her house. In both cases, this laughter is a form of resistance to the powerlessness of their own marginalization. In the first case, Mona laughs at the social norms that proscribe women's role. There, she also responds lovingly to the outcast Assoun, whom the foreman's wife calls "dirty." In the second case, Mona and Lydie laugh at the very structure that makes Lydie powerless: her nephew Jean-Pierre and his wife Elaine have control over Lydie's life; they make her decisions for her; her house will go to her nephew almost regardless of what she does.

This subversive laughter is not the only characteristic that makes these outlaw relationships. Like Mona, both Assoun and Lydie are themselves marginal figures. As a foreigner and a Tunisian among Moroccans, Assoun is doubly excluded. He is alone among foreigners who dictate his lifestyle. Lydie is an old woman who has little say in her own lifestyle. For the most part, she has been left alone to die. Her nephew visits only because he stands to inherit her house. And, Yolanda treats her like a piece of the furniture that she needs to dust. The foreigner, the elderly, and the vagabond are all misfits, outsiders, marginal figures excluded by the social laws of a system that abjects them all so that it might sustain itself. In an important sense, it is their perceived otherness in relation to the social norms or laws that brings them together. In both cases, it is the interference, or reappearance, of the social order that abruptly separates them from each other. The Moroccan workers cannot allow a woman in their barracks. Yolanda is outraged when she sees the old woman and Mona drinking together; old women are not allowed to get tipsy.

The philosopher-goatherder suggests that it is Mona's freedom that leads to loneliness. Perhaps, however, it is not her freedom but her lack of freedom that leads to loneliness. To have relations and maintain them, they must be socially sanctioned and inscribed by social laws and norms. Outlaw relationships are not allowed. Yet, any relationship with the "vagabond," the abjected other, is outlawed. So, it is not because Mona is free from the system that she rejects, as the goatherder says, that she is isolated and excluded; rather, the laws of the system continually interfere with her relationships and require her isolation and exclusion. Even those relationships with other marginal figures are eventually regulated by social expectations and laws.

Perhaps what is more interesting to consider is how or why some relationships with other marginal figures are affirming and compassionate and others are negating and oppressive (e.g., Mona's relationship with the train station grifter who wants to put her in porn films, or even her relationship with the philosopher-goatherder). Also, is it possible to imagine an affirming and compassionate relationship between a marginal figure and one safely inscribed within the social center of the law (if one such person exists)? These concerns bring me back to the questions that I deferred earlier: What does it mean to witness (to) the other? What does it mean to recognize someone? How does someone become recognizable?

Witnessing and Recognition

Kristeva's theory of abjection is promising in that it describes a relationship with what is not recognizable as myself. It is limiting, however, in that it describes that relationship as one of exclusion that can be overcome only through a proper recognition and assimilation—if always only tentative—of abjection through psychoanalytic elaboration. Although Kristeva opens up the space prior to the recognition or misrecognition of the Lacanian mirror stage, ultimately she too accepts the role of recognition or misrecognition (two sides of the same process) in self-identity and ego formation. Following in the Hegelian wake of Lacanian psychoanalysis, other contemporary feminist theorists incorporate theories of recognition into their explanations of the politics of identity and exclusion.[1] While it would distract me from my purpose here to go into the details of those theories, I do want to suggest some general problems with notions of identity or relationship based on recognition.

In general, theories dependent on notions of recognition reinscribe a type of master-slave relationship within the very act of recognition of the other. First, recognition presupposes a recognizer who has the authority and power to determine who is in and who is out. This rational or merciful subject grants legitimacy to the other through its recognition of the other. Second, insofar as recognition presupposes a recognizer, even the act of inclusion reinscribes the exclusion of the other who is still dependent on the subject who recognizes. As history has shown, it is not enough that women or blacks, for example, be recognized as human beings, persons, or citizens by rational or merciful white men to end discrimination against them. Third, what is recognized in the act of recognition is nothing other than sameness, which continues to reinscribe the position of mastery by requiring that the other be assimilated in order to be recognized. The other can be recognized only insofar as it exhibits those qualities recognized by the dominant subjects, whether those be the qualities attributed to human beings, persons, citizens, or rational agents. Finally, as I suggested in the last chapter, recognition presupposes a faulty notion of vision that separates the very persons or things that it purports to bring together.

While I leave a sustained analysis of theories of recognition for another context, I want to turn to how Varda's *Vagabond* and its notion of witnessing might provide alternatives to recognition-based relationships. In general, a notion of witnessing might provide an alternative to the problematic notion of recognition used in contemporary liberation theories. *Witnessing* is an interesting word because it can mean *observing,* but it can also mean *testifying.* It can mean testifying to that which you *observe,* but it can also mean testifying to that which you *do not observe.* In a courtroom, a witness is one who observes something *and* one who testifies. To bear witness, however, with its religious connotations, means to testify to something that cannot be observed, to testify to your faith in God. To bear witness has connotations of testifying but also of listening to the testimony of others. To bear witness can mean telling about an experience in order to make sense out of it for yourself and/or for another. So, what could it mean to bear witness to the other?

The voice-over at the beginning of *Vagabond* says that the people Mona recently met remembered her and that "those witnesses helped me tell the last weeks of her last winter" because "she left her mark on them." Here *witness* has both the sense of observe and testify. These people saw Mona in the last few weeks of her life, and they describe what they saw of her in their testimony. But, insofar as Mona left her mark on these people, they are testifying to her impact; they are bearing witness to her and her affect on them; they are testifying to that which cannot be observed. Ultimately, what these people *see* in Mona cannot be observed. In fact, by juxtaposing testimony with action the film shows us that what people *see* in Mona when they observe her is very different depending on the context and their own perspectives.

There is no expert witness who has some objective perspective. Rather, the film multiplies perspectives. It invites, even demands, the viewer's own testimony from her own perspective, a testimony that can vary as much as those represented in the film. The viewer is drawn into the film as a third party in every relationship. Since the characters often speak directly to the camera, the viewer is put into the position of the documentarian, analyst, or confessor, who bears witness in the sense of listening to the testimony of others. But, insofar as the action scenes often complicate these testimonies, the viewer is put in the position of a witness who can corroborate or deny the testimony of the participants. Varda's style of moving between testimony and action both legitimates and challenges all perspectives, including that of the viewer/analyst.

There is no authorized subject position in the film. Even as subjective authority is displaced onto the third, the documentarian or viewer, this authority is constantly challenged. In this way, the film refuses to reproduce a master-slave relationship. It valorizes neither the center nor the margin, the dominant nor the victim, the familiar nor the unfamiliar; rather, it makes those distinctions ambiguous by presenting so many different perspectives. It does not attempt to identify with Mona and show us her perspective; we never see the world through her eyes. It does not presume to know her. Yet, it does not merely invert the master-slave or subject-object opposition by representing Mona as a victim to barbarous, inhuman, or animal-like torturers or institutions. Still, it does not justify the abjection or exclusion of Mona to legitimate some clean and proper self.

By opening the space of the witness, Varda creates an alternative to subject-object or master-slave relationships. This position of the third who is never quite equivalent to the other two complicates any simple equations of domination or oppression. We can interpret this third position as something like Kristeva's psychoanalytic elaboration that opens the subject to infinite analysis. In the film it is a space that is constantly transformed by its different inhabitants, who in turn transform the viewer's relation to the film. Beyond the subject-object relation, the space of elaboration maintains the infinite analysis that allows for the continual self-overcoming of the subject in relationships, not as mastery but as vigilance. Bearing witness to the other connotes a vigilance that requires guarding the openness of subjectivity to otherness.

Bearing witness to the other in the sense of testifying to that which cannot be known, observed, or completely understood requires a vigilance toward the other and a constant awareness of one's own limitations in recognizing the other. Unlike recognition, which maintains the mastery of the subject over itself and the other by presuming the primacy of the subject, witnessing admits that the other comes first. Testifying to the other, in both the sense of telling yourself to the other and of telling of the other to others, presumes the primacy of the other. Unlike recognition, which maintains a telos in that moment of recognition or seeing, witnessing has no such telos or moment. Bearing witness to the other is an infinite process that never reaches its *goal,* since, as Assoun realizes in *Vagabond,* it is impossible to testify to the other. Yet, it is necessary to try, hence the vigilance inherent in bearing witness.

We are, in fact, dependent on others to make sense out of our own lives. Communication is essential to subjectivity; our subjective identities are supported by listeners. We are by virtue of the stories that we tell about ourselves to others. We require witnesses and witnessing to survive, especially the most difficult times. Psychoanalyst Dori Laub has described the necessity of witnessing for Holocaust survivors:

> What ultimately matters in all processes of witnessing, spasmodic and continuous, conscious and unconscious, is not simply the information, the establishment of facts, but the experience itself of *living through* testimony, of giving testimony. The testimony is, therefore, the process by which the narrator (the survivor) reclaims his position as a witness: reconstitutes the internal "thou," and thus the possibility of a witness or a listener inside himself. (1992, 85)

Laub argues that the horrors of the Holocaust eliminated witnesses to its events, and this elimination of witnesses made its annihilation of human life complete. He suggests that only by reinstating the witness, by witnessing and thereby reconstituting the internal witness, can the annihilation of subjectivity in survivors be contained. Laub's analysis suggests that subjectivity is dependent on a sympathetic listener, an interlocutor, who functions to set in motion the internal dialogue that makes subjective experience possible. Communication with an other is vital to human life.

Although the other cannot be seen or known, this does not mean that communication or communion is impossible. But, communication as communion cannot begin with recognition. Recognition at the same time denies the differences necessary for two people to communicate and forces a separation that prohibits the communion necessary for communication. Recognition requires that we be the same in order to communicate even while it reinstitutes a master-slave relationship that contaminates any real communion between us. Whereas recognition maintains the universality of the rational or merciful subject, witnessing continually calls into question that subjectivity by opening it to infinite testimony and analysis.

Infinite analysis, analysis without dogma, or analysis that continually asserts its own nonuniversality opens subjectivity to otherness and to experiencing the other otherwise. More than this, infinite analysis, without distinction between analyst and analysand, opens the borders between subjectivity and otherness. But this ambiguity, seen from a perspective beyond subject-object restrictions, is not abject or excluded. It is not subject to the restrictions of an economy of identity that necessarily preserves itself through abjection and exclusion. Perhaps it is necessary to have the perspective of the *othered* to see beyond abjection. Perhaps Kristeva is right that it takes a woman or other others to elaborate abjection, not for the sake of purification or the reinscription of boundaries for the clean and proper self but for the rebirth of subjectivity otherwise.

Certainly a philosophy that starts from the perspective of the *othered* would not talk of recognition, which would require its own unrecognizability. In spite of the conflicts in identity because of her marginal position, the othered does not see herself as invisible. Only from the perspective of the othering subject can we talk about the invisible or unrecognizable other. Recognition relies on a distinction between truth and falsity when it sheds light on the other and acknowledges that it really exists and is therefore not invisible. By giving up illusions as it recognizes the truth, the subject of recognition can maintain the borders between truth and falsity, between history and fiction.

It is these borders, however, that Varda's film calls into question. *Vagabond* presents the illusion of an oscillation between history and fiction; where each of these is located, however, becomes problematic. The documentary style is used when witnesses present their testimony to the camera. These moments appear as history, as the retelling of past events, while the events themselves are represented through the narrative fiction of the action sequences, more familiar to the audience. The authority of the testimony of what should be the history endowed with the objectivity and authority of documentary is undermined by the fictional story of the film. Yet, the story of the film appears to give us a more accurate representation of the history of events. Of course, the film is not a documentary, and Varda's style also reminds us of this when, for example, characters address the camera in the middle of an action scene. The distinction between history and story cannot be maintained. The borders between the legitimacy of history and the illegitmacy of fiction become blurred.

It is necessary to challenge the borders of fiction and history to imagine a theory of liberation or a philosophy that starts from the perspective of the othered. After all, from the perspective of the dominant subject, the truth of the other is the falsity of the subject. More than this, to imagine an elaboration that does not proclaim itself universal, history and fiction cannot be separated. In other words, we need more than the enlightenment notion that as rational beings we can recognize truth and make progress toward overcoming oppression. To maintain infinite analysis, the truth can never shut out or abject fiction. Inverting the binary, however, is not enough since it merely ascribes universal status to the other rather than the one.

One effect of Varda's *Vagabond* is to throw the subject—both the characters in the film and the viewer of the film—into infinite analysis by giving up any universal perspective and by displacing the authority of truth onto a third position beyond truth or fiction—the position of infinite analysis itself. Fiction and history, falsity or truth, cannot be separated, one taking priority over the other. In *Vagabond* truth is not a banner that can be waved in the face of injustice. Rather, by displaying something of the way in which its borders are set up and by showing various relationships to its borders, Varda's film bears witness not only to the necessity for vigilance in our relationships but also the possibilities opened up beyond recognition and abjection.

Notes

Chapter 1

1. In *Family Values* I argue that Locke and Rousseau engage in the contradictory move of claiming that the father's authority is based on nature and that patriarchal government is grounded in the authority of the father, and that the government's authority does not derive from nature. See chapter 3's section on "Paternal Authority" (Oliver 1997).

2. In his book *Making the American Self* (Cambridge, Mass.: Harvard University Press, 1997), Daniel Walker Howe shows how Platonic philosophy influenced early American philosophy and religious thinking.

3. See Howe's analysis of the American notion of self-improvement in *Making the American Self,* chapter 4.

4. See Howe, *Making the American Self,* 153.

5. Quoted in "Bonding in the Bleachers: A Visit to the Promise Keepers" by John Spalding, in *Christian Century* 113, no. 8 (March 6, 1996): 260.

6. See also Goode (1997, 48); Rosin (1997, 11); Higgins (1997, 19); New men for Jesus (1995, A21); Gilbreath (1995, 20).

7. See Allen (1997, 10); Miller (1996, 46); Gilbreath (1995, 20).

8. At a Promise Keepers rally in Buffalo, one of the speakers, David Castro, "shouted that faith in Jesus can cure men of their 'homosexual tendencies'—something he put in the same sinful category as 'sexual impurity,' 'lust,' 'pornography,' 'sexual abuse,' and 'the filth on the internet' " (Hetherly 1997, 14). A writer for the *Economist* reports that "just in case any guys should show up, counsellors are on hand to help them convert" (New men for Jesus 1995, A21).

9. See Spalding (1996); Phillips (1997); Gilbreath (1995); Hetherly (1997); Higgins (1997).

10. Following Levinas's description of virility, in *Family Values* I develop a notion of virile subjectivity as subjectivity founded on an "I can" and the will to possess and control one's environment (Oliver 1997).

11. See especially Spalding (1996, 260) and New men for Jesus (1995, A21).

12. To be fair, Patterson does go on to talk about the prevalance of racism among white Americans.

13. "1985 saw Louis Farrahkan initiate a nationwide tour to promote

POWER (People Organized and Working for Economic Rebirth), his plan for the economic development of Black Americans. Funded by a five million dollar loan from Libya, the aim of POWER is to develop an economically independent Black population as the Honorable Elijah Muhammad attempted through the Nation's business enterprises in the 1960's" (Lee 1996, 84–85).

14. For a more developed account of the absent male body, see my *Family Values* (Oliver 1997).

15. See The Farrakhan distraction (1995); Patterson (1995).

Chapter 2

1. The word *piety* is an early form of *pity*. The English word *piety* comes from the Old French *piete*. The popular form in France was *pité*, pity. The word *pity* can mean compassion, to be sorry for, to grieve or regret, to feel remorse for one's own wrongdoing, to repent; in modern usage it implies contempt for someone inferior to oneself.

2. John Brenkman points out that Ricoeur assumes that contracts take place between equals (1993, 45).

3. Thanks to Lisa Walsh who pointed out that whereas in the United States the mother identifies the father at the hospital for the birth certificate record, in France the father has the legal right to "recognize" (*reconnaître*) the child as his or not; in France the mother's recognition of the father has no legal hold.

4. Although I cannot develop issues around child custody laws here, I present a more detailed analysis of child custody laws in this same context in *Family Values: Subjects between Nature and Culture* (Oliver 1997).

5. In *Family Values,* I diagnose the attempts of both Ricoeur and Levinas to cover over the contingent and chance aspects of paternity as a fear of what I call an *abject father.*

6. Some of his contemporaries have criticized Levinas for sacrificing the feminine for the masculine subject's ascent into the ethical relationship through paternity. See especially Luce Irigaray, "The Fecundity of the Caress" (1993a) and "Questions to Emmanuel Levinas" (1991b).

7. In the last section of *Marine Lover of Friedrich Nietzsche,* "When the Gods Are Born," Luce Irigaray (1991a) argues that Christ's suffering on the cross and his bleeding side are masculine appropriations of the mother's suffering and the blood of childbirth through which she gives life.

8. Irigaray (1993b) makes this argument in "Belief Itself."

9. Responsibility is a matter of response. In both German (*Verantwortung*) and French (*responsabilité*), *responsibility* comes from *respond* (*antworten, répondre*) and has a stronger sense of *answer* than in English, in which *respond* and *answer* are different words. The Latin *respondeo* means to answer and in the legal sense means to answer one's name or be present before the law.

Chapter 3

1. See my *Family Values* (Oliver 1997).

Chapter 4

1. Compare this to a passage in Lacan's 1953–54 seminar in which he claims that the symbol opens up the world of negativity (1988a, 1: 173–74).

2. Lacan also identifies a negativization that is prior to the no (1988a, 1: 173–74). Kristeva suggests that this is already a symbolic operation. Although I am not convinced that her interpretation of Lacan is the most useful, I will not take that problem up here.

3. In *Tales of Love,* Kristeva (1987c) describes this mimicry as a transference and not as an imitation.

4. I think that Kristeva's writings can themselves be read as an oscillation between the semiotic and symbolic, between rejection and identification. For example, in *Revolution in Poetic Language* and *Powers of Horror* she emphasizes rejection and the semiotic. In *Tales of Love* and *Black Sun* she emphasizes identification and the symbolic. In *Strangers* and *Lettre ouverte* she emphasizes the ways in which one is always implicated in the other. See my *Reading Kristeva* (Oliver 1993).

5. Kristeva argues that becoming abject is the body's defense against cannibalism. If it is disgusting, it will not be eaten (1980b, 78–79).

6. "Between birth and birth" is the place that Lyotard describes as the object of our longing. It is the space between our birth and our realization that we were born, a place forever lost to us.

7. This is why, for Freud, fetishism is not a denial of *woman's* castration, but a denial of the *mother's* castration—"If mom is castrated and I was once her, then I too am castrated."

8. Kristeva's position with regard to the phallus in *Tales of Love* is a bit confusing. Later in the text she suggests that there are advantages to a nonphallocentric explanation of primary identification. She suggests that there are fathers other than the father of the law, and she maintains a strict identification between the father of the law (law of the father) and the symbolic.

9. Within the framework of traditional psychoanalytic theory, it is possible to read Kristeva's thesis that the logic of the symbolic is already at work in the maternal body as a form of fetishism.

10. Although Kristeva insists that this analysis applies to homosexual couples as well as heterosexual couples, she does not explain how. It seems, however, that it may be much easier for a woman to find her mother in relation with another woman's body. The primary identification that supports the archaic regression would be more straightforward (cf. 1987c, 226). However, Kristeva has been criticized because she relegates homosexuality, especially female homosexuality, to the borders of intelligibility, psychosis. For example, Judith Butler (1990) argues that because Kristeva accepts the structuralist assumption that society is founded on heterosexual exchanges of women, she maintains that homosexuality is capable only of psychotic sexual expression. It seems to me, however, that Kristeva is more concerned with a pre-Oedipal relation to the mother, which for females requires a kind of homosexuality. Also, despite those aspects of her writings that privilege heterosexuality and take up a traditional psychoanalytic framework, Kristeva does explicitly claim that every individual has his or her own sexuality. She wants to move away from the dualism between hetero- and homosexuality (Kristeva 1984).

11. Kristeva complains that the "break up of Christianity" has left the three terms of the *prefigured* Oedipal operation in "suspense." She argues that without the Virgin Mary, abjection turns to social representation. Also, without the loving father, she argues, contemporary discourse is "incapable of assuming primary identification" (1987c, 374). These kinds of claims suggest Kristeva's own longing for the Christian (or more specifically Catholic) imaginary or something to replace it. Psychoanalysis, then, works to replace the broken Christian imaginary. Thus, the analyst, Kristeva herself, takes the place of the Virgin Mother, the loving father, and the priest of the secular post-Christian imaginary.

12. Kristeva criticizes existential feminist notions of motherhood without mentioning Simone de Beauvoir, thus covering over one of her own foremothers.

13. Kristeva's discussion of the pregnant maternal body is the central focus, around the time of her own pregnancy and the birth of her son in 1976, in two essays: "Motherhood According to Giovanni Bellini" and "Stabat Mater."

14. Even this is problematic: witness Kristeva's account of the cult of the virgin mother and, I might add, the rhetoric of antiabortion crusaders in the United States who argue that the fetus is a unified subject in its own right.

15. This, of course, poses problems for feminist mothers who hope to change the status quo. Do they raise their children with traditional patriarchal values and sacrifice the feminist struggle? Or do they raise them with countercultural values and risk their being misfits?

Chapter 5

1. In *Volatile Bodies,* Elizabeth Grosz (1994) describes how upon reaching the age of sexual maturity, girls face shame and guilt while boys face pride and joy.

2. In *Family Values* (1997), I argue that virility and property are inseparable in that the virile subject relates to everything and everybody as his property.

3. In *Family Values,* I argue that the absent father is the patriarchal father.

4. For example, in the 1976 Supreme Court case *Gilbert vs. General Electric,* the Court used equal rights jargon to defend its ruling in favor of GE's exclusion of pregnancy-related disabilities from its insurance coverage. The justices' rationale was that pregnancy-related disabilities were denied equally to everyone, including men. We can infer from this the absurd conclusion that if men were mothers, they would not be allowed pregnancy-related disabilities, either.

Chapter 7

1. For a critique of Derrida's position on his own subjectivity, see Paul Smith's *Discerning the Subject* (Minneapolis: University of Minnesota Press,

1988). Also, Smith reminds us of the useful distinction between "the subject" and agency.

2. See, for example Nancy Fraser, "Michel Foucault: A 'Young Conservative'?" *Ethics* 96 (1985): 165–84, and "Foucault on Modern Power: Empirical Insights and Normative Confusions," *Praxis International* 1 (1981): 272–87; Jurgen Habermas, "Taking Aim at the Heart of the Present" in *Foucault: A Critical Reader,* ed. David Hoy (New York: Basil Blackwell, 1986); Richard Rorty, "Foucault and Epistemology" in *Foucault,* ed. Hoy; Charles Taylor, "Foucault on Freedom and Truth," *Political Theory* 12, no. 2 (1984): 152–83; Michael Walzer, "The Politics of Michel Foucault" in *Foucault,* ed. Hoy.

3. Linda Alcoff, "The Unhappy Marriage of Feminism and Foucault" presented at the 1988 Eastern American Philosophical Association meeting; a version entitled "Feminist Politics and Foucault: The Limits of Collaboration" appears in *Selected Studies in Phenomenology and Existential Philosophy,* series vol. 16, *Crises in Continental Philosophy,* ed. A. Dallery and C. Scott (Albany: State University of New York Press, 1990).

4. For example, both Freud and Kolhberg suggest that females have an inferior sense of justice or an underdeveloped morality. Both suggest that females are not "normal, healthy, individuals."

5. In her latest work (in preparation), Elizabeth Grosz challenges the view of nature as static and permanent and suggests an alternative notion of nature as unstable and becoming. In this regard, we could talk about the naturalization of nature.

6. Stephen Kellert has pointed out to me that it is important to emphasize that the butterfly effect does not describe a traditional notion of causality. Rather, as Kellert poignantly says, "one of the important ways chaos theory makes us rethink the physical world is to relinquish a simplistic causal picture. Small events can have big effects, but not because they *cause* them. Rather, small events can alter the geometry of the situation—pushing a system into a very different type of behavior" (1990 unpublished letter).

7. See Judith Butler's analysis of Beauvoir's notion of freedom: "Sex and Gender in Simone de Beauvoir's *Second Sex,*" *Yale French Studies* 72 (1986).

8. This statement is of the type powerfully employed by Nietzsche that is self-undermining or, as Nietzsche might say, self-overcoming. Nietzsche is famous for metaphysical statements that work to undermine metaphysics—for example, "the truth is that there is no truth." Of course, this immediately involves us in the paradox of skepticism—how can the skeptic say anything even about her own doubt? This type of statement can be both enabling and disabling in positive ways. To say that "we must continually ask, 'Who is this we?' " allows me to enable some "we," some identification between oppressed peoples, and yet at the same time call into question that very "we" and thereby possibly disable its totalizing effects. This constant questioning of identity defers identity even while presupposing it.

Chapter 8

1. In the history of philosophy, the distinction between body and soul has also been discussed as a distinction between body and mind, or the mind-body problem.

2. For a more developed account of Kristeva's theory of drives, see my *Womanizing Nietzsche: Philosophy's Relation to the "Feminine"* (1995), chapter 6, "Save the Mother."

3. Kristeva's theory also challenges the narrow conception of material as it is opposed to social or linguistic.

4. Traditional theories have tried to address these problems in various ways. Referential theories of meaning have held that the meaning of a word is its reference to something extralinguistic, something in the world. The meaning of a word is either what it refers to (some thing) or the relationship between the word and its referent. But as Frege pointed out, meaning and reference are not the same since there are many different ways of referring to the same thing, and not all of these linguistic expressions necessarily have the same meaning even if they have the same referent. The most famous example is the reference to Venus as both the morning star and the evening star. Some theorists (e.g., Locke, Husserl, Saussure) have tried to avoid some of the problems of referential theories by supposing that the meaning of a word is determined by the thought that corresponds to that word. The referent in this case becomes an idea or concept and not a material thing in the world. These theories, however, merely displace the problems of reference from the material world to the world of ideas. All of the problems of correspondence still obtain. Some contemporary theorists (Austin, Wittgenstein, Searle) propose that meaning is determined by the use of words and that the use of words must be analyzed as a type of activity with certain rules and regulations. The way in which words are used, however, varies as much as the thoughts or ideas associated with them and their possible material referents.

5. The attempt to find meaning through New Age religions is particularly interesting. Before the scientific revolution, religion with its sacred mysteries provided meaning for people's lives. After the scientific revolution, science replaced religion and demystified religion. Recently, science has lost the ability to explain our world. The experts present such conflicting data on everything from oat bran to ozone that people have lost faith in science. New Age religion is a synthesis of sorts of science and religion. It uses the rhetoric of science, with talk of harnessing energies and forces, to promote self esteem and a better future. Whereas Nancy Reagan consulted an astrologer, Hillary Clinton consults a New Age psychologist, a "global midwife" (*New York Times*, June 24, 1996, p. 1).

6. Veroff et al. (1981) indicate that the number of people going to therapy has dramatically increased since World War II (166–67, 176–77). Bellah et al. (1985) suggest that people go to therapy looking for love.

7. For a developed version of this argument, see my *Family Values: Subjects between Nature and Culture* (1997).

8. For substantiation of this reading of Kristeva's imaginary father, see my *Reading Kristeva: Unraveling the Double-Bind* (1993), chapter 3.

9. Freud, *Jokes and Their Relation to the Unconscious* (1953–1974, 205).

10. Although she does not develop her criticism, Elizabeth Grosz challenges Kristeva's exemption for semen in *Volatile Bodies* (1994, 206–7).

11. "The Biggest Evolutionary Challenge May Be the Other Half of the Species," *New York Times*, June 18, 1996, pp. B5, B10.

12. I am not suggesting that we accept these biologists' conclusions that semen is toxic and the sexes are engaged in a deadly evolutionary war. In fact, I want to challenge these metaphors of war and battle and the experimental methods (tying the hand of female fruit flies) that produce "toxic semen." Rather, my point is that semen is invisible and purified in our culture.

13. See the discussion of the theories of Aristotle and Galen in chapter 1, the section "Biological Imaging," in my *Family Values* (1997).

14. See Grosz's analysis in *Volatile Bodies* (1994), especially at 205.

Chapter 10

1. The recent work of Judith Butler and Nancy Fraser are notable examples of theories of recognition put to different purposes. I present a critical analysis of their theories in *Beyond Recognition: Toward a Theory of Othered Subjectivity* (forthcoming).

Bibliography

Alcoff, Linda. 1988. The unhappy marriage of feminism and Foucault. Paper presented at the Eastern American Philosophical Association meeting. (A version entitled "Feminist Politics and Foucault: The Limits of Collaboration" is reprinted in *Selected Studies in Phenomenology and Existential Philosophy,* series vol. 16, *Crises in Continental Philosophy,* ed. A. Dallery and C. Scott [Albany: State University of New York Press, 1990].)

Allen, L. Dean. 1997. Breaking down the wall? *Church & State* 50, no. 1 (July): 10–14.

Alter, Jonathan. 1995. The long march home. *Newsweek,* October 19, 44.

Bellah, Robert, et al. 1985. *Habits of the heart.* Berkeley: University of California Press.

Bellant, Russ. 1995. Mania in the stadia. *Free Inquiry* 16, no. 1 (Winter): 28–31.

Bergman, Ingmar. 1972. *Persona and shame: The screenplays of Ingmar Bergman.* Trans. Keith Bradfield. New York: Boyars.

Brenkman, John. 1993. *Straight male modern.* New York: Routledge.

Brennan, Teresa. 1992. *The interpretation of the flesh: Freud and femininity.* New York: Routledge.

———. 1993. *History after Lacan.* New York: Routledge.

Butler, Judith. 1989. The body politics of Julia Kristeva. *Hypatia* 3 (winter): 104–118.

———. 1990. *Gender trouble.* New York: Routledge.

———. 1993. *Bodies that matter: On the discursive limits of "sex."* New York: Routledge.

———. 1997. *The psychic life of power.* Stanford, Calif.: Stanford University Press.

Chernikov, Alexander, et al. 1988. Chaos: How regular can it be? *Physics Today,* November, 27–35.

Conason, Jason. 1996. The Promise Keepers are coming. *The Nation* 263, no. 10 (October 7).

Connith, Ruth. 1997. Invasion of the Promise Keepers. *Progressive* 61, no. 11 (November): 10.

Cornell, Drucilla. 1991. *Beyond accommodation: Ethical feminism, deconstruction, and the law.* New York: Routledge.
———. 1992. *The philosophy of the limit.* New York: Routledge.
———. 1993. *Transformations: Recollective imagination and sexual difference.* New York: Routledge.
———. 1995. *The imaginary domain: Abortion, pornography and sexual harrassment.* New York: Routledge.
———. 1996. Re-thinking consciousness raising: Citizenship and the law and politics of adoption. *Southern Journal of Philosophy* 35 (supple.): 109–27.
Cose, Ellis. 1997. Promises . . . promises. *Newsweek* 130, no. 15 (October 13, 1997): 28–32.
Crutchfield, James, et al. 1984. Chaos. *Scientific American,* November, pp. 46–57.
Deleuze, Gilles. 1988. *Foucault.* Trans. Sean Hand. Minneapolis: University of Minnesota Press.
Derrida, Jacques. 1973. *Speech and Phenomenon.* Trans. D. Allison. Evanston, Ill.: Northwestern University.
———. 1977. *Spurs Nietzsche's styles.* Trans. Barbara Harlow. Chicago: University of Chicago Press.
———. 1978. *Writing and Difference.* Trans. Alan Bass. Chicago, Ill.: University of Chicago Press.
———. 1980. Interview. *Literary Review* (London) 14: 21.
———. 1991. At this very moment here I am. . . . Trans. R. Berezdivin. In *Re-Reading Levinas,* ed. R. Bernasconi and S. Critchley. Bloomington: Indiana University Press.
———. 1992a. The force of law: The "mystical foundation of Authority." In *Deconstruction and the possibility of justice,* ed. D. Cornell et al. New York: Routledge.
———. 1992b. Psyche: Inventions of the other. In *Acts of literature,* ed. D. Attridge. New York: Routledge.
———. 1995. *The gift of death.* Trans. David Wills. Chicago: University of Chicago Press.
Dickerson, Debra. Queen for a day? *New Republic* 213, no. 19 (November 6, 1995): 22.
Douglas, Mary. 1969. *Purity and danger.* New York: Routledge.
Douglass, Fredrick. 1994. *The Autobiographies,* ed. Henry Louis Gates, Jr. New York: Library of America.
Dreier, Peter. 1995. What Farrakhan left out. *Commonweal* 122, no. 22 (December 15): 10–12.
Dyson, Michael Eric. 1995. Words unsaid. *Christian Century* 112, no. 34 (November 22): 1100.
Edwards, Jonathan. 1959. Charity and its fruits. In *Works,* vol. 8, *Ethical writings,* ed. Paul Ramsey.
An elegy for integration. 1995. *Time,* 146, no. 18 (October 30): 108.
The Farrakhan distraction. 1995. *Economist,* 337, no. 7936 (October 14): 36.
Fineman, Howard. 1995a. An angry charmer. *Newsweek* (October 30): 32–37.
———. 1995b. Grappling with race. *Newsweek* 126, no. 17 (October 23): 30–34.

Ford, Joseph. 1983. How random is a coin toss? *Physics Today,* April, 40–47.

Foucault, Michel. 1977. *Language, counter-memory, practice.* Ed. Donald Bouchard, trans. Donald Bouchard and Sherry Simon. Ithaca, N.Y.: Cornell University Press.

———. 1979. *Discipline and punish: The birth of the prison.* Trans. Alan Sheridan. New York: Random House.

———. 1980a. *The history of sexuality: Vol. I. An introduction.* Trans. Robert Hurley. New York: Random House.

———. 1980b. *Power/knowledge: Selected interviews and other writings.* Ed. Collin Gordon. New York: Pantheon.

———. 1983a. On the genealogy of ethics. In *Beyond structuralism and hermeneutics,* ed. Hubert Dreyfus and Paul Rabinow. Chicago: University of Chicago Press.

———. 1983b. The subject and power. In *Beyond structuralism and hermeneutics,* ed. Hubert Dreyfus and Paul Rabinow. Chicago: University of Chicago Press:

Fraser, Nancy. 1981. Foucault on modern power: Empirical insights and normative confusions. *Praxis International* 1: 272–87.

———. 1985. Michel Foucault: A "young conservative"?: *Ethics* 96: 165–84.

Freud, Sigmund. 1913. *Totem and taboo.* In *The standard edition of the complete psychological works of Sigmund Freud,* vol. 13, ed. and trans. James Strachey, in collaboration with Anna Freud. London: Hogarth.

———. 1953–1974. *Jokes and their relation to the unconscious.* In *The standard edition of the complete psychological works of Sigmund Freud,* vol. 8, ed. and trans. James Strachey. London: Hogarth.

———. 1961. *Civilization and its discontents,* trans. James Strachey. New York: Norton.

———. 1961. *Group psychology.* In *The standard edition of the complete psychological works of Sigmund Freud,* trans. J. Strachey. London: Hogarth.

———. 1967. *The Interpretation of Dreams,* trans. James Strachey. New York: Avon Books.

Gilbreath, Edward. Manhood's great awakening: Promise Keepers ambitious agenda for transforming Christian men. *Christianity Today* 39, no. 2 (February 6, 1995): 20–28.

Gleick, James. 1987. *Chaos: The making of a new science.* New York: Penguin.

Goode, Stephen. 1997. The Christian soldiers march on Washington. *Insight on the News* 13, no. 39 (October 27): 48.

Grosz, Elizabeth. 1994. *Volatile bodies: Toward a corporeal feminism.* Bloomington: Indiana University Press.

Habermas, Jurgen. 1986. Taking aim at the heart of the present. In *Foucault: A critical reader,* ed. David Hoy. New York: Basil Blackwell.

Hegel, G. W. F. 1952. *The philosophy of right.* Trans. T. M. Knox. London: Oxford University Press.

———. 1977. *Phenomenology of spirit.* Trans. A. V. Miller. Oxford: Clarendon.

Hetherly, Marian. 1997. PK publicity and production. *Humanist* 57, no. 5 (September–October): 14–19.

Higgins, John M. 1997. A humanist among the faithful. *Humanist* 57, no. 5 (September–October): 19–25.

Hoff-Wilson, Joan. 1987. The unfinished revolution. *Signs: Journal of Women in Culture and Society* 13, no. 1 (Autumn): 7–36.

Hoffer, Richard. 1996. Putting his house in order. *Sports Illustrated.*

Howe, Daniel Walker. 1997. *Making the American self.* Cambridge, Mass.: Harvard University Press.

Irigaray, Luce. 1991a. *Marine lover of Friedrich Nietzsche.* Trans. Gillian Gill. New York: Columbia University Press.

———. 1991b. Questions to Emmanuel Levinas. In *The Irigaray reader*, ed. Margaret Whitford.

———. 1993a. The fecundity of the caress. In *An ethics of sexual difference,* trans. Carolyn Burke and Gillian Gill. Ithaca, N.Y.: Cornell University Press.

———. 1993b. *Sexes and genealogies.* Trans. Gillian Gill. New York: Columbia University Press.

Jardine, Alice. 1985. Introduction to Julia Kristeva's "Women's Time." *Signs* 7, no. 1: 5–12.

Kierkegaard, Soren. 1954. *Fear and trembling.* Trans. Walter Lowrie. Princeton, N.J.: Princeton University Press.

King, Florence. 1997. The misanthrope's corner. *National Review* 49, no. 21 (November 10): 68.

Klein, Joe. 1995. Can Powell reach them? *Newsweek* (October 30): 48.

Kristeva, Julia. 1974. *Revolution in poetic language.* Trans. Margaret Waller. New York: Columbia University Press.

———. 1975. Motherhood according to Giovanni Bellini. Trans. Thomas Gora, Alice Jardine, and Leon Roudiez. In *Desire in language,* ed. Leon Roudiez. New York: Columbia University Press.

———. 1977. Le sujet en procès. In *Polylogue.* Paris: Seuil.

———. 1980a. *Desire in language.* Ed. Leon Roudiez. New York: Columbia University Press.

———. 1980b. *Powers of horror.* Trans. Leon Roudiez. New York: Columbia University Press.

———. 1982. Women's time. In *Feminist theory: A critique of ideology,* ed. N. Keohane, M. Z. Rosaldo, and B. C. Gelpi. Brighton: Harvester.

———. 1984. Julia Kristeva in conversation with Rosalind coward. *Desire, ICA Documents,* pp. 22–27.

———. 1986. *The Kristeva reader.* Ed. Toril Moi. New York: Columbia University Press.

———. 1987a. *Black sun.* Trans. Leon Roudiez. New York: Columbia University Press.

———. 1987b. La femme tristesse. *L'Infini* 17: 5–9.

———. 1987c. *Tales of love.* Trans. Leon Roudiez. New York: Columbia University Press.

———. 1987d. La vierge de Freud. *L'Infini* 18: 23–30.

———. 1988. *In the beginning was love,* trans. A. Goldhammer. New York: Columbia University Press.

———. 1988. Interview with Julia Kristeva. In *Women Analyze Women,* ed. Elaine Baruch and Lucienne Serrano. New York: New York University Press.
———. 1990. *Lettre ouverte à Harlem Désir.* Paris: Rivages.
———. 1991. *Strangers to ourselves.* Trans. Leon Roudiez. New York: Columbia University Press.
———. 1995. *New maladies of the soul.* Trans. Ross Guberman. New York: Columbia University Press.
———. 1996. *Time and sense: Proust and the experience of literature.* Trans. Ross Guberman. New York: Columbia University Press.
Lacan, Jacques. 1977. *Écrits.* Trans. Alan Sheridan. New York: Norton.
———. 1988a. *The seminar of Jacques Lacan: Book 1. Freud's papers on technique, 1953–54,* trans. John Forrester. Cambridge: Cambridge University Press.
———. 1988b. *The seminar of Jacques Lacan: Book 2. The ego in Freud's theory and in the technique of psychoanalysis, 1954–1955,* trans. Sylvana Tomaselli. Cambridge: Cambridge University Press.
Lacayo, Richard. 1995. I, too, sing America. *Time* 146, no. 18 (October 30).
Laub, Dori. 1992. *Testimony: Crises of witnessing in literature, psychoanalysis, and history,* ed. with Shoshana Felman. New York: Routledge.
Lee, Martha F. 1996. *The Nation of Islam: An American millenarian movement.* Syracuse, N.Y.: Syracuse University Press.
Leo, John. 1997. Men behaving well. *U.S. News & World Report* 123, no. 17 (November 3): 16.
Levinas, Emmanuel. 1969. *Totality and infinity.* Trans. Alphonso Lingis. Pittsburgh: Duquesne University Press.
Lewis, John. 1995. Why we marched in '63. *Newsweek* 126, no. 17 (October 23): 33.
Lincoln, Abraham. 1953–1955. "Address before the Young Men's Lyceum. In *The collected works of Abraham Lincoln,* vol. 1, ed. Roy P. Basler. New Brunswick, N.J.: Rutgers University Press.
Locke, John. 1980. *Second treatise on government,* ed. C. B. MacPherson. Cambridge, Mass.: Hackett.
Manning, Marable. 1995. *New Statesmen & Society* 8, no. 376 (October 27): 14–17.
Marchers make pledge. 1995. *Christian Century* 112, no. 31 (November 1): 1008–10.
Marty, Martin E. 1995. Supporting religion. *Christian Century* 112, no. 31 (November 1): 1031.
Merleau-Ponty, Maurice. 1968. *The visible and the invisible.* Trans. A. Lingis. Evanston, Ill.: Northwestern University Press.
McKissack, Fredrick. 1995. Thanks a million. *Progressive* 59, no. 12 (December): 23–36.
Miller, Holly G. 1996. Real men keep promises. *Saturday Evening Post* 268, no. 4 (July–August): 46–49.
Miller, Kevin A. 1995. McCartney preaches reconciliation. *Christianity Today* 39, no. 7 (June 19): 43.
Minebrook, Scott. 1995. Mission on the mall. *U.S. News & World Report* 119, no. 17 (October 30): 10–12.

Mollins, Carl. 1995. The new main man: Louis Farrakhan marches to power. *Maclean's* 108, no. 44 (October 30): 36–38.
Murchison, William. 1996. Promises are for keeps. *Human Life Review* 22, no. 1 (Winter): 5–13.
New men for Jesus. 1995. *Economist,* 335, no. 7917 (June 3): A21–A23.
Nietzsche, Friedrich. 1967. *On the genealogy of morals.* Trans. Walter Kaufmann. New York: Random House.
Oliver, Kelly. 1993. *Reading Kristeva: Unraveling the double-bind.* Bloomington: Indiana University Press.
———. 1995. *Womanizing Nietzsche: Philosophy's relation to the "feminine."* New York: Routledge.
———. 1997. *Family values: Subjects between nature and culture.* New York: Routledge.
Outmarching the hatred. 1995. *Nation,* 261, no. 15 (November 6): 521–24.
Patterson, Orlando. 1995. The paradox of integration. *New Republic* 213, no. 19 (November 6): 24–28.
Phillips, Andrew. 1997. Christian men on the march: A movement preaching male dominance angers feminists. *Macleans* 110, no. 40 (October 6): 52–54.
Philp, Mark. 1983. Foucault on power: A problem in radical translation? *Political Theory* 11: 29–52.
Raine, Harrison. 1995. A new awakening. *U.S. News & World Report* 119, no. 17 (October 30): 32.
Ricoeur, Paul. 1974. *The Conflict of interpretations.* Trans. Robert Sweeney, ed. Don Idhe. Evanston, Ill.: Northwestern University Press.
Robinson, Sally. 1989. Misappropriations of the "feminine." *SubStance* 59.
Rorty, Richard. 1986. Foucault and epistemology. In *Foucault: A critical reader,* ed. David Hoy. New York: Basil Blackwell.
Rosin, Hanna. 1997. Promise weepers: The Right embraces sentimentality. *New Republic* 217, no. 17 (October 27): 11–13.
Rousseau, Jean-Jacques. 1987. Discourse on political economy. In *The basic political writings.* Ed. and Trans. Donald Cress. Cambridge: Hackett Publishing.
Rudder, Chantal de. 1996. Daddy come home. *World Press Review* 43, no. 7 (July): 44–46.
Schmidt, Carl Crawford. 1994. Message to men. *Christian Century* 111, no. 25 (September 7): 805–7.
Smith, Paul. 1988. *Discerning the subject.* Minneapolis: University of Minnesota Press.
Snyder, Howard A. 1994. Will the Promise Keepers keep their promises? *Christianity Today* 38, no. 13 (November 14): 20–22.
Sophocles. 1967. *Electra.* In *The plays of Sophocles,* trans. Sir Richard Claverhouse Jebb. New York: Bantam.
Spalding, John D. 1996. Bonding in the bleachers: A visit to the Promise Keepers. *Christian Century* 113, no. 8 (March 6): 260–66.
Spivak, Gayatri Chakravorty. 1983. Displacement and the discourse of woman. In *Displacement: Derrida and after,* ed. Mark Krupnick. Bloomington: Indiana University Press.

———. 1987. *In other words.* New York: Methuen.

———. 1989. Feminism and deconstruction, again: Negotiating with unacknowledged masculinism. In *Between feminism and psychoanalysis,* ed. Teresa Brennan. London: Routledge.

Swomley, John M. 1997. Storm troopers in the culture war. *The Humanist* 57, no. 5 (September–October): 8–14.

Taylor, Charles. 1984. Foucault on freedom and truth. *Political Theory* 12, no. 2: 152–83.

Van Brema, David. 1995. Full of promise. *Time* 146, no. 19 (November 6): 62.

Veroff, Joseph, et al. 1981. *Mental health in America.* New York: Basic Books.

Wall, James M. 1995. Message and messenger: The Million Man March. *Christian Century* 112, no. 31 (November 1): 1003.

Walzer, Michael. 1986. The politics of Michel Foucault. In *Foucault: A critical reader,* ed. David Hoy. New York: Basil Blackwell.

Warren, Kenneth. 1995. Marching in place. *The Nation* 261, no. 15 (November 6): 524.

Wieseltier, Leon. 1995. Brothers. *New Republic* 213, no. 19 (November 6): 56.

Wycliff, Don. 1995. Why Farrakhan appeals. *Commonweal* 122, no. 20 (November 17): 8.

Ziarek, Eva. 1992. At the limits of discourse: Heterogeneity, alterity and the maternal body. *Hypatia* 7, no. 2 (Spring 1992): 91–108.

Zuckerman, Mortimer B. 1995. Louis Farrakhan's white noise. *U.S. News & World Report* 119, no. 18 (November 6): 96.

Index

About the Author

Kelly Oliver is associate professor of philosophy at the University of Texas at Austin. She is the author of *Reading Kristeva: Unraveling the Double Bind* (1993); *Womanizing Nietzsche: Philosophy's Relation to "the Feminine"* (1995); and *Family Values: Subjects between Nature and Culture* (1997). She has edited several books, including *The Portable Kristeva* (1997) and *Feminist Interpretations of Friedrich Nietzsche* (1998, with M. Pearsall).